Usborne Children's
World
Atlas

Stephanie Turnbull and Emma Helbrough
Designers: Stephen Moncrieff and Andrea Slane
Consultant cartographic editor: Craig Asquith

Cartography by European Map Graphics Ltd
Additional map design by Laura Fearn and Keith Newell
Consultant: Dr. Roger Trend, Senior Lecturer in Earth Science
and Geography Education, University of Exeter

CONTENTS

Here you can see dramatic cloud formations at sunset over a desert in California, U.S.A. Below is a large sandstone arch, shaped by the weather over many years.

USBORNE QUICKLINKS

Throughout this book, we have
recommended websites where
you can find out more about
the topics covered in this book.

Internet links

At the Usborne Quicklinks website,
you'll find links to all the best websites
on the internet, from interactive games
and activities, video clips and animations,
to photo galleries, puzzles and quizzes.

To visit the sites, go to Usborne Quicklinks
at **www.usborne.com/quicklinks**
and type the keyword "atlas".

Internet links

Look out for internet links boxes with descriptions of the
websites you can visit. To visit the recommended sites,
go to **www.usborne.com/quicklinks**, enter the keyword
"atlas" and then the number of the page you are reading.

What you can do

Here are some of the things you can do at
the websites recommended for this book:

- Explore online maps of all the countries
  in the world.

- See satellite images of the Earth and
  find out how satellites work.

- Go on virtual tours and find sightseeing
  guides to places around the world.

- See inside an Egyptian pyramid, watch
  a video clip about the Great Wall of China
  or take an underwater tour of the Great
  Barrier Reef.

- Try lots of map games, activities and
  test-yourself quizzes.

- Browse fact files and guides to all the
  countries in the world.

Internet safety

When using the internet, please make sure you follow our three basic rules:

• Always ask an adult's permission before using the internet.

• Never give out personal information, such as your name, address, the name of your school or telephone number.

• If a website asks you to type in your name or email address, check with an adult first.

For more information about using the internet safely and securely, go to the Help and advice area at the Usborne Quicklinks website.

Site availability

The websites described in this book are regularly checked and reviewed by Usborne editors and the links at Usborne Quicklinks are updated. If a website closes down, we will replace it with a new link. Sometimes we add extra links too, so when you visit Usborne Quicklinks, the links may be slightly different from those described in your book.

Notes for parents

We recommend that children are supervised while using the internet, and that you ensure they read and follow our three basic rules for internet safety shown on this page.

You may also wish to use the parental controls provided in most web browsers and search engines, and by Internet Service Providers. These can help you restrict access to particular websites, set time limits and monitor the sites visited by children.

For more information about using the internet and parental controls, go to the section for adults in the Help and advice area at the Usborne Quicklinks website.

The websites described in this book are regularly reviewed and the links at Usborne Quicklinks are updated. However, please note that the content of a website may change at any time and Usborne Publishing is not responsible for the content or availability of any website other than its own.

Computer not essential
If you don't have use of the internet, don't worry. This book is a complete, self-contained reference book on its own.

WHAT IS AN ATLAS?

An atlas is a collection of maps. This atlas helps you explore our world and find out more about its varied landscapes, famous cities and amazing sights.

What maps show

A map is an image that represents an area of the Earth's surface, usually from above. Unlike a photograph, which shows exactly what an area looks like, a map can show features of the area in a clear, simplified way. It can also give different information, such as place names. Symbols are often used to mark features such as volcanoes and waterfalls.

Which way is up?

Although the Earth doesn't have a top and a bottom, north is usually at the top of maps. But it is sometimes more convenient to reposition a map, so north might not necessarily be at the top. Some maps have a compass symbol that indicates where north lies.

Wolf volcano

Darwin volcano

Fernandina

San Salvador

Alcedo volcano

La Cumbre volcano

Isabela

Santa Cruz

Sierra Negra volcano

Cerro Azul volcano

This simple map of the central Galapagos Islands names the main islands and their volcanoes.

Floreana

This is a satellite image of part of the Galapagos Islands. Using the map on this page, can you identify the islands shown in the photograph?

Physical and political

Physical maps indicate natural features such as mountains, deserts, rivers and lakes. Political maps focus on the division of the Earth's surface into different countries. Look on pages 18–19 for a political map of the world, and on pages 20–21 for a physical map. Most of the maps in this atlas show physical features as well as country borders, cities and towns.

Map scales

The size of a map in relation to the area it shows is called its scale. Some maps have a scale bar, which is a rule with measurements. It tells you how many miles or km are represented by a certain distance on the map. Other maps show these relative distances just as numbers. For example, the figure 1:100 means that 1cm on the map represents 100cm on the Earth's surface.

The scale of a map depends on its purpose. A map showing the whole world is on a very small scale, but a town plan is on a much larger scale so that features such as roads can be shown clearly.

1:72,300,000

| 0 | 1,000 | 2,000 | 3,000km |

| 0 | 1,000 | 2,000 miles |

This map of Europe is on a small scale so that it all fits onto one small map.

Internet links

For links to websites where you can see different kinds of maps and find out more about them, go to **www.usborne.com/quicklinks**

1:6,400,000

| 0 | 100 | 200 | 300km |

| 0 | 100 | 200 miles |

This map of Denmark is on a larger scale to show more detail.

Using this atlas

The maps in this atlas are grouped by continent. There are seven continents, which are (from largest to smallest): Asia, Africa, North America, South America, Antarctica, Europe and Australasia and Oceania. Each map section is accompanied by photographs and satellite images showing some of the continent's most impressive sights. You can look up many of these places on the maps.

This is Mount Rushmore, a huge sculpture of four U.S. presidents, which is one of the most famous sights in the U.S.A. Throughout this atlas you will see pictures of many more well known landmarks from around the world.

THE EARTH FROM SPACE

Modern technology has enabled scientists to make more accurate maps of the world than ever before. Even remote places, such as deserts, ocean floors and mountain ranges, have been mapped in detail, using information from satellites that observe the Earth from space.

What is a satellite?

Artificial satellites are machines that orbit, or travel around, the Earth. They observe the Earth using a technique called remote sensing. Instruments on the satellite monitor the Earth from a distance, and send back pictures of its surface. Satellites also monitor moons and other planets.

This satellite monitors the Earth 24 hours a day. It uses powerful radar that pierces through clouds. This means that the satellite can provide images of the Earth in all weather conditions.

Satellite movement

Some satellites orbit the Earth at a height of between 5km (3 miles) and 1,500km (930 miles), providing views of different parts of the planet. Others stay above the same place all the time, moving at the same speed as the Earth rotates to give a constant view of a particular area. These are called geostationary satellites. They travel at a height of around 36,000km (22,370 miles).

Internet links

For links to websites where you can zoom into satellite images of the Earth and find out how satellites work, go to **www.usborne.com/quicklinks**

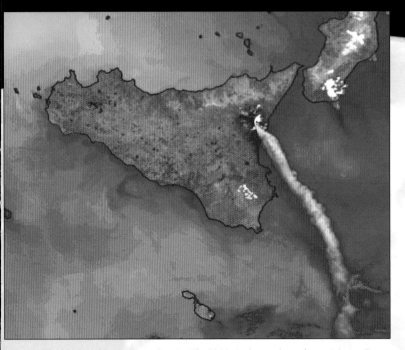

This satellite image of Sicily was taken in July 2001. It shows the volcano Mount Etna erupting. You can see smoke from the volcano on the right of the picture.

Satellite uses

Satellite pictures can be used to help predict and monitor natural hazards such as volcanic eruptions. They can also help scientists to observe the effects people have on the environment, for example the destruction of rainforests in South America. Satellite images are often artificially shaded to highlight relevant features, for example forests, so that they are easier to see.

Remote sensing

Satellites use a range of remote sensing techniques. One type is radar, which can provide images of the Earth even when it is dark or cloudy. Radar works by reflecting radio waves off a target object. The time it takes for a wave to bounce back indicates how far away the object is.

Powerful cameras provide pictures of the Earth's surface. Often, infrared cameras are used. Different surfaces reflect infrared rays differently, so infrared images of the Earth are able to show its various types of land surfaces, such as deserts, grasslands and forests.

This satellite image of the Earth is shaded to show different types of land. Deserts and other dry regions are red, and areas with lots of vegetation are orange.

DIVIDING LINES

The Earth is divided up with imaginary lines that help us measure distances and find where places are. There are two sets of lines, called latitude and longitude.

This arctic fox lives in northern Canada, very near the Arctic Circle line of latitud

Latitude lines

Lines of latitude run around the globe. They are parallel to each other and get shorter the closer they are to the two poles. The latitude line that runs around the middle of the Earth is called the Equator. It is the most important line of latitude as all other lines are measured north or south of it.

Longitude lines

Lines of longitude run from the North Pole to the South Pole. All the lines are the same length, and they all meet at the North and South Poles.

The most important line of longitude is the Prime Meridian Line, which runs through Greenwich, in England. All other lines of longitude are measured east or west of this line.

Other lines

The Equator is not the only named line of latitude. The Tropic of Cancer is a line north of the Equator, and the Tropic of Capricorn is at the same distance south of the Equator. Between these lines are the hottest, wettest parts of the world. This region is called the tropics.

The Arctic Circle is a latitude line far north of the Equator. The area north of this includes the North Pole and is called the Arctic. On the other side of the globe is the Antarctic Circle. The area south of this includes the South Pole and is known as the Antarctic.

Internet links

For links to websites where you can find out about lines of latitude and longitude, go to **www.usborne.com/quicklinks**

Latitude lines

Longitude lines

This drawing of the Earth shows some of the main latitude and longitude lines.

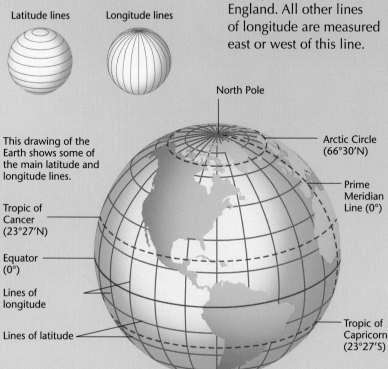

North Pole

Arctic Circle (66°30'N)

Prime Meridian Line (0°)

Tropic of Cancer (23°27'N)

Equator (0°)

Lines of longitude

Lines of latitude

Tropic of Capricorn (23°27'S)

Using the lines

Lines of latitude and longitude are measured in degrees (°). The positions of places are described according to which lines of latitude and longitude are nearest to them. For example, a place with a location of 50°S and 100°E has a latitude 50 degrees south of the Equator, and a longitude 100 degrees east of the Prime Meridian Line.

Exact locations

The distance between degrees is divided up to give even more precise measurements. Each degree is divided into 60 minutes ('), and each minute is divided into 60 seconds ("). The subdivisions allow us to locate any place on Earth. For example, the city of New York, U.S.A., is at 40°42′51″N and 74°00′23″W.

The steamy rainforests of Malaysia lie near the Equator. Many apes, like the one shown here, live in these rainforests.

This is a map of New Zealand, with a grid formed by lines of latitude and longitude.

Using a grid

Lines of latitude and longitude form grids on maps. The maps in this book look similar to the one on the left. The columns that run from top to bottom are formed by lines of longitude and marked with letters. The rows running across the page are formed by lines of latitude and are numbered.

All the places listed in the map index on page 130 have a letter and a number reference that tell you where to find them on a particular page. For example, on the map on the left, the city of Christchurch would have a grid reference of C3.

HOW MAPS ARE MADE

The process of making maps is called cartography. Map-makers, or cartographers, compile each map by gathering information about the area and representing it as an image as accurately as possible.

Internet links

For links to websites where you can find out how maps are made with online activities, go to **www.usborne.com/quicklinks**

Creating maps

Many sources are used to create maps. These include satellite images and aerial photographs. Cartographers often visit the area to be mapped, where they take many extra measurements.

In addition, cartographers use statistics, such as population figures, from censuses and other documents. As the maps are being made, many people check them to make sure they are accurate and up-to-date.

Map projections

Cartographers can't draw maps that show the world exactly as it is, because it is impossible to show a curved surface on a flat map without distorting (stretching or squashing) some areas. A representation of the Earth on a map is called a projection. Projections are worked out using complex mathematics.

There are three basic types of projections – cylindrical, conical and azimuthal, but there are also variations on these. They all distort the Earth's surface in some way, either by altering the shapes or sizes of areas of land or the distance between places.

A cartographer uses an electronic distance measurer to check the measurements of an area of land.

Cylindrical projections

A cylindrical projection is similar to the image created by wrapping a piece of paper around a globe to form a cylinder and then shining a light inside the globe. The shapes of countries would be projected onto the paper. Near the middle they would be accurate, but farther away they would be distorted.

Cartographers often alter the basic cylindrical projection to make the distortion less obvious in certain areas, but they can never make a map that is completely accurate.

This picture of a piece of paper wrapped around a globe illustrates how a cylindrical projection is made.

Below is a type of cylindrical projection called the Mercator projection, which was invented in 1596 by a cartographer named Gerardus Mercator. It makes countries the right shape, but makes those near the poles too big.

This cylindrical projection makes countries the right size in relation to each other, but some parts are too long. The projection was created in 1973 by Arno Peters. It is called the Peters Projection.

Conical projections

A conical projection is similar to the image you would get if you wrapped a cone of paper around part of a globe, then shone a light inside the globe. Where the cone touches the globe, the projection will be most accurate.

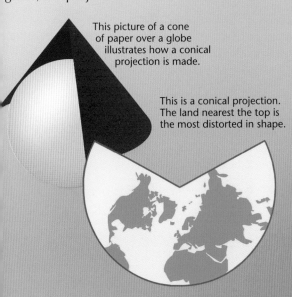

This picture of a cone of paper over a globe illustrates how a conical projection is made.

This is a conical projection. The land nearest the top is the most distorted in shape.

Azimuthal projections

An azimuthal projection is like an image made by holding paper in front of a globe, and shining a light through it. Land projected onto the middle of the paper would be accurate, but areas farther away would be distorted.

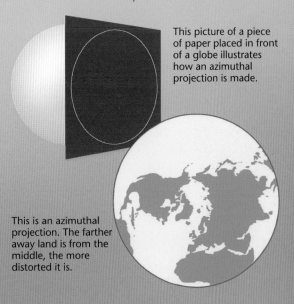

This picture of a piece of paper placed in front of a globe illustrates how an azimuthal projection is made.

This is an azimuthal projection. The farther away land is from the middle, the more distorted it is.

THEMATIC MAPS

Maps that represent information on particular themes, like the ones on these pages, are known as thematic maps. They help you to identify patterns and make comparisons between the features of different areas.

Earth's resources

The Earth contains all kinds of useful resources. Rocks and minerals can be used as building materials, and fuels such as coal, oil and gas contain energy that can be turned into heat and electricity.

Countries with large amounts of natural resources can become very rich. For example, Saudi Arabia, in western Asia, has large oil and gas reserves, which it exports all over the world.

This is an oil field, where oil is extracted from the ground using pumps. It is then piped to refineries and turned into products such as motor fuel.

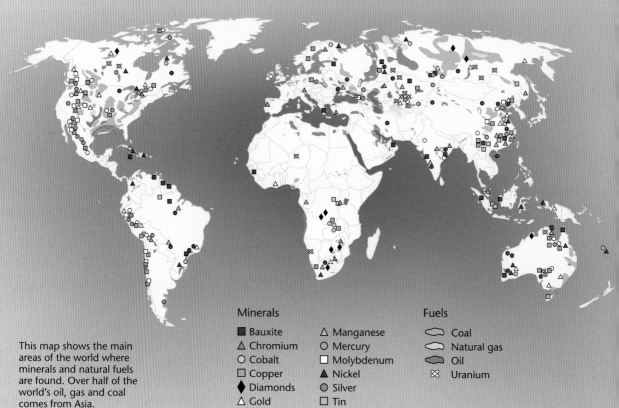

This map shows the main areas of the world where minerals and natural fuels are found. Over half of the world's oil, gas and coal comes from Asia.

Minerals

■ Bauxite	△ Manganese
△ Chromium	○ Mercury
○ Cobalt	□ Molybdenum
□ Copper	▲ Nickel
◆ Diamonds	○ Silver
△ Gold	□ Tin
● Iron	△ Tungsten
▥ Lead	○ Zinc

Fuels

▭ Coal
▭ Natural gas
▭ Oil
⊠ Uranium

Different climates

The long-term or typical pattern of weather in a particular area is known as its climate. Climates vary across the world and depend largely on each area's latitude. The hottest parts of the world are those closest to the Equator.

Climate is also affected by other factors, such as wind and the height of the land. Oceans influence climate too – places near the sea normally have a milder, wetter climate than areas farther inland.

In this map, land is divided into five climate types. Dry areas are generally hot, but temperatures there can fall very low too. Some dry places, such as the Gobi Desert in eastern Asia, are extremely cold in winter.

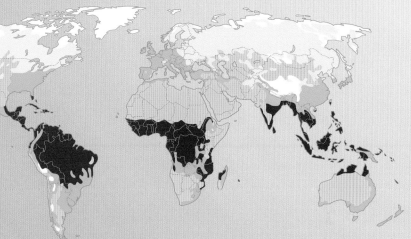

☐ Polar
☐ Cold
☐ Temperate
☐ Dry
■ Tropical

World population

There are more than six billion people in the world, and the population is still growing. Experts think it may reach more than nine billion by 2050. The number of people living in a given area is known as its population density. Europe and Asia are the most densely populated continents in the world. About a third of the world's population lives in China and India alone.

Internet links

For links to websites where you can find thematic maps of the world and see the Earth's population when you were born, go to **www.usborne.com/quicklinks**

This map shows the average population density by country. The shading indicates the number of people per sq km (0.4 sq miles).

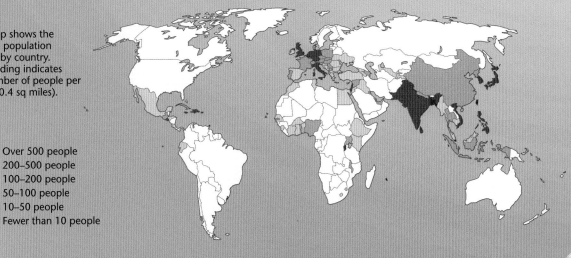

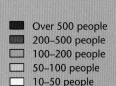

■ Over 500 people
■ 200–500 people
☐ 100–200 people
☐ 50–100 people
☐ 10–50 people
☐ Fewer than 10 people

HOW TO USE THE MAPS

Each continent section in this atlas begins with a political map showing the whole continent. The rest of the maps are larger scale maps showing the various parts of the continent in more detail.

Political maps

The shading on the political maps in this book is there to help you see clearly the different states, or countries, that make up each continent. The main purpose of these maps is to show country borders and capital cities. Alongside them there are facts and figures about the continents and their features.

This is a section of the political map of South America. You can see the whole map on pages 36–37.

Environmental maps

The majority of the maps in this book are environmental maps, like the one on the right. The shading on these maps shows different types of land, or environments, such as desert, mountain or wetland.

The main key on the opposite page shows what the different shading means. It also shows the symbols used to represent towns, cities and other features. There is a smaller key on each environmental map repeating the most important information from this key.

Finding places

To find a particular place or feature on the environmental maps, look up its name in the index on pages 130–143. Its page number and grid reference is given next to the name. You can find out how to use the grid on page 11.

The map on the right is part of the environmental map of the U.S.A. The numbered labels at the top explain some important features of these maps.

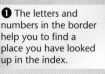

❶ The letters and numbers in the border help you to find a place you have looked up in the index.

❷ Lines of latitude and longitude are shown as thin blue lines.

❸ The names of countries are shown in large, bold type with capital letters.

❹ The thick purple lines are country boundaries.
❺ The thinner purple lines are boundaries of internal regions within a country.

Main key

Land cover:
- Boreal forest
- Temperate forest
- Tropical forest
- Temperate grassland
- Savanna
- Semi-desert and scrub
- Hot desert
- Wetland
- Mountain (Only high mountains are marked.)
- Tundra
- Ice
- Cultivation
- Urban

Cities and towns:
- ■ National capital
- ● Internal capital
- ⊙ Major city or town
- ○ Other town

Boundaries:
- International boundary
- --- International boundary through water
- Internal boundary
- --- Internal boundary through water

Water features:
- Sea
- Lake or reservoir
- Seasonal lake
- Dry lake/salt pan
- River
- Seasonal river
- Waterfall/dam

Other features:
- ▲ 2,490m (8,169ft) Height above or below sea level (Only a selection of elevation points are given. Places below sea level have a minus sign in front of the height.)
- ∴ Ruin or other place of interest
- ⊓⊓⊓ Ancient wall

Scale:
This tells you the size of the map in relation to the area it represents. For example:

1:13,800,000

0   200   400km

0   100   200   300 miles

C   115°   D   110°   E   105°   F   100°   G   85°

BIA

ALBERTA

Lethbridge

Coeur d'Alene

Missoula

wiston

ROCKY

Great Falls

Missouri

Helena

MONTANA

Yellowstone

Billings

IDAHO

oise

Idaho Falls

Twin Falls

Yellowstone Lake

Grand Teton 4,197m (13,770ft)

WYOMING

Casper

Great Salt Lake Desert

Great Salt Lake

Ogden

Salt Lake City

Provo

Kings Peak 4,123m (13,527ft)

M O U N T A I N S

St. George

Grand Junction

UTAH

Colorado

Grand Canyon

Colorado Plateau

Flagstaff

ARIZONA

Phoenix

Baldy Peak 3,476m (11,404ft)

NEW MEXICO

Tucson

Nogales

Agua Prieta

Hermosillo

Ciudad Obregon

California

Los Mochis

Swift Current

Moose Jaws ❷ Regina

SASKATCHEWAN

Estevan

Fort Peck Lake

❹

Minot

NORTH DAKOTA

Bismarck

Yellowstone

Great Plains

Rapid City

❺

Pierre

SOUTH DAKOTA

Missouri

Cheyenne

Denver

COLORADO

Colorado Springs

Pueblo

NEBRASKA

Platte

Grand Island

KANSAS

Wichita

❸ U N I T E D

Farmington

Rio Grande

Santa Fe

Albuquerque

Canadian

Amarillo

Lubbock

Red

S T A T E S

Oklahoma City

Pecos

El Paso

Ciudad Juarez

Ojinaga

Chihuahua

Western Sierra Madre

MEXICO

Monclova

Abilene

Fort Worth

TEXAS

Edwards Plateau

Austin

Del Rio

San Antonio

Rio Grande

Corpus Christi

Laredo

Eastern Sierra Madre

Lake Manitoba

MANITOBA

Brandon

C A N

ONTAR

Marath

rior

Lake Michigan

aukee

Gr Ra

South Bend

INDIA

India

Evansv

deau

Kentucky Lake

A

TENN

Jackson

Cha

his

Huntsv

Po

T

PI

AL

an

M

on

Mobile

Orleans

Mississip Delta

f Me

Gulf

GREENLAND
(Denmark)

ICELAND

Arctic Circle

ALASKA
(U.S.A.)

C A N A D A

IRELAND UN
KIN

UNITED STATES
OF AMERICA

PORTUGAL SPA

Azores
(Portugal)

MOROCCO

Canary Islands
(Spain)

WESTERN SAHARA
(Morocco)

Tropic of Cancer

THE BAHAMAS

CUBA
DOMINICAN
HAITI REPUBLIC

MAURITANIA

Ma

MEXICO

JAMAICA

Hawaiian
Islands
(U.S.A.)

BELIZE
GUATEMALA HONDURAS
EL SALVADOR NICARAGUA

DOMINICA

SENEGAL

CAPE VERDE

THE GAMBIA
GUINEA-BISSAU

Caribbean Sea

BUR
FA

GUINEA

COSTA RICA
PANAMA

TRINIDAD AND TOBAGO

SIERRA LEONE
LIBERIA

IVORY
COAST

P A C I F I C

VENEZUELA

GUYANA
SURINAME

COLOMBIA

FRENCH GUIANA
(France)

SAO TO
PRIN

O C E A N

Galapagos Islands
(Ecuador)

ECUADOR

A T L A N T I C

Equator

KIRIBATI

PERU

B R A Z I L

O C E A N

Cook
Islands
(New Zealand)

BOLIVIA

French
Polynesia
(France)

20°
S

Tropic of Capricorn

Pitcairn
Islands
(U.K.)

PARAGUAY

CHILE

ARGENTINA

URUGUAY

40°

1:92,000,000

0 1,000 2,000 3,000 4,000 5,000km

0 1,000 2,000 3,000 miles

Falkland Islands
(U.K.)

South Georgia
(U.K.)

60°

Antarctic Circle

Weddell
Sea

80°

160° 140° 120° 100° 80° 60° 40° 20° W

Abbreviations used on map:

ALB.	ALBANIA
ARM.	ARMENIA
AUST.	AUSTRIA
AZER.	AZERBAIJAN
BELG.	BELGIUM
B.H.	BOSNIA AND HERZEGOVINA
CRO.	CROATIA
CZECH REP.	CZECH REPUBLIC
KOS.	KOSOVO
LEB.	LEBANON
LUX.	LUXEMBOURG
MAC.	MACEDONIA
MONT.	MONTENEGRO
NETH.	NETHERLANDS
SERB.	SERBIA
SLOV.	SLOVENIA
SWITZ.	SWITZERLAND
U.A.E.	UNITED ARAB EMIRATES

The shading on this map is there to help
you see the different countries clearly.

160° 140° 120° 100° 80° 60° 40° 20° W

80°

Beaufort
Sea

*Ellesmere
Island*

*Victoria
Island*

*Queen
Elizabeth
Islands*

*Baffin
Island*

*Baffin
Bay*

Greenland

Gree
Se

Icelar

Arctic Circle

Alaska
Mount McKinley

6,194m
(20,321ft)

60°

Yukon

*Hudson
Bay*

*Labrador
Sea*

*British
Isles*

Aleutian Islands

Gulf of Alaska

Rocky Mountains

**NORTH
AMERICA**

Great plains

40°

Newfoundland

*Great
Lakes*

Appalachian Mountains

Azores

Mississippi

*Canary
Islands*

Atlas

Tropic of Cancer

Gulf of
Mexico

Cuba

West Indies

Greater Antilles

*Cape Verde
Islands*

20°
N

*Hawaiian
Islands*

Caribbean
Sea

*Lesser
Antilles*

*Guiana
Highlands*

*Galapagos
Islands*

*Amazon
Basin*

Amazon

A T L A N T I C

0° Equator

P A C I F I C

Selvas

O C E A N

O C E A N

P o l y n e s i a

**SOUTH
AMERICA**

20°
S

Tahiti

A n d e s

Tropic of Capricorn

Atacama Desert

Easter Island

Aconcagua

6,961m
(22,837ft)

Pampas

40°

1:92,000,000

0   1,000 2,000 3,000 4,000 5,000km

0   1,000   2,000   3,000 miles

Patagonia

Falkland Islands

South Georgia

Cape Horn

60°

Antarctic Circle

*Antarctic
Peninsula*

*W e d d e l l
S e a*

80°

160° 140° 120° 100° 80° 60° 40° 20° W

ARCTIC OCEAN

40° 60° 80° 100° 120° 140° 160° 180° 80°

Novaya Zemlya
Kara Sea
Severnaya Zemlya
Laptev Sea
New Siberia Islands
East Siberian Sea

Barents Sea

Arctic Circle

European Plain
Ob
Ural Mountains
Yenisey
Siberia
Verkhoyansk Range

60°

Volga
ASIA
Altai Mountains
Lake Baikal
Sea of Okhotsk
Kamchatka Peninsula

EUROPE
Mount Elbrus
5,642m (18,510ft)
Aral Sea
Caspian Sea
Gobi Desert
Huang He (Yellow)
Hokkaido

Black Sea
40°

Mediterranean Sea
Zagros Mountains
Himalayas
Chang Jiang (Yangtze)
Yellow Sea
Honshu

▲ **Mount Everest**
8,848m (29,029ft)
East China Sea

Ganges
Taiwan
Chang Jiang
Tropic of Cancer

Nile
Red Sea
Arabian Peninsula
Deccan Plateau
Bay of Bengal
Mekong

20° N

AFRICA
Arabian Sea
Philippine Islands
Micronesia
PACIFIC OCEAN

Ethiopian Highlands
Sri Lanka
South China Sea

Lake Victoria
Celebes Sea
Equator 0°

▲ **Kilimanjaro**
5,895m (19,341ft)
Seychelles
Sumatra
Borneo
New Guinea
▲ **Mount Wilhelm**
4,509m (14,793ft)
Melanesia

Congo basin
Comoro Islands
Greater Sunda Islands
Java
Arafura Sea
Solomon Islands

Rift Valley
INDIAN OCEAN
Lesser Sunda Islands
Coral Sea
New Caledonia
Fiji Islands

Madagascar
Mauritius
Reunion
Great Barrier Reef
20° S

Kalahari Desert
Great Sandy Desert
Tropic of Capricorn

Drakensberg
AUSTRALASIA AND OCEANIA
Great Victoria Desert
Great Dividing Range
Tasman Sea
North Island

Hope
Tasmania
South Island

40°

Kerguelen Islands

60°

SOUTHERN OCEAN

Antarctic Circle

ANTARCTICA

80°

See page 17 for key.

40° 60° 80° 100° 120° 140° 160° 180°

21

NORTH AMERICA

The name "North America" can be used to mean several different things. In this atlas, North America includes Greenland, Canada, the U.S.A., the Caribbean, and the countries of Central America, which run along the narrow strip of land between the U.S.A. and South America. The continent has over 20 countries, including Canada, the second-largest country in the world.

These are columns of rock called hoodoos in Bryce Canyon National Park, U.S.A.

Arctic Circle

ARCTIC OCEAN

Beaufort Sea

Bering Sea

Yukon

ALASKA
(U.S.A.)

Anchorage

Vic
Isl

CAN

Vancouver

Columbia

PACIFIC

OCEAN

Hawaiian
Islands
(U.S.A.)

UNITED ST

Colorado

Los Angeles

Rio Gra

Tropic of Cancer

ME

Mex

The shading on this map is there to help you see clearly the different countries that make up the continent.

GREENLAND
(Denmark)

Arctic Circle

Baffin
Island

Nuuk

Hudson
Bay

Newfoundland

St. Lawrence

Montreal
Ottawa

Great
Lakes

icago

New York

Washington D.C.

AMERICA

Mississippi

ATLANTIC

OCEAN

Bermuda
(U.K.)

Tropic of Cancer

uston

THE
BAHAMAS

Nassau

Gulf of
Mexico

Havana

CUBA

Port-au-
Prince

Kingston

HAITI

JAMAICA

DOMINICAN
REP.

Santo
Domingo

Puerto
Rico
(U.S.A.)

Guadeloupe
(France)

DOMINICA

Martinique (France)

BARBADOS

BELIZE

Belmopan

ATEMALA
nala City

HONDURAS

Tegucigalpa

Salvador

SALVADOR

NICARAGUA

Managua

San Jose

COSTA RICA

PANAMA

Panama City

Caribbean Sea

Port-of-Spain

TRINIDAD
AND TOBAGO

Facts

Total land area *24,709,000 sq km (9,540,198 sq miles)*

Total population *565 million*

Biggest city New York City, U.S.A.

Biggest country Canada *9,984,670 sq km (3,855,103 sq miles)*

Smallest country Saint Kitts and Nevis *261 sq km (101 sq miles)*

Highest mountain Mount McKinley, Alaska, U.S.A. *6,194m (20,321ft)*

Longest river Mississippi/Missouri, U.S.A. *6,019km (3,740 miles)*

Biggest lake Lake Superior, between the U.S.A. and Canada *82,100 sq km (31,700 sq miles)*

Highest waterfall Yosemite Falls, on the Yosemite Creek, California, U.S.A. *739m (2,425ft)*

Biggest desert Great Basin Desert, U.S.A. *492,000 sq km (189,962 sq miles)*

Biggest island Greenland *2,166,086 sq km (836,330 sq miles)*

Main mineral deposits Silver, gold, copper, lead, zinc, graphite, molybdenum, nickel

Main fuel deposits Oil, coal, natural gas, uranium

The bald eagle is the national bird of the U.S.A. It is not really bald, but has white feathers on its head.

23

North America covers a huge area, from just south of the North Pole to just north of the Equator. The land in the far north is icy and barren, while southern areas are lush and tropical. The west is dominated by the snow-capped Rocky Mountains.

Enormous parks

North America has many vast national parks. These are specially-protected natural areas where all kinds of animals live. One of the most famous parks is Yellowstone Park in Wyoming, U.S.A., which is home to wolves, black bears and many other animals. The park also has natural hot springs and geysers.

This satellite image of North America shows dry areas in brown, vegetation in green and icy regions in white.

Erupting island

Half of the island of Hawaii is covered by Mauna Loa, the biggest volcano on Earth, and one of the most active. The volcano is monitored constantly to check for impending eruptions. Its biggest eruption was in 1950, when a wide river of red-hot lava flowed 24km (15 miles) to the sea, destroying roads and houses in its path.

This satellite image shows part of Mauna Loa volcano. The dark, round hole at the top is one of the volcano's craters, out of which lava and gases regularly explode.

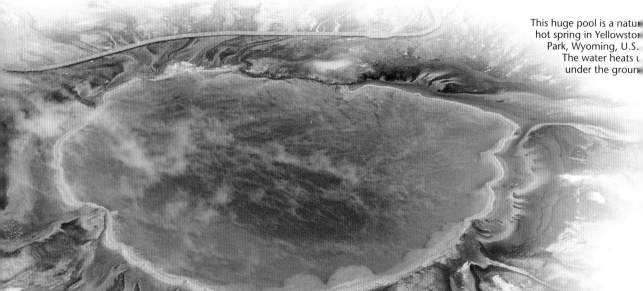

This huge pool is a natural hot spring in Yellowstone Park, Wyoming, U.S. The water heats up under the ground.

Internet links

For links to websites where you can explore Yellowstone National Park, the Grand Canyon and other American landscapes, go to **www.usborne.com/quicklinks**

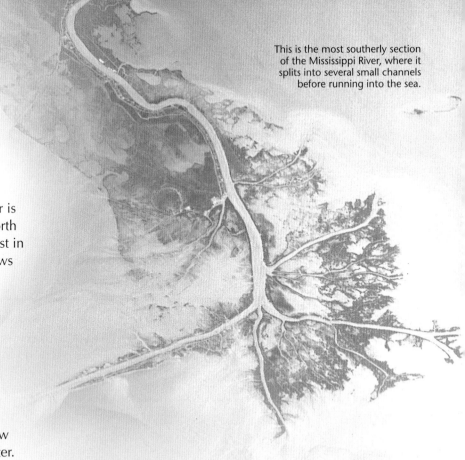

This is the most southerly section of the Mississippi River, where it splits into several small channels before running into the sea.

Mighty Mississippi

The Mississippi/Missouri River is the longest river system in North America and the fourth-longest in the world. The Mississippi flows from Minnesota in northern U.S.A. to the Gulf of Mexico in the south. The Missouri begins in Montana, in the west, and joins the Mississippi in the state of Missouri. The river system is a busy shipping route, and is also vital for wildlife – migratory birds follow it as they fly south in the winter.

The deepest valley

The Grand Canyon, in Arizona, U.S.A., is the world's largest gorge, a deep valley that stretches over 400km (250 miles). In some parts it is 1.6km (1 mile) deep, and up to 29km (18 miles) wide.

The Grand Canyon was carved out by the Colorado River, which eroded the rocky land over many thousands of years. It is possible to hike down the sides of the Canyon, but they are so steep that it takes a whole day to get to the bottom.

Running from top left to bottom right of this satellite image is the jagged Grand Canyon, in the flat, dry state of Arizona, U.S.A. Smaller valleys join the main canyon.

The northern part of North America consists mainly of Canada and the U.S.A. and has many large, dynamic cities as well as forests, deserts and other vast natural spaces.

Huge clouds of spray and mist rise from Horseshoe Falls, one of the two spectacular waterfalls that form Niagara Falls. The falls divide the U.S.A. (left) and Canada (right).

Cold country

Canada has extremely cold, snowy winters, especially in northern and eastern areas. In the city of Montreal, an amazing 1m (40in) of snow once fell in a single day. Not surprisingly, Canada is famous for its many winter sports, such as skiing, ice-skating and ice hockey.

On the border

The border between Canada and the U.S.A. is the longest in the world, covering 6,416km (3,987 miles). In the east, the border runs through several huge lakes, known as the Great Lakes. This section of the border includes Niagara Falls, where water from Lake Erie crashes over two enormous waterfalls.

Big cities

The largest city in the U.S.A. is New York, which is also the country's financial capital. Other big cities include Los Angeles, home of the movie-making area Hollywood, and Las Vegas, which boasts the largest number of hotel rooms of any U.S. city.

At night, the casinos and hotels of Las Vegas are lit up in a blaze of neon lights.

Desert heat

Death Valley in California is the driest place in the U.S.A., and one of the hottest places in the world. The temperature in this vast wilderness has been known to reach a sweltering 57°C (134°F). The desert is generally barren, though when rain does occasionally fall, beautiful wild flowers spring up between the rocks.

An American alligator lazes in one of Florida's coastal swamps. Alligators eat birds, frogs and other animals – sometimes even small alligators.

In the foreground of this Las Vegas skyline is a replica of the Chrysler Building, a New York skyscraper. It is part of an extravagant hotel that has 12 towers, each in the shape of a famous New York building.

The sunshine state

Florida, in southeastern U.S.A., has a hot, tropical climate and is nicknamed "the sunshine state". Southern Florida is covered in swampy wetlands called the Everglades. All kinds of wildlife live there, including Florida panthers and American alligators.

Internet links

For links to websites where you can find map games, slide shows and activities about Canada, the U.S.A. and North American wildlife, go to **www.usborne.com/quicklinks**

Central America is dominated by the country of Mexico, with its ancient ruins and crowded cities. Farther south, the countries near the border with South America have beautiful beaches, tropical rainforests and fiery volcanoes.

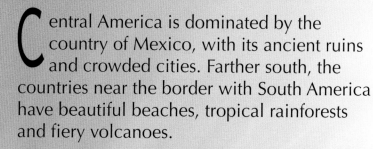

Here a bright wall mural is being painted in the coastal town of Cancun, one of Mexico's lively tourist spots.

City living

Mexico has a huge population, and also has millions of visitors every year. Its biggest city is the capital, Mexico City, where almost a quarter of Mexico's total population lives. The city is so overcrowded that the air is heavily polluted, and many people have poor living conditions and inadequate water supplies.

These statues are in Tula, Mexico. They were built by the ancient Toltec people, and were probably columns that held up a roof.

Ancient remains

In Mexico and nearby areas there are many remains of ancient cities. These were built by people from ancient civilizations, such as the Maya and the Toltec. The Maya had a powerful empire around AD200–900, while the Toltec ruled from about 900 to 1200. These peoples were excellent builders, and created many impressive temples and elaborately carved statues.

Land of volcanoes

Along the Pacific coast of Central America are more than 40 volcanoes. Lava from volcanic eruptions helps make the soil fertile, which is good for growing crops such as bananas and coffee. The volcanoes erupt regularly, and can be very dangerous. For example, the Arenal volcano in Costa Rica wiped out a whole town in a 1963 eruption, and has produced frequent lava flows ever since.

A white-nosed coati raids a banana tree in Costa Rica. These Central American mammals eat all kinds of fruit.

This is the Arenal volcano during an eruption. Lava can flow more than 2km (1.5 miles) from the volcano's base.

Sun and storms

The Caribbean islands have stunning sandy beaches and a hot climate. But their position in the Atlantic Ocean means that they are often hit by tropical storms and hurricanes. Some hurricanes reach wind speeds of 250kph (155mph).

Internet links

For links to websites where you can take virtual tours of Central American countries and explore ancient sites, go to **www.usborne.com/quicklinks**

Linking oceans

The Panama Canal is one of the world's busiest shipping routes. It cuts through the country of Panama and is a short cut for ships sailing between the Atlantic and Pacific oceans. Before the canal opened, ships had to sail around South America, an extra 12,500km (7,800 miles).

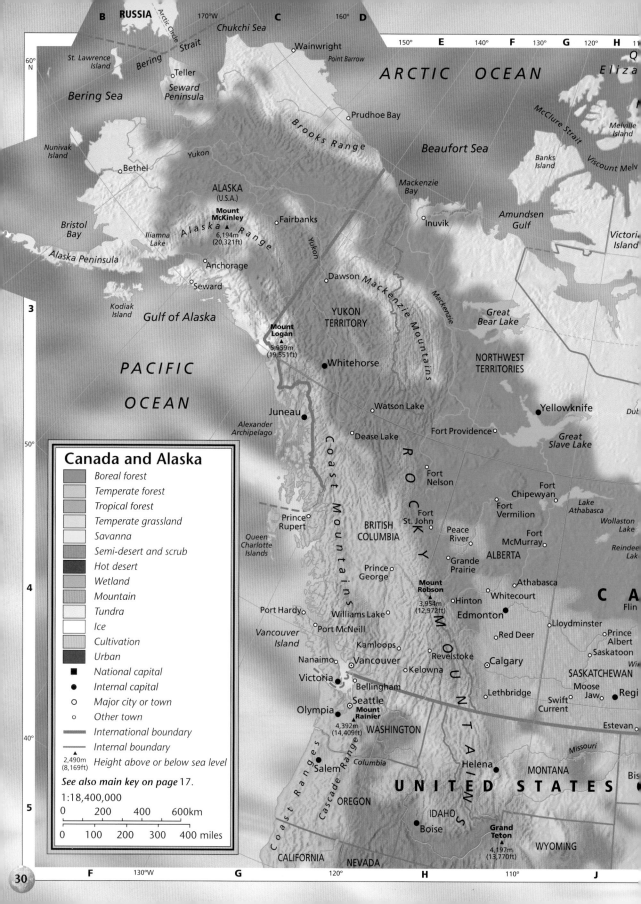

Canada and Alaska

	Boreal forest
	Temperate forest
	Tropical forest
	Temperate grassland
	Savanna
	Semi-desert and scrub
	Hot desert
	Wetland
	Mountain
	Tundra
	Ice
	Cultivation
	Urban
■	National capital
●	Internal capital
○	Major city or town
○	Other town
	International boundary
	Internal boundary
▲ 2,490m (8,169ft)	Height above or below sea level

See also main key on page 17.

1:18,400,000

0   200   400   600km

0   100   200   300   400 miles

RUSSIA

Chukchi Sea

Wainwright

ARCTIC OCEAN

Point Barrow

St. Lawrence Island

Bering Strait

Teller

Seward Peninsula

Bering Sea

Prudhoe Bay

Beaufort Sea

Brooks Range

McClure Strait

Melville Island

Banks Island

Viscount Melv

Nunivak Island

Bethel

Yukon

Mackenzie Bay

Amundsen Gulf

Victoria Island

ALASKA (U.S.A.)

Mount McKinley ▲ 6,194m (20,321ft)

Fairbanks

Inuvik

Bristol Bay

Iliamna Lake

Alaska Range

Yukon

Anchorage

Seward

Dawson

Mackenzie Mountains

Great Bear Lake

NORTHWEST TERRITORIES

Alaska Peninsula

Kodiak Island

Gulf of Alaska

YUKON TERRITORY

Mackenzie

PACIFIC OCEAN

Mount Logan ▲ 5,959m (19,551ft)

Whitehorse

Juneau

Watson Lake

Yellowknife

Dub

Alexander Archipelago

Dease Lake

Fort Providence

Great Slave Lake

Coast Mountains

Fort Nelson

Fort Chipewyan

Lake Athabasca

Wollaston Lake

Prince Rupert

BRITISH COLUMBIA

Fort St. John

Fort Vermilion

Fort McMurray

Reindeer Lak

Queen Charlotte Islands

Prince George

Peace River

Grande Prairie

ALBERTA

R O C K Y

Mount Robson ▲ 3,954m (12,972ft)

Athabasca

Port Hardy

Williams Lake

Hinton

Whitecourt

Flin

Vancouver Island

Port McNeill

Edmonton

Lloydminster

Prince Albert

Kamloops

Red Deer

Saskatoon

Nanaimo

Vancouver

Revelstoke

Calgary

SASKATCHEWAN

Wi

Victoria

Kelowna

Bellingham

Lethbridge

Moose Jaw

Regi

Seattle

M O U N T A I N S

Swift Current

Estevan

Olympia

Mount Rainier ▲ 4,392m (14,409ft)

WASHINGTON

Missouri

Coast Ranges

Cascade Range

Columbia

Helena

MONTANA

Bis

Salem

UNITED STATES

OREGON

IDAHO

Boise

Grand Teton ▲ 4,197m (13,770ft)

WYOMING

Coast Ranges

CALIFORNIA

NEVADA

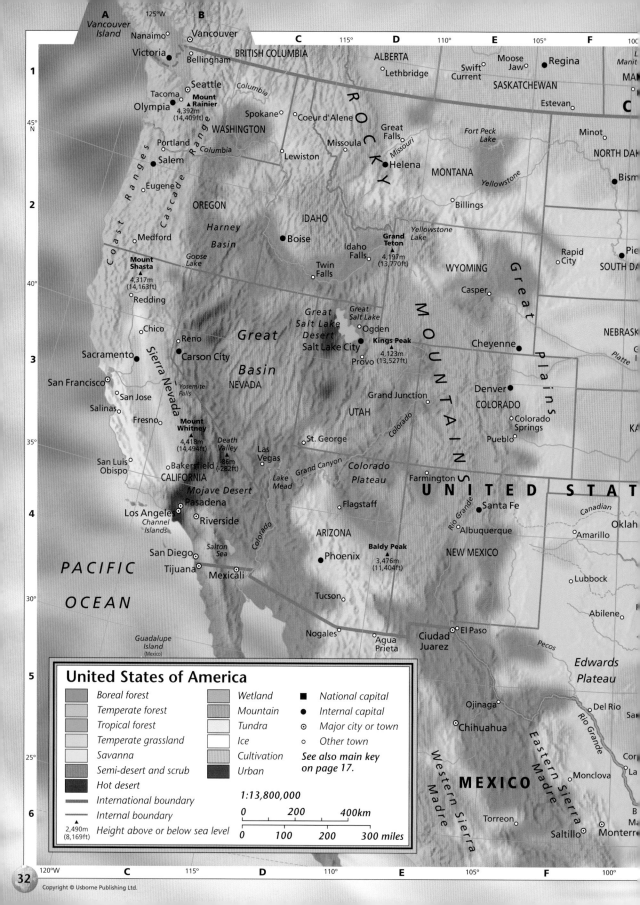

United States of America map (western portion)

Grid references (top): A B C 115° D 110° E 105° F 100°

Latitude markers (left): 45°N, 40°, 35°, 30°, 25°

Longitude: 125°W, 120°W, 115°, 110°, 105°, 100°

Places and features:

Vancouver Island, Nanaimo, Vancouver, Victoria, Bellingham, BRITISH COLUMBIA, ALBERTA, Lethbridge, Swift Current, Moose Jaw, Regina, SASKATCHEWAN, Manit, MA

Tacoma, Seattle, Mount Rainier 4,392m (14,409ft), Olympia, Mount, Spokane, Coeur d'Alene, Great Falls, Missouri, Fort Peck Lake, Minot, NORTH DAK

Portland, Columbia, Salem, Eugene, WASHINGTON, Lewiston, Missoula, Helena, MONTANA, Yellowstone, Billings, Bism

OREGON, Medford, Harney Basin, IDAHO, Boise, Idaho Falls, Yellowstone Lake, Grand Teton 4,197m (13,770ft), WYOMING, Rapid City, Pie, SOUTH DA

Mount Shasta 4,317m (14,163ft), Goose Lake, Twin Falls, Casper, ROCKY, MOUNTAINS, Great Plains

Redding, Chico, Reno, Carson City, Great Salt Lake Desert, Great Salt Lake, Ogden, Kings Peak 4,123m (13,527ft), Salt Lake City, Provo, Cheyenne, NEBRAS

Sacramento, Sierra Nevada, Great Basin, NEVADA, Yosemite Falls, Grand Junction, Denver, COLORADO, Colorado Springs, KA

San Francisco, San Jose, Salinas, Fresno, UTAH, Colorado, Pueblo

Mount Whitney 4,418m (14,494ft), Death Valley -86m (-282ft), Las Vegas, St. George, Grand Canyon, Colorado Plateau, Farmington, UNITED STAT

San Luis Obispo, Bakersfield, CALIFORNIA, Mojave Desert, Lake Mead, Flagstaff, Santa Fe, Canadian, Oklah

Pasadena, Los Angeles, Channel Islands, Riverside, Colorado, ARIZONA, Baldy Peak 3,476m (11,404ft), Phoenix, NEW MEXICO, Albuquerque, Amarillo

San Diego, Salton Sea, Tijuana, Mexicali, Tucson, Rio Grande, Lubbock

PACIFIC OCEAN, Nogales, Agua Prieta, Ciudad Juarez, El Paso, Pecos, Abilene, Edwards Plateau

Guadalupe Island (Mexico), Ojinaga, Del Rio, Rio Grande

Chihuahua, Western Sierra Madre, Eastern Sierra Madre, MEXICO, Monclova, La, Cor

Torreon, Saltillo, Monterre, Ma

Legend:

United States of America

- Boreal forest
- Temperate forest
- Tropical forest
- Temperate grassland
- Savanna
- Semi-desert and scrub
- Hot desert
- ——— International boundary
- ——— Internal boundary
- ▲ 2,490m (8,169ft) Height above or below sea level

- Wetland
- Mountain
- Tundra
- Ice
- Cultivation
- Urban

- ■ National capital
- ● Internal capital
- ⊙ Major city or town
- ○ Other town

See also main key on page 17.

1:13,800,000

0 200 400km
0 100 200 300 miles

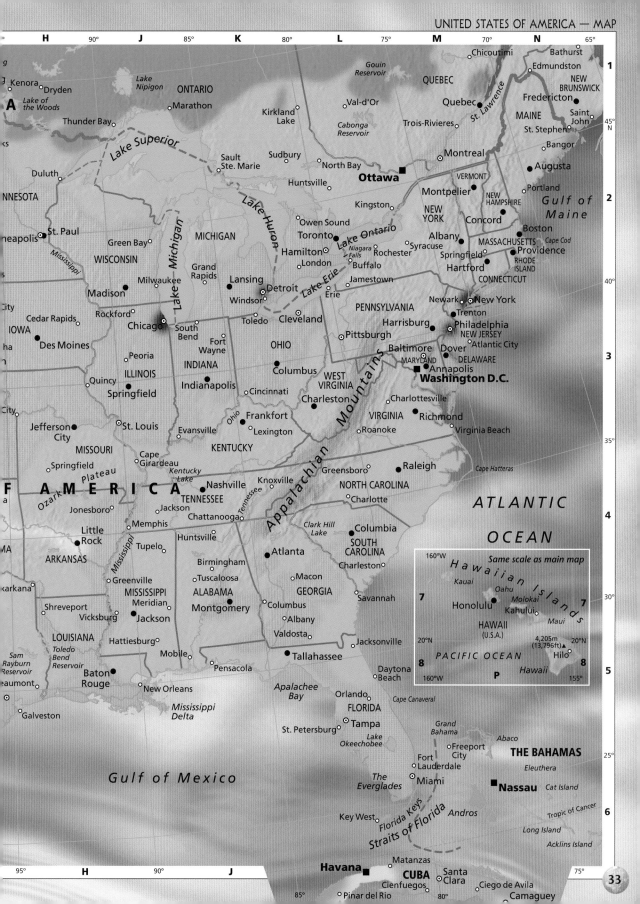

120°W **A** 115° **B** 110° **C** 105° **D** 100° **E** 95° **F** 90

CALIFORNIA
San Diego
Tijuana
Mexicali
Phoenix
ARIZONA
NEW MEXICO
OKLAHOMA
Little Rock
ARKANSAS
MISS

1
30°N
Nogales
Agua Prieta
Tucson
Ciudad Juarez
El Paso
UNITED STATES OF AMERICA
Lubbock
Fort Worth
Abilene
Texarkana
Dallas
TEXAS
Waco
Shreveport
LOUISIANA
Hattie

Guadalupe Island (Mexico)
Cedros Island
Point Eugenia
Hermosillo
Ciudad Obregon
Ojinaga
Chihuahua
Edwards Plateau
Rio Grande
Pecos
Austin
Houston
San Antonio
Galveston
Baton Rouge

2
25°
Tropic of Cancer
Los Mochis
La Paz
Culiacan
Plateau of Mexico
Durango
Torreon
Saltillo
Monclova
Laredo
Monterrey
Matamoros
Brownsville
Corpus Christi

3
Cape San Lucas
Mazatlan
MEXICO
Durango
Matehuala
San Luis Potosi
4,054m (13,300ft)
Ciudad Victoria
Tampico
Gulf of Mex

4
20°
Revillagigedo Islands (Mexico)
Puerto Vallarta
Guadalajara
Aguascalientes
Colima
Morelia
Uruapan
Celaya
Leon
Teotihuacan
Puebla
Mexico City
Orizaba 5,610m (18,405ft)
Tehuacan
Veracruz
Coatzacoalcos
Villahermosa
Bay of Campeche
Merida
Ciudad del
Can

Acapulco
Southern Sierra Madre
Oaxaca
Juchitan
Isthmus of Tehuantepec
Tuxtla Gutierrez
Tikal
Belmo

Gulf of Tehuantepec
Tapachula
Tajumulco 4,220m (13,845ft)
Quetz
Guatemala City
San Salvador
EL S
GUATE

PACIFIC OCEAN

Galapagos Islands (Ecuador)
Puerto Ayora

Inset map

L 65°W M 60° N

Virgin Islands (U.K.)
Anguilla (U.K.)
ATLANTIC OCEAN
Leeward Islands

San Juan
Puerto Rico (U.S.A.)
Virgin Islands (U.S.A.)
St. Martin (France and Netherlands)
ANTIGUA AND BARBUDA
St. John's

Basseterre
ST. KITTS AND NEVIS
Montserrat (U.K.)
Guadeloupe (France)
Basse-Terre
Windward Islands

1:9,200,000
0   100   200km
0   50   100 miles

DOMINICA
Roseau
Martinique (France)
Fort-de-France

Caribbean Sea
Lesser Antilles
ST. LUCIA
Castries
BARBADOS
Bridgetown
Kingstown
ST. VINCENT AND THE GRENADINES

St. George's **GRENADA**

Margarita Island
Porlamar
Tobago
Port-of-Spain **TRINIDAD AND TOBAGO**

Cumana
L 65°W **VENEZUELA** M Trinidad 60° N
Equator

34

115°W **B** 110° **C** 105° **D** 100° **E** 95° 90°

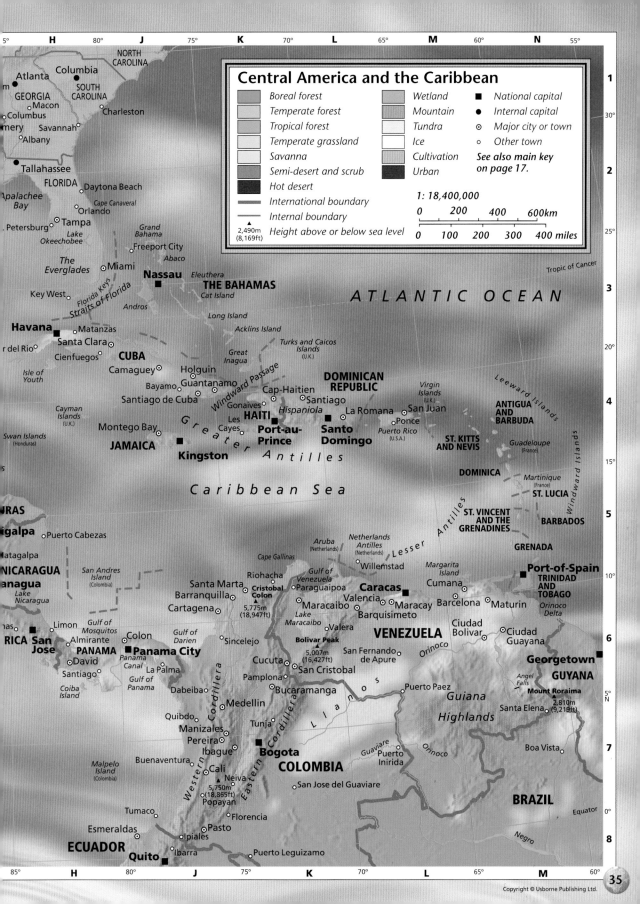

Central America and the Caribbean

SOUTH AMERICA

South America is made up of 12 independent countries, along with French Guiana, which belongs to France. The continent's biggest and most industrialized country is Brazil, which covers about half of the total land. Brazil is also home to half of South America's population.

This is a guanaco. Guanacos are members of the camel family that live in South America. Guanaco hair is used to make textiles.

Caribbean Sea

Cara

VENEZU

Medellin° ■ Bogota

COLOMBIA

Orinoco

Quito ■

ECUADOR

Galapagos
Islands
(Ecuador)

Guayaquil°

Equator

PERU

Lima ■

BOL

La Pa ■

Tropic of Capricorn

CHILE

PACIFIC

OCEAN

Santiago ■ ° Mend

ARG

Ca

Drake

The shading on this map is there to help you see clearly the different countries that make up the continent.

town
Paramaribo
■ Cayenne
E FRENCH
GUIANA
(France)

Equator

○Recife

R A Z I L

■ Brasilia

○Belo Horizonte

Parana

AY   Sao Paulo   ○Rio de Janeiro
ion   Tropic of Capricorn

○Porto Alegre

ATLANTIC

tevideo
Aires   OCEAN

Islands
K.)

This is a red-eyed tree frog. These frogs live in rainforests in South and Central America.

Facts

Total land area *17,840,000 sq km (6,888,063 sq miles)*
Total population 407 million
Biggest city Sao Paulo, Brazil
Biggest country Brazil *8,514,877 sq km (3,287,612 sq miles)*
Smallest country Suriname *163,820 sq km (63,251 sq miles)*

Highest mountain Aconcagua, Argentina *6,961m (22,837ft)*
Longest river Amazon, mainly in Brazil *6,437km (4,000 miles)*
Biggest lake Lake Maracaibo, Venezuela *13,210 sq km (5,100 sq miles)*
Highest waterfall Angel Falls, on the Churun River, Venezuela *979m (3,212ft)*
Biggest desert Patagonian Desert, Argentina *673,000 sq km (259,847 sq miles)*
Biggest island Tierra del Fuego *47,401 sq km (18,302 sq miles)*

Main mineral deposits Copper, tin, molybdenum, bauxite, emeralds
Main fuel deposits Oil, coal

37

South America has a varied and dramatic landscape. In the north there are lush, tropical rainforests, and in central areas are grassy plains, called pampas. In the far south there are glaciers, which are huge, slow-moving masses of ice.

The big picture

The Andes mountain range stretches more than 7,250km (4,500 miles) down the whole length of western South America. It is the longest chain of mountains on Earth.

South America also has the second-longest river in the world, the Amazon. It snakes through the northern half of the continent, from the Andes in Peru to the coast of Brazil, and carries around one-fifth of the world's fresh water.

On this satellite image of South America the Andes mountains are clearly visible in the west. The range contains many active volcanoes.

This flock of large birds, called scarlet ibises, is flying over fish 'farms' in Venezuela.

Icy lands

The southern tip of South America is near Antarctica, which means that the climate is extremely cold. There are glaciers in the mountainous regions, and icebergs in the area's many lakes. South America's most southerly point is Cape Horn. The seas around it are rough and stormy, which can make sailing around Cape Horn very dangerous.

The bluish-white shape in the middle of this image is part of a huge glacier. Melting ice gradually flows into Lake Viedma, shown in the bottom right.

Internet links

For links to websites where you can find online maps, facts and virtual tours of South America, go to www.usborne.com/quicklinks

Water source

On the border of Brazil and Paraguay is a vast expanse of water, about 1,350 sq km (520 sq miles) in size. This is the Itaipu reservoir, a man-made water source which provides water for homes, farms and factories in many areas of Brazil and Paraguay. In the past there had been many droughts, so the reservoir was built to provide a reliable supply of water.

This large blue area is part of the huge Itaipu reservoir, which forms part of the border between Paraguay (left) and Brazil (right).

The river running down the lower part of this image is the Parana River. It flows southward on the eastern side of South America.

This is a mountainous part of the Atacama Desert. In the middle are two snow-capped volcanoes, and on the right are white areas of salt from evaporated salt lakes.

The driest desert

Running down the western coast of Chile is the Atacama Desert, the driest place on Earth. Many areas of the desert go for decades without rain and in some parts rainfall has never been recorded.

Vast areas of the desert are covered in salt, which is all that is left of evaporated saltwater lakes. The rocky landscape looks like the Moon's surface, and NASA vehicles have been tested there in preparation for crossing the Moon's rugged terrain.

One of South America's main features is the Amazon rainforest. This is the largest rainforest in the world, covering an area nearly the size of Europe. The continent also has fascinating cities, both ancient and modern.

Parrot snakes live in trees in the Amazon rainforest. They often open their mouths wide like this to scare off predators.

Machu Picchu

High in the Andes Mountains of Peru lies the ancient, ruined city of Machu Picchu. It was built by the Incas, the South American people who ruled the western part of the continent from about 1400 to 1530. The city contains the ruins of many stone buildings, such as temples, palaces and storerooms, which were built around large central courtyards.

This is Machu Picchu, in the Andes. The city's buildings were constructed on wide steps cut into the sloping ground.

Amazing Amazon

The Amazon rainforest spreads across northern South America and is home to one-third of all the world's animal species. The rainforest contains over 100 species of snakes, from rare boa constrictors to common green parrot snakes.

Here is part of the wealthy, crowded financial district in Santiago, Chile.

City sprawl

South America has many huge cities, such as Sao Paulo in Brazil and Santiago in Chile. The growth of business and industry in these cities has led to the creation of towering skyscrapers, but also causes extra traffic and pollution. The cities are so overcrowded that many people live in poor, run-down suburbs.

Island animals

The Galapagos Islands are a cluster of small, rocky islands that lie in the Pacific Ocean, about 1,000km (600 miles) off the coast of Ecuador.

The islands are home to all kinds of unusual animals, such as giant tortoises. These enormous creatures weigh up to 250kg (550lb), and can live for more than a hundred years. Many tropical birds live on the islands too, including Galapagos penguins and frigate birds.

Fantastic falls

South America's mountainous landscape has led to the formation of many waterfalls, including Angel Falls in Venezuela, which is the world's biggest waterfall. It is 979m (3,212ft) high, just over three times the height of the Eiffel Tower in Paris, France.

A male frigate bird puffs out his bright red pouch to attract females. Frigate birds live on many of the Galapagos Islands.

Internet links

For links to websites where you can watch video clips about Amazon wildlife and the ancient site of Machu Picchu, go to **www.usborne.com/quicklinks**

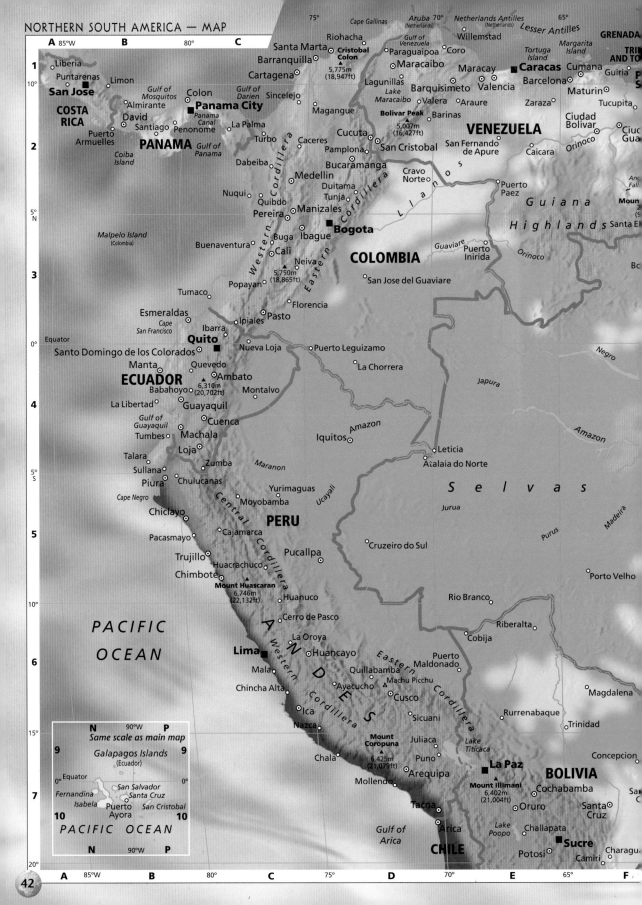

NORTHERN SOUTH AMERICA — MAP

A 85°W   B   80°   C

1
10°   Liberia
Puntarenas
San Jose
COSTA
RICA
Limon
Gulf of
Mosquitos
Almirante
David
Santiago
Colon
Panama City
Panama
Canal
Penonome
La Palma
Gulf of
Darien
Turbo
Caceres
Santa Marta
Barranquilla
Cartagena
Sincelejo
Riohacha
Cape Gallinas
Cristobal
Colon
5,775m
(18,947ft)
Paraguaipoa
Maracaibo
Lagunillas
Lake
Maracaibo
Aruba 70°
(Netherlands)
Coro
Maracay
Netherlands Antilles
(Netherlands)
Willemstad
Barquisimeto
Valencia
Caracas
Barcelona
Lesser Antilles
GRENADA
TRI
AND TO
Cumana
Guiria
Maturin
Tucupita

2
Puerto
Armuelles
Coiba
Island
PANAMA
Gulf of
Panama
Dabeiba
Magangue
Cucuta
Pamplona
San Cristobal
Bolivar Peak
5,007m
(16,427ft)
San Fernando
de Apure
Barinas
VENEZUELA
Araure
Valera
Zaraza
Ciudad
Bolivar
Caicara
Orinoco
Ciuc
Gua

Nuqui
Quibdo
Pereira
Medellin
Bucaramanga
Duitama
Tunja
Manizales
Bogota
Cravo
Norteo
Llanos
Puerto
Paez
Guiana
Highlands
Santa E
Moun
(9

3
5°
N
Malpelo Island
(Colombia)
Buenaventura
Buga
Cali
Ibague
Neiva
5,750m
(18,865ft)
Popayan
Tumaco
Florencia
COLOMBIA
San Jose del Guaviare
Guaviare
Puerto
Inirida
Orinoco
Negro
B

Esmeraldas
Cape
San Francisco
Ipiales
Pasto
Santo Domingo de los Colorados
Ibarra
Quito
Nueva Loja
Puerto Leguizamo
La Chorrera
Japura

0°
Equator

4
Manta
Quevedo
Ambato
6,310m
(20,702ft)
Babahoyo
Montalvo
ECUADOR
La Libertad
Guayaquil
Tumbes
Cuenca
Machala
Iquitos
Amazon
Leticia
Atalaia do Norte
Amazon

5°
S
Gulf of
Guayaquil
Talara
Sullana
Piura
Loja
Zumba
Maranon
Cape Negro
Chulucanas
Yurimaguas
Moyobamba
Ucayali
Selvas

5
Chiclayo
Pacasmayo
Cajamarca
PERU
Pucallpa
Cruzeiro do Sul
Jurua
Purus
Madeira
Porto Velho

Trujillo
Chimbote
Huacrachuco
Mount Huascaran
6,746m
(22,132ft)
Huanuco
Rio Branco
Riberalta

10°
Cerro de Pasco
La Oroya
Cobija
PACIFIC
OCEAN
Western Cordillera
Central Cordillera
Eastern Cordillera
ANDES

6
Lima
Mala
Chincha Alta
Huancayo
Quillabamba
Ayacucho
Machu Picchu
Cusco
Sicuani
Puerto
Maldonado
Magdalena
Rurrenabaque
Trinidad

Ica
Nazca
Chala
Mount
Coropuna
6,425m
(21,079ft)
Juliaca
Puno
Lake
Titicaca
Concepcion

15°
Mollendo
Arequipa
La Paz
BOLIVIA
Cochabamba
Santa
Cruz
Sa

7
Tacna
Mount Illimani
6,402m
(21,004ft)
Oruro
Potosi
Challapata
Sucre
Charagu

Arica
Gulf of
Arica
Lake
Poopo
CHILE
Camiri

20°
A 85°W   B 80°   C   75°   D 70°   E 65°   F

Galapagos Islands inset:
N 90°W P
Same scale as main map
9   9
Galapagos Islands
(Ecuador)
0° Equator   0°
Fernandina
Isabela
San Salvador
Santa Cruz
Puerto
Ayora
San Cristobal
10   10
PACIFIC OCEAN
N 90°W P

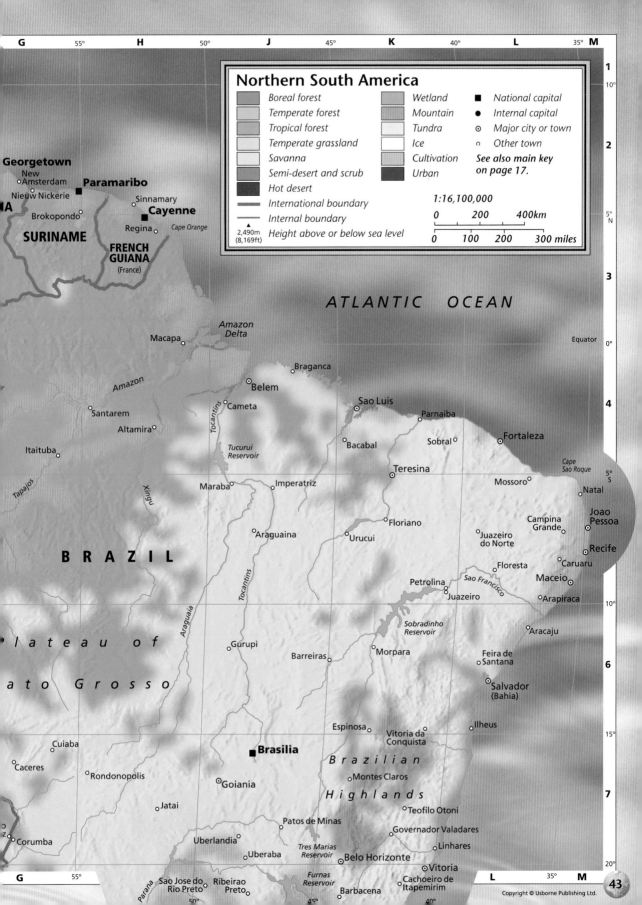

Northern South America

Boreal forest
Temperate forest
Tropical forest
Temperate grassland
Savanna
Semi-desert and scrub
Hot desert
International boundary
Internal boundary
2,490m (8,169ft) Height above or below sea level

Wetland
Mountain
Tundra
Ice
Cultivation
Urban

■ National capital
● Internal capital
⊙ Major city or town
○ Other town

See also main key on page 17.

1:16,100,000

0 200 400km
0 100 200 300 miles

Sobradinho
Reservoir

Feira de Santana
Morpara
Ilheus
Vitoria da
Conquista
Espinosa
Montes Claros
Teofilo Otoni
Linhares
Governador
Valadares
Vitoria
Cachoeiro
de Itapemirim
Campos
Barreiras
B r a z i l i a n
Belo Horizonte
Barbacena
Juiz
de Fora
Macae
Nova Iguacu
Rio de Janeiro
Tropic of Capricorn
H i g h l a n d s
Patos de Minas
Tres Marias
Reservoir
Furnas
Reservoir
Mount
Agulhas
Negras
2,787m
(9,144ft)
Sao Paulo
Brasilia
Goiania
Uberaba
Ribeirao
Preto
Pocos de
Caldas
Campinas
Gurupi
Jatai
Uberlandia
Sao Jose do Rio Preto
Araraquara
Marilia
Itapetininga
Curitiba
Paranagua
B R A Z I L
Rondonopolis
Campo Grande
Presidente
Prudente
Londrina
Guarapuava
Itajai
Florianopolis
Criciuma
Porto Alegre
Caxias do Sul
Patos
Lagoon
Rio Grande
Cuiaba
Dourados
Ponta Pora
Cascavel
Foz do Iguacu
Eldorado
Passo Fundo
Santa Maria
P l a t e a u   o f
Caceres
Corumba
Pedro Juan
Caballero
Concepcion
Ciudad
del
Este
Iguacu
Falls
Posadas
Uruguaiana
Rivera
Tacuarembo
URUGUAY
M a t o   G r o s s o
Puerto Suarez
Paraguay
Asuncion
PARAGUAY
Villarrica
Formosa
Encarnacion
Reconquista
Concordia
Salto
Paysandu
Gualeguaychu
Melo
Concepcion
Santa Cruz
San Jose de
Chiquitos
G r a n   C h a c o
Pilcomayo
Corrientes
Parana
Santa Fe
Rosario
Mirim
Magdalena
Camiri
Charagua
Tartagal
San Miguel de Tucuman
Santiago del Estero
Salado
San Francisco
Villa Maria
Rio Cuarto
Trinidad
Tarija
San Salvador
de Jujuy
Cordoba
Merlo
San Luis
Riberalta
BOLIVIA
Cochabamba
Oruro
Challapata
Potosi
Uyuni
Tupiza
Salta
A N D E S
La Rioja
Catamarca
San Juan
Aconcagua
6,959m
(22,831ft)
Mendoza
Rio Branco
Cobija
Rurrenabaque
La Paz
Mount
Illimani
6,404m
(21,004ft)
Sucre
Ollague
Calama
San Pedro de Atacama
Mount
Ojos del Salado
6,908m
(22,664ft)
Puerto
Maldonado
Juliaca
Puno
Lake
Titicaca
Arica
Lake
Poopo
Pica
Iquique
Antofagasta
Tropic of Capricorn
C H I L E
Coquimbo
Ovalle
Illapel
San Luis
PERU
Tacna
Atacama Desert
Taltal
Chanaral
Copiapo
Vallenar
Valparaiso

Tocantins
Araguaia
Parana

D 70°W
10°
S
65°
15°
20°
60°
55°
25°
50°
30°
45°
40°

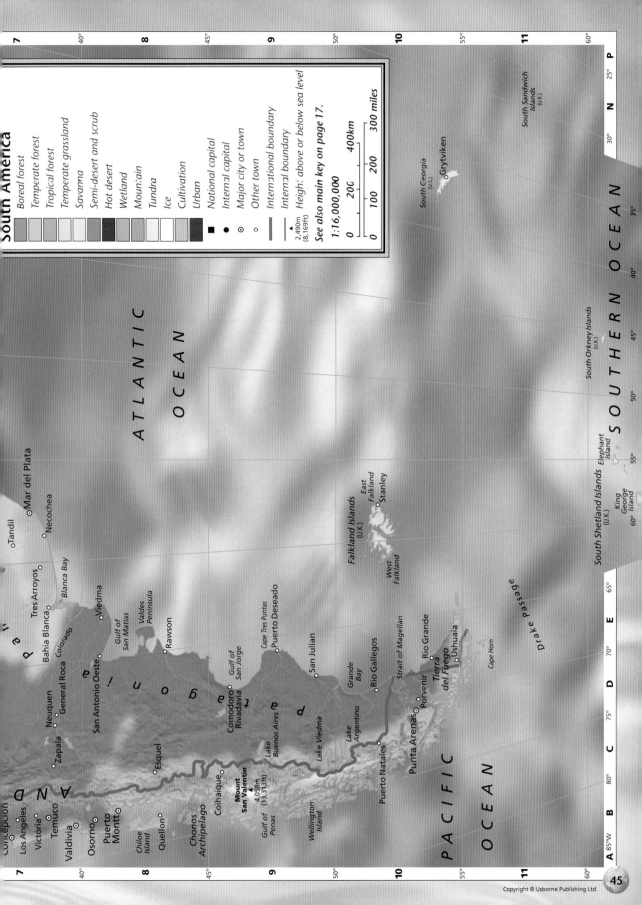

South America

Boreal forest
Temperate forest
Tropical forest
Temperate grassland
Savanna
Semi-desert and scrub
Hot desert
Wetland
Mountain
Tundra
Ice
Cultivation
Urban

■ National capital
● Internal capital
⊙ Major city or town
○ Other town

— International boundary
Internal boundary

▲ 2,490m (8,169ft) Height: above or below sea level

See also main key on page 17.

1:16,000,000

0   100   200   300 miles
0   200   400km

AUSTRALASIA AND OCEANIA

Australasia is made up of Australia, New Zealand and Papua New Guinea. Oceania is a collection of over 20,000 islands stretching out into the Pacific Ocean.

International Date Line

Northern Mariana Islands (U.S.A.)

Guam (U.S.A.)

MARSHALL ISLANDS

Melekeok ■

Palikir ■

Majuro ■

FEDERATED STATES OF MICRONESIA

PALAU

Bairiki ■

Equator

■Yaren

PAPUA NEW GUINEA

New Guinea

NAURU

KIR

INDIAN

Port Moresby ■

SOLOMON ISLANDS

TUVALU

Funafuti ■

Arafura Sea

Honiara ■

S.

OCEAN

Wallis and Futuna (France)

Coral Sea Islands Territory (Australia)

VANUATU

FIJI

Coral Sea

Port Vila ■

■Suva

T

New Caledonia (France)

Nukualofa

○Noumea

Tropic of Capricorn

AUSTRALIA

Brisbane ■

NEW ZEALAND

Darling

Perth ⊙

Adelaide ⊙

⊙Sydney

Auckland ⊙

North Island

Murray

■Canberra

Melbourne ⊙

Tasmania

Tasman Sea

■Wellington

⊙Christchurch

South Island

This small island is part of Papua New Guinea.

The shading on this map is there to help you see clearly the different countries that make up the continent.

PACIFIC OCEAN

Line Islands

Equator

Marquesas Islands

French Polynesia (France)

Society Islands

Cook Islands (New Zealand)

Pitcairn Islands (U.K.)

Tropic of Capricorn

Facts

Total land area *8,564,400 sq km (3,306,733 sq miles)*

Total population 38 million

Biggest city Sydney, Australia

Biggest country Australia *7,741,220 sq km (2,988,902 sq miles)*

Smallest country Nauru *21 sq km (8 sq miles)*

Highest mountain Mount Wilhelm, Papua New Guinea *4,509m (14,793ft)*

Longest river Murray/Darling River, Australia *3,718km (2,310 miles)*

Biggest lake Lake Eyre, Australia *9,500 sq km (3,668 sq miles)*

Highest waterfall Sutherland Falls, on the Arthur River, New Zealand *580m (1,903ft)*

Biggest desert Great Victoria Desert, Australia *348,750 sq km (134,653 sq miles)*

Biggest island New Guinea *786,000 sq km (303,476 sq miles)* (Australia is counted as a continental land mass and not as an island.)

Main mineral deposits Iron, nickel, precious stones, lead, bauxite

Main fuel deposits Oil, coal, uranium

The Moorish idol fish is found in shallow waters throughout the Pacific. It has a long, distinctive dorsal fin.

Australasia and Oceania's climate is generally very hot. New Zealand and Papua New Guinea are both lush, while Australia is mostly barren. The tiny tropical islands that make up Oceania are surrounded by vast areas of open sea.

This image shows a section of the Southern Alps of South Island, New Zealand. The two turquoise patches are Lake Pukaki and Lake Tekapo.

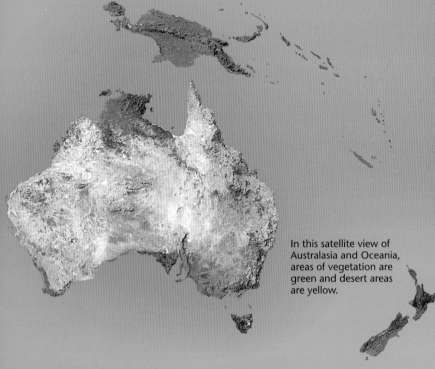

In this satellite view of Australasia and Oceania, areas of vegetation are green and desert areas are yellow.

Milky waters

New Zealand has two main islands, North Island and South Island, and several smaller ones. On South Island there is a mountain range called the Southern Alps, which has some dramatic milky-turquoise lakes. Their cloudy appearance is caused by rock dust, which is collected, finely ground and then deposited in the lake by glaciers. The rock dust is so fine, it stays suspended in the water, instead of sinking.

Land of bushfires

Most of Australia is hot, dry desert and the country suffers badly from bushfires almost every year. The fires are usually caused by lightning striking dry vegetation. Some species of trees found in Australia have adapted to cope with the constant outbreaks of fire. Eucalyptus trees can withstand fire, and some types of banksia trees actually need fire to open their seed pods.

Internet links

For links to websites with photo galleries, video clips and tours of Australia and Oceania, go to **www.usborne.com/quicklinks**

These are the Palau Rock Islands of Micronesia, Oceania. There are over 200 rock islands in total. Each one is made of limestone rock and covered with thick forest.

Tropical islands

Lots of the small islands in the South Pacific are volcanoes. Coral reefs (dense colonies of tentacled sea animals) often grow in shallow waters around the islands. They form barriers which trap water between the reef and the island's coast. The trapped water is known as a lagoon.

Many of the volcanoes are inactive, and are slowly sinking back into the sea. Sometimes, a volcano sinks entirely into the sea, leaving behind a shallow lagoon surrounded by a coral reef. This is called an atoll.

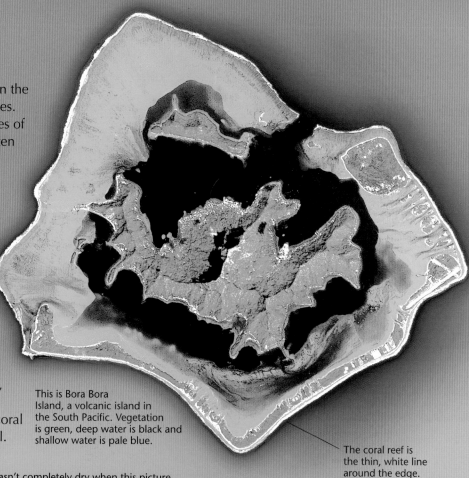

This is Bora Bora Island, a volcanic island in the South Pacific. Vegetation is green, deep water is black and shallow water is pale blue.

The coral reef is the thin, white line around the edge.

This is Lake Eyre in Australia. It wasn't completely dry when this picture was taken – dry areas are pale pink and wet areas are dark pink.

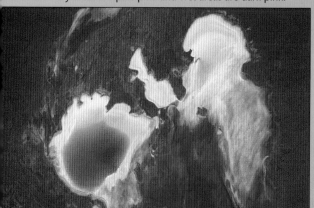

A vanishing lake

Australia's largest salt lake, Lake Eyre, is in the dry, central part of the country. Most of the year it is virtually dry, and you can see a glistening sheet of white salt on the lake bed. When the lake fills, it spreads out over 9,500 sq km (3,670 sq miles), but this usually only happens about once every eight years. The lake has two main sections, Lake Eyre North and Lake Eyre South, which are joined by a channel called the Goyder Channel.

Australasia and Oceania's attractions include a group of huge stone carvings, a strange tree formation and animals equipped with their own baby-carriers.

Great Barrier Reef

Around the coast of Queensland, Australia, lies the Great Barrier Reef, an enormous coral reef structure. It is made up of over 2,800 coral reefs covering 345,000 sq km (133,200 sq miles) and is home to more than 1,500 species of fish.

Coral reefs are very fragile. They are found in clear, shallow waters with a constant, warm temperature. Global warming might make the sea too hot for coral reefs to survive, and the Great Barrier Reef could die out.

Easter Island

Easter Island is a remote island, far east of Australia, famous for its large stone carvings of human figures with large heads The carvings are thought to be between 400 and 1,000 years old, and are believed to represent the spirits of important chiefs and ancestor. of the island. A Dutch navigator named Jacob Roggeveen gave Easter Island its name when he first visited it on Easter day in 1722.

These sculptures on Easter Island were carved out of volcanic rock. They are about 4m (13ft) tall, and some are partly buried.

Internet links

For links to sites about the Great Barrier Reef, Easter Island, the Olgas and marsupials, go to www.usborne.com/quicklinks

The Olgas

In Uluru National Park, in Australia's Northern Territory, there is a group of 36 enormous rocks known as the Olgas. The rocks are a type of sandstone, which means they were formed by loose sand that has become hardened and folded by the Earth's movements to produce layered rocks. The rocks were gradually eroded by wind and rain into the rounded hills we see today. The sand grains that make up the sandstone are mostly made of a pink mineral called feldspar.

These rounded rocks are the Olgas. The aboriginals, who were the first people to settle in Australia, named the site "Kata Tjunta" meaning "many heads".

This is a tree kangaroo, a type of animal only found in Queensland, Australia, and Papua New Guinea. Tree kangaroos can leap great distances from tree to tree.

Marsupials

Australasia and Oceania are home to lots of unusual animals, including a group of mammals called marsupials. As soon as marsupials are born, they crawl into a pouch of skin on their mother's tummy. They stay inside the pouch for the first few months of their lives. Kangaroos, koalas, wombats and possums are all marsupials.

The seven-in-one tree

On the island of Rarotonga, in the Cook Islands, there is a group of seven coconut trees which have grown naturally in a perfect circle. Local history tells that the seven trees grew from a single seed planted in 1907, so they are known as the "seven-in-one tree".

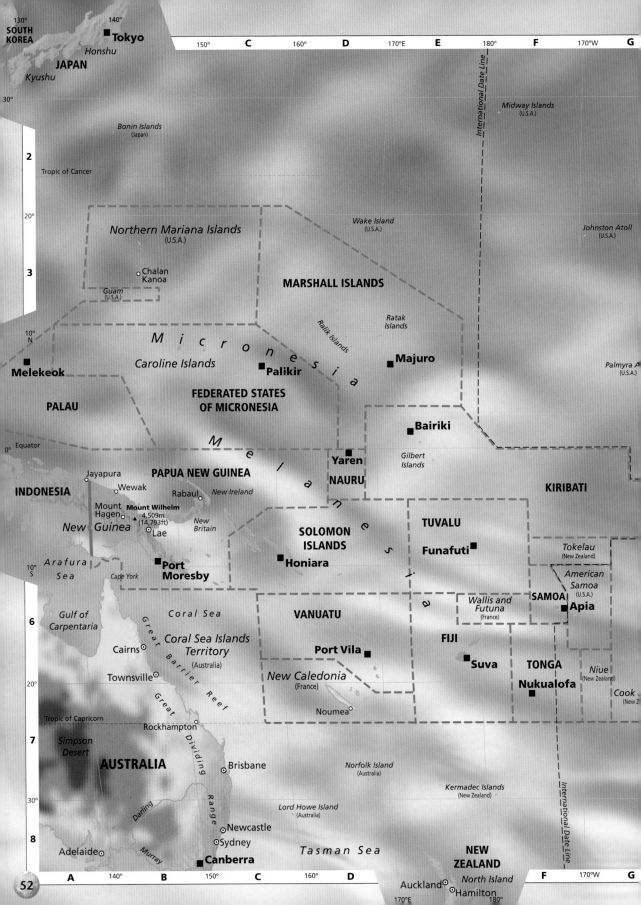

SOUTH
KOREA

Honshu

Tokyo

JAPAN

Kyushu

30°

International Date Line

30°

Bonin Islands
(Japan)

Midway Islands
(U.S.A.)

2

Tropic of Cancer

20°

Wake Island
(U.S.A.)

Johnston Atoll
(U.S.A.)

Northern Mariana Islands
(U.S.A.)

3

○ *Chalan*
Kanoa

Guam
(U.S.A.)

MARSHALL ISLANDS

Ratak
Islands

10°
N

M i c r o n e s i a

Ralik Islands

■ **Majuro**

Palmyra A
(U.S.A.)

Caroline Islands

■ **Palikir**

■
Melekeok

FEDERATED STATES
OF MICRONESIA

PALAU

M e l a

■ **Bairiki**

0° Equator

Gilbert
Islands

Yaren
■

KIRIBATI

○ Jayapura

PAPUA NEW GUINEA

○ Wewak

NAURU

INDONESIA

Mount
Hagen ○

Mount Wilhelm
▲ 4,509m
(14,793ft)
○ Lae

○ Rabaul

New Ireland

n e s

New
Guinea

New
Britain

SOLOMON
ISLANDS

TUVALU

Funafuti ■

Tokelau
(New Zealand)

10°
S

Arafura
Sea

Cape York

■ **Port**
Moresby

■ **Honiara**

i a

Wallis and
Futuna
(France)

SAMOA

American
Samoa
(U.S.A.)

■ **Apia**

6

Gulf of
Carpentaria

Coral Sea

VANUATU

a

Coral Sea Islands
Territory
(Australia)

Cairns ○

FIJI

Townsville ○

■ **Port Vila**

■ **Suva**

TONGA

Niue
(New Zealand)

20°

New Caledonia
(France)

■ **Nukualofa**

Cook
(New Z)

Tropic of Capricorn

○ Rockhampton

Noumea ○

Simpson
Desert

7

AUSTRALIA

○ Brisbane

Norfolk Island
(Australia)

30°

Kermadec Islands
(New Zealand)

Lord Howe Island
(Australia)

International Date Line

○ Newcastle

8

Adelaide ○

○ Sydney

Tasman Sea

NEW
ZEALAND

Murray

■ **Canberra**

Auckland ○

North Island

170°E   ○ Hamilton   180°

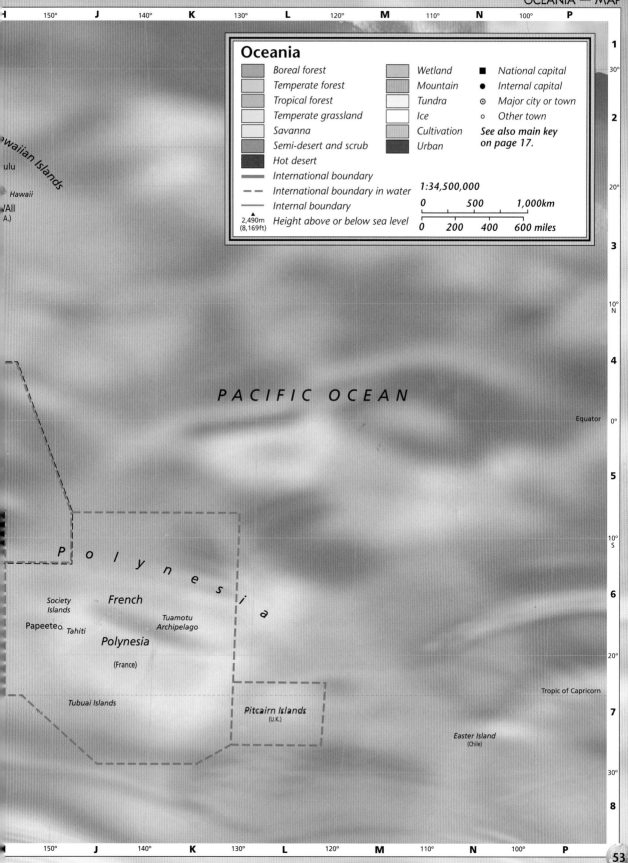

H 150° J 140° K 130° L 120° M 110° N 100° P

1
30°
2
20°
3
10° N
4
Equator 0°
5
10° S
6
20°
Tropic of Capricorn
7
30°
8

Oceania

Boreal forest		Wetland	■ National capital
Temperate forest		Mountain	● Internal capital
Tropical forest		Tundra	⊙ Major city or town
Temperate grassland		Ice	○ Other town
Savanna		Cultivation	**See also main key**
Semi-desert and scrub		Urban	**on page 17.**
Hot desert			

International boundary

International boundary in water

Internal boundary

▲ 2,490m (8,169ft) Height above or below sea level

1:34,500,000

0   500   1,000km

0   200   400   600 miles

Hawaiian Islands

ulu

Hawaii

VAII
A.)

PACIFIC OCEAN

P o l y n e s i a

Society Islands

French

Papeete○ Tahiti

Tuamotu Archipelago

Polynesia

(France)

Tubuai Islands

Pitcairn Islands
(U.K.)

Easter Island
(Chile)

H 150° J 140° K 130° L 120° M 110° N 100° P

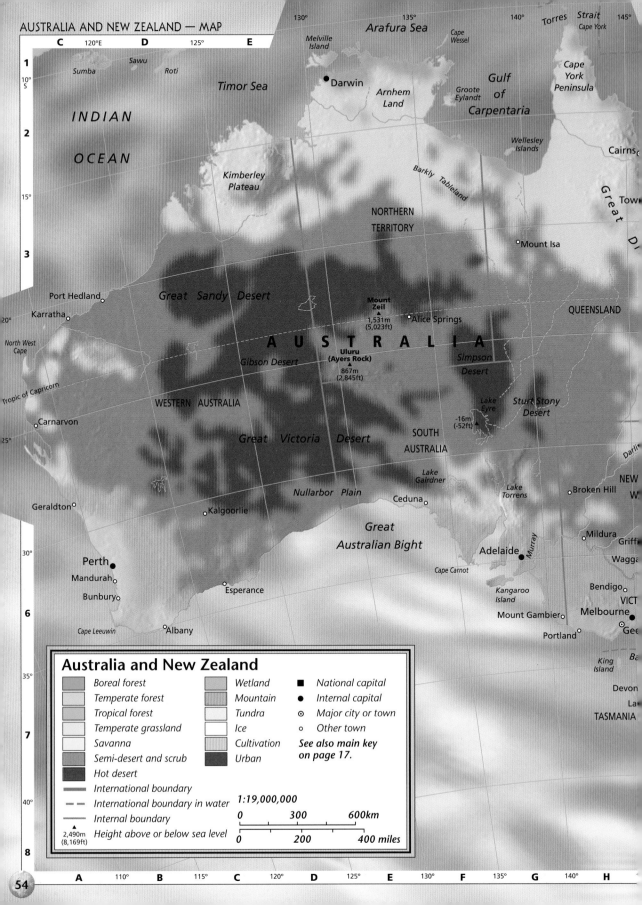

C 120°E   D   125°E   E

130°   135°   140°   Torres Strait   145°
Cape York

Arafura Sea
Cape Wessel

1
10°S   Sumba   Sawu   Roti
Melville Island

INDIAN   Timor Sea   Darwin   Arnhem Land   Groote Eylandt   Gulf of Carpentaria   Cape York Peninsula

2
OCEAN   Wellesley Islands   Cairns

Kimberley Plateau   Barkly Tableland   Great Di

15°   NORTHERN TERRITORY   Tow

3   Mount Isa

Port Hedland   Great Sandy Desert   Mount Zeil   QUEENSLAND
Karratha   1,531m (5,023ft)   Alice Springs

20°   A U S T R A L I A
North West Cape   Gibson Desert   Uluru (Ayers Rock)   Simpson Desert

Tropic of Capricorn   867m (2,845ft)   Sturt Stony Desert
Lake Eyre

Carnarvon   WESTERN AUSTRALIA   -16m (-52ft)   Darli
25°   SOUTH AUSTRALIA
Great Victoria Desert

Lake Gairdner   Broken Hill   NEW

Geraldton   Nullarbor Plain   Ceduna   Lake Torrens   W
Kalgoorlie   Mildura   Griff
30°   Great   Adelaide   Murray   Wagga
Australian Bight   Cape Carnot
Perth   Bendigo
Mandurah   Esperance   Kangaroo Island   VICT
Bunbury   6   Mount Gambier   Melbourne
Cape Leeuwin   Albany   Portland   Gee
King Island   Ba

35°   Devon
La
TASMANIA

40°

8

A   110°   B   115°   C   120°   D   125°   E   130°   F   135°   G   140°   H

K   150°   155°   L   160°   M   165°   N   170°   P   175°   Q

Coral Sea

SOLOMON ISLANDS

Rennell
Island

Santa Cruz
Islands

TUVALU

10°
S

1

Coral Sea
Islands
Territory
(Australia)

VANUATU

Banks Islands

Espiritu
Santo

○Luganville

Malakula

2

15°

Port Vila

FIJI

Efate ■ Port Vila

Vanua Levu

Chesterfield
Islands

New Caledonia
(France)

Lautoka○

Viti Levu   ■Suva

Noumea○

Loyalty
Islands

20°

■Mackay

○stone

Bundaberg○

Fraser Island

Gympie○

oomba○

●Brisbane
○Gold Coast

PACIFIC OCEAN

Tropic of Capricorn

4

○Grafton

25°

○ding Range

Norfolk Island
(Australia)

Port Macquarie○

Lord Howe
Island
(Australia)

5

●Newcastle

●Sydney
○Wollongong

Kermadec Islands
(New Zealand)

nberra
RALIAN CAPITAL
TERRITORY

30°

North Cape

6

Tasman Sea

○Whangarei

35°

○Auckland

North Island

Hamilton○

New Plymouth○

○Rotorua
Lake
Taupo

East Cape

Cape
Farewell

○Napier

7

Nelson○

Cook Strait

■ Wellington

South Island

Aoraki
(Mount Cook)
▲
3,754m
(12,316ft)

○Christchurch

NEW
ZEALAND

Sutherland Falls

40°

Cape Providence

○Dunedin

Invercargill○

Chatham Islands
(New Zealand)

Stewart Island

South West Cape

8

K   155°   L   160°   M   165°   N   170°   P   175°E   Q   180°   R   175°W   S   170°

55

ASIA

Asia is the largest continent and has 49 countries, including Russia, the biggest country in the world. As well as large land masses, it has thousands of islands and inlets, giving it over 160,000km (100,000 miles) of coastline. Turkey and Russia are part in Europe and part in Asia, but both are shown in full on the map on the right.

The shading on this map is there to help you see clearly the different countries that make up the continent.

This is a type of Chinese boat called a junk, sailing in the sea off Singapore.

ARCTIC OCE

Franz Josef Land

Novaya Zemlya

Barents Sea

■ Moscow

R U

Volga

Ob

Black Sea

■ Ankara

TURKEY

GEORGIA

CYPRUS

ARMENIA

Caspian Sea

AZERBAIJAN

Aral Sea

Astana ■

KAZAKHSTAN

UZBEKISTAN

■ Bishkek

LEBANON
Beirut ■

SYRIA
■ Damascus

TURKMENISTAN

Tashkent ■

KYRGYZSTAN

Jerusalem ■
ISRAEL

■ Amman

Ashgabat ■

Dushanbe ■

JORDAN

■ Baghdad

■ Tehran

TAJIKISTAN

IRAQ

IRAN

Kabul ■

■ Islamabad

Tropic of Cancer

KUWAIT

AFGHANISTAN

PAKISTAN

SAUDI
ARABIA

BAHRAIN
QATAR

Riyadh ■

Doha ■

■ Abu Dhabi

UNITED ARAB
EMIRATES

■ Muscat

New Delhi ■

NEP
Kathma

Indus

Ganges

BA

■ Sana

OMAN

YEMEN

Arabian
Sea

INDIA

Socotra
(Yemen)

INDIAN OCEAN

Equator

SRI L

Sri Jayewardenepura Kotte ■

■ Colomb

MALDIVES
■ Male

56

Wrangel
Island

Bering Sea

New Siberia
Islands

East
Siberian
Sea

aya
a

Laptev
Sea

Lena

Sea of
Okhotsk

Hokkaido

Lake
Baikal

Ulan Bator ■

MONGOLIA

NORTH
KOREA

JAPAN
■Tokyo

Pyongyang■

■Seoul

Beijing ■

Honshu

SOUTH
KOREA

C H I N A

Huang He (Yellow)

East China
Sea

Tropic of Cancer

Chang Jiang (Yangtze)

Taiwan

PACIFIC

OCEAN

RMA
NMAR)

Hanoi ■

LAOS
■Vientiane

South China
Sea

PHILIPPINES

Taw

■Manila

THAILAND

VIETNAM

Philippine
Sea

angkok■

CAMBODIA

man
ds
a)

Phnom ■
Penh

Equator

obar
nds
dia)

MALAYSIA

BRUNEI

■Kuala Lumpur

Putrajaya■

New Guinea

SINGAPORE

Borneo

Celebes

Sumatra

INDONESIA

Dili ■

Arafura Sea

■Jakarta

■EAST
TIMOR

Java

Facts

Total land area 44,537,920 sq km
(17,196,187 sq miles)
Total population 4.3 billion (including
all of Russia)
Biggest city Tokyo, Japan
Biggest country Russia *Total area:*
17,075,200 sq km (6,592,772 sq miles)
Area of Asiatic Russia: 12,780,800 sq km
(4,934,694 sq miles)
Smallest country Maldives *300 sq km*
(116 sq miles)

Highest mountain Mount Everest,
Nepal/China border *8,848m (29,029ft)*
Longest river Chang Jiang (Yangtze),
China *6,380km (3,964 miles)*
Biggest lake Caspian Sea, western Asia
386,400 sq km (149,190 sq miles)
Highest waterfall Jog Falls, on the
Sharavati River, India *253m (830ft)*
Biggest desert Arabian Desert, in and
around Saudi Arabia *2,330,000 sq km*
(900,000 sq miles)
Biggest island Borneo *748,168 sq km*
(288,869 sq miles)

Main mineral deposits Zinc, mica, tin,
chromium, iron, nickel
Main fuel deposits Oil, coal, uranium,
natural gas

These are lotus flowers, a type of
water lily. In China they are
associated with purity and for
Buddhists they are sacred.

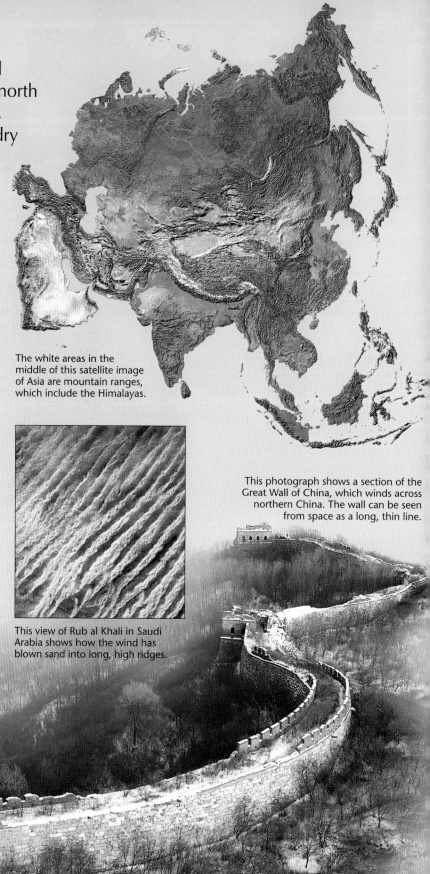

Asia is made up of all kinds of rugged terrain. In the far north are vast, frozen plains, and farther south are dry deserts. Asia also has enormous mountain ranges, including the Himalayas, the world's highest range. Most of Asia's population lives in the far south, which is hot and humid, with lush rainforests.

The white areas in the middle of this satellite image of Asia are mountain ranges, which include the Himalayas.

Empty land

Southern Saudi Arabia has a sandy desert that covers an area about the size of France. It is called Rub al Khali, and is often nicknamed the Empty Quarter as it has hardly any plants or animals and no permanent human settlements. Strong winds blow the sand into mounds that can be more than 330m (1,000ft) high, taller than the Eiffel Tower in Paris.

This view of Rub al Khali in Saudi Arabia shows how the wind has blown sand into long, high ridges.

This photograph shows a section of the Great Wall of China, which winds across northern China. The wall can be seen from space as a long, thin line.

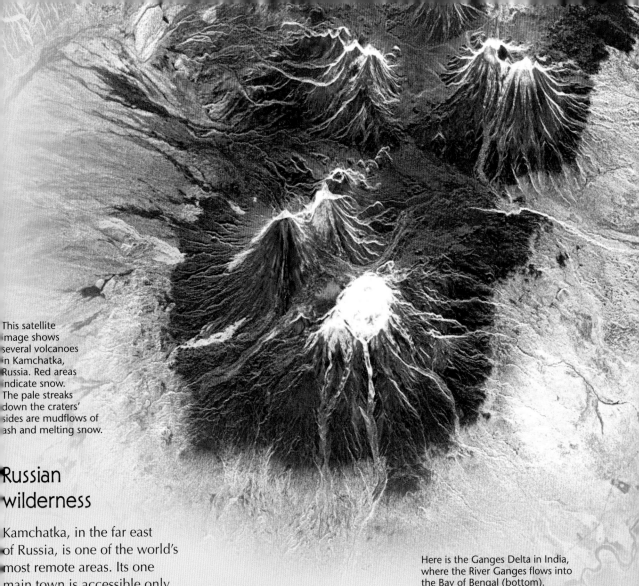

This satellite image shows several volcanoes in Kamchatka, Russia. Red areas indicate snow. The pale streaks down the craters' sides are mudflows of ash and melting snow.

Russian wilderness

Kamchatka, in the far east of Russia, is one of the world's most remote areas. Its one main town is accessible only by air or sea. Much of the land is mountainous, with more than 300 volcanoes. Some of these are active, and they regularly eject boiling rivers of mud and great plumes of steam from their rocky craters.

Internet links

For links to websites where you can find maps and facts about Asia and see panoramic views of the Great Wall of China, go to **www.usborne.com/quicklinks**

A sacred river

The River Ganges begins in the Himalayas and flows through India and Bangladesh to the Indian Ocean. The river is regarded as holy by followers of the Hindu religion. Every day thousands of Hindus bathe in the Ganges, which they believe washes away their sins. People often worship the river by throwing flowers into it or floating oil lamps on its surface.

Here is the Ganges Delta in India, where the River Ganges flows into the Bay of Bengal (bottom).

Much of central and southern Asia is densely populated, so there are many large cities, including Tokyo, the world's most populous city. There are beautiful natural areas too, such as the forests and mountain ranges of China.

A panda climbs a tree in China. Pandas are good climbers, and often rest or sleep high in trees.

Pandas of China

Wild pandas live in the mountainous forests of China. Pandas depend on the bamboo that grows there, as their diet consists almost exclusively of bamboo shoots. But forests are being cut down, so pandas are losing their habitat and food source. There may be as few as 1,000 wild pandas left.

A floating market

Near Bangkok, in Thailand, there is a famous floating market which is held on a canal. Farmers go there daily with fresh fruit and vegetables piled high on narrow boats. Customers weave their way along the busy canal in similar boats, looking for bargains. They must come early, though, as the market begins at about 8 a.m., and everything is sold by 11 a.m.

These women have brought fruit and vegetables to sell at Bangkok's floating market.

Japanese capital

One of Asia's most vibrant cities is Tokyo, the capital of Japan. This big, sprawling city has been rebuilt twice, first in the 1920s when an earthquake destroyed vast areas, and then after the Second World War, when bombs devastated the city. Modern Tokyo is a mixture of a few old streets and many new, towering skyscrapers.

Enormous department stores with glaring neon signs line a street in central Tokyo.

Forbidden City

In the middle of the city of Beijing, in China, is an ancient, walled city. For hundreds of years it was the palace of China's kings, or emperors. It was known as the Forbidden City because no one but the emperor, his family and guests was allowed in its grounds.

China no longer has a royal family, and the Forbidden City is a popular tourist attraction. The city has 800 buildings, including huge temples and elaborate arches, decorated with ornate carvings and grand bronze statues.

Internet links

For links to websites where you can watch video clips about China and Japan, go to **www.usborne.com/quicklinks**

This bronze tortoise stands in Beijing's Forbidden City. According to ancient Chinese beliefs, tortoises were divine animals, and tortoise statues were said to bring good luck.

The countries of western Asia are full of important cultural and historical sights, such as places of worship and the remains of ancient civilizations. The Asian part of Russia stretches far across the continent. It is dominated by the region of Siberia, where the climate is so harsh that most of the land is uninhabited.

This museum in Jerusalem, Israel, houses ancier manuscripts known as the Dead Sea Scrolls.

The Dead Sea

The Dead Sea, in Israel, gets its name because it is so salty that nothing can live in it. However, many people swim in the sea, as its water contains health-giving minerals.

The Dead Sea is also famous for the Dead Sea Scrolls. These are 2,000-year-old Jewish handwritten papers that were discovered in caves by the sea. The scrolls cover mainly religious topics, and have helped historians to learn what life was like in ancient times.

Homes of rock

The region of Cappadocia, near Ankara in central Turkey, has a strange landscape of rocky cones, made of soft volcanic rock. Many hundreds of years ago, people carved caves in the rock, creating whole towns and villages that included houses, stables and even churches. They also built an amazing network of underground tunnels that linked the houses.

These rocky peaks ir Cappadocia, Turkey, were carved out to create rocl houses. Today, they are crumbling away

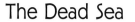

Holy places

Many different religions are followed in Asia, and their various places of worship and study, such as Muslim mosques and Hindu temples, are found in towns and cities all over the continent. Many of these buildings are intricately decorated, for example with huge domes covered in thousands of patterned tiles.

This is the Trans-Siberian Express in Serbia. The train runs from Moscow to Vladivostok, stopping at other stations on the way.

This elaborate, domed building in Esfahan, Iran, is a school for Muslim students.

Russian train trip

Crossing the enormous country of Russia is the Trans-Siberian rail line. This is the longest rail line in the world, running more than 9,000km (5,600 miles) between Moscow in the west and Vladivostok in the east. The line passes through the plains of Siberia, which freeze over in winter. The fastest train trip along the line takes about seven days.

Reindeers

Siberia is home to many reindeers. They have thick fur that keeps them warm in winter, and also have such a good sense of smell that they can sniff out plants to eat that are buried deep under the snow.

Internet links

For links to websites where you can see places of worship and remains of ancient civilizations in Asia, go to **www.usborne.com/quicklinks**

These reindeers are being driven by Siberian herders through western Siberia. Reindeers can easily pull heavy, loaded sleds.

Southern Southeast Asia

▢	Boreal forest
▢	Temperate forest
▢	Tropical forest
▢	Temperate grassland
▢	Savanna
▢	Semi-desert and scrub
▢	Hot desert
▬	International boundary
—	Internal boundary
▲ 2,490m (8,169ft)	Height above or below sea level

▢	Wetland
▢	Mountain
▢	Tundra
▢	Ice
▢	Cultivation
▢	Urban

■	National capital
●	Internal capital
⊙	Major city or town
○	Other town

See also main key on page 17.

1:13,800,000

0   200   400km
0   100   200   300 miles

Grid references: A 100°E, B 105°, C 110°, D 115°

VIETNAM

Qui Nhon
Nha Trang

South Ch... Sea

Spratly Islands

THAILAND
Andaman Sea
Hat Yai
Yala
Alor Setar
Kota Bharu
Banda Aceh
Lhokseumawe
George Town (Penang)
Kuala Terengganu
Taiping
Gunung Tahan ▲ 2,187m (7,175ft)
Ipoh
Langsa
Kuantan
Medan
MALAYSIA
Pematangsiantar
Putrajaya ■
Kuala Lumpur ■
Seremban
Lake Toba
Melaka
Sibolga
Strait of Malacca
Johor Bahru
Singapore ■
SINGAPORE
Simeulue
Nias
Pekanbaru
Riau Islands
Equator 0°
Sumatra
Padango
Gunung Kerinci ▲ 3,805m (12,483ft)
Jambi
Bangka
Pangkalpinang
Mentawai Islands
Palembang
Belitung
Bengkulu
Lahat
Baturaja
Tanjungkarang-Telukbetung
Krakatoa ▲ 813m (2,667ft)
Serang
Jakarta ■
Bogor
Bandung
Cilacap
Java

Natuna Islands
Anambas Islands
Kuching
Borneo
Pontianak
Palangkaraya
Banjarmasin
Martapura

Kota Kinabalu
Bandar Seri Begawan
BRUNEI
Miri
Bintulu
Sibu
Tanju...
▲ 2,988m (9,803ft)
Sama...
Balikpa...

Greater Sunda Islan...
INDONESI...
Java Sea
Tegal
Semarang
Surakarta
Surabaya
Yogyakarta
Jember
Malang
Bali
Denpasar
Le...
Lor...

INDIAN OCEAN

Christmas Island (Australia)

A 100°E   B 105°   C 110°   D 115°

A 90°E B 95° C 100° D 105° E

Brahmaputra o Lhasa *Chengdu* o Wanxian

H i m a l a y a s **Gongga Shan** ▲ Leshan o Neijiang o o Chongqir

2 **Mount Everest** 7,556m o Luzhou o Chongqir
8,848m (24,790ft) o Xichang Yibin o
(29,029ft) **Thimphu** o Zhaotong o Zunyi
NEPAL o Darjeeling **BHUTAN** o Panzhihua o Guiyang
o Biratnagar **INDIA** *Brahmaputra* o Dibrugarh o Anshun

o Darbhanga o Rangpur o Jorhat o Guwahati o Kunming
25° o Bhagalpur o Shillong *Red* o Kaiyuan
N Rangpur *Ganges* o Rajshahi Sylhet o o Dali o Gejiu
o Asansol **BANGLADESH** o Imphal o Baoshan o Ha Giang Lao Cai o
o Jamshedpur **Dhaka** ■ o Myitkyina o Phongsali Thai Nguyen o Qinzho
o Kolkata o Khulna o Aizawl Son La o o Qinzho
(Calcutta) o Chittagong o Lashio o Simao o Son La
3 *Mouths of the Ganges* o Monywa **Mandalay** o Louangphrabang ■ **Hanoi**
o Mandalay **Mount** o Meiktila o Taunggyi Hai Phong
20° **Victoria** o Sittwe ▲ o Thanh Hoa
3,053m **BURMA** (10,016ft) **(MYANMAR)** *Mekong* **LAOS** *Gulf of*
Nay Pyi Taw ■ o Pye *Salween* o Chiang Mai *Tonkin*
o Sandoway *Irrawaddy* **Vientiane** ■ o Vinh
4 o Henzada o Pegu o Thaton o Udon Thani o Savannakhet
o Pathein o Moulmein o Phitsanulok o Khon o Hue
Rangoon ■ Kaen o Pakxe D
15° *Mouths of the* o Nakhon Sawan o Ubon
Irrawaddy **THAILAND** Ratchathanio o Attapu
o Tavoy o Nakhon Ratchasima

I N D I A N o Pattaya ■ **Bangkok** Angkor ☩ Stoeng Treng o **VIE**
O C E A N *Tonle Sap* Qui
5 *Andaman* o Mergui o Batdambang **CAMBODIA** Bu
Islands *Andaman* o Pattaya Kampong o Th
(India) *Sea* Chhnang Kampong o o Da Lat
o Port Blair o Prachuap Cham o Bien Hoa
Little Khiri Khan Krong **Phnom** o Ho Chi Mir
Andaman o Kaoh Kong **Penh** ■ (Saigor
10° *Ten Degree Channel* o Chumphon o Kampong Saom o Long Xuyen *Mekong*
Mergui o Can Tho
Archipelago *Gulf of Thailand* o Bac Lieu

6 *Nicobar Islands* o Nakhon Si *Con Son*
(India) Thammarat

o Hat Yai
o Yala
5° o Banda Aceh o Alor Setar o Kota Bharu
o Lhokseumawe o George Town o Kuala Terengganu
7 *Sumatra* (Penang) **Gunung**
INDONESIA o Langsa o Taiping o Ipoh **Tahan** ▲ **MALAYSIA** Nat
2,187m Isla
(7,175ft) (Indo

A 90°E B 95° C 100° D 105° E

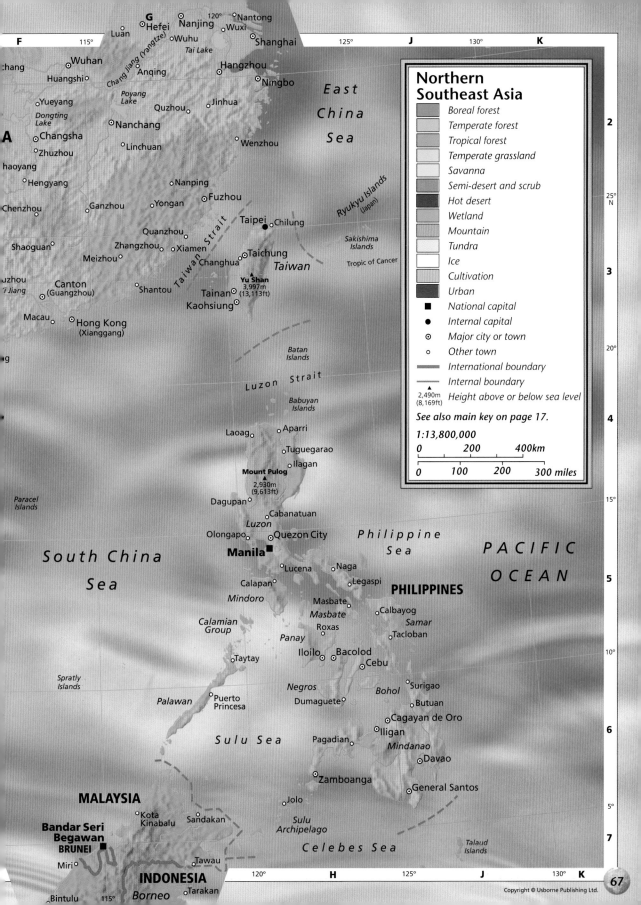

A 80°E B 85° C 90° D 95° E 100° F 105° G

KAZAKHSTAN

Bulgan

Ulan Bat

Karamay

Almaty

Yining

Kuytun

Dzungarian Basin

Altay

MONGOLIA

Lake Issyk

Shihezi

Urumqi

KYRGYZSTAN

▲ Pik Pobedy
7,439m
(24,406ft)

Aksu

Turpan

Bosten Lake

▲ -154m
(-505ft)

Turpan Depression

Hami

T i e n   S h a n

Altai Mountains

Korla

Gobi Desert

Baotou

Wuhai

Tarim Basin

Lop Lake

Mogao Caves

Yumen

The Great Wall of China

Taklimakan Desert

Hotan

Altun Mountains

▲ 5,547m
(18,199ft)

Yinchuan

Kunlun Mountains

Qaidam Basin

Golmud

Qinghai Lake

Xining

Huang He (Yellow)

Lanzhou

CHINA

Plateau of Tibet

Baoji

Mour (Terra

Xian

Siling Lake

Yushu

TIBET

Nam Lake

Brahmaputra

Shiyar

NEPAL

Himalayas

Lhasa

Chang Jiang (Yangtze)

Salween

Mekong

Kathmandu

Chengdu

Yicha

▲ Mount Everest
8,848m
(29,029ft)

Thimphu

Gongga Shan
▲ 7,556m
(24,790ft)

Chongqing

Darbhanga

Darjeeling

BHUTAN

Leshan

Cha

Patna

Biratnagar

Brahmaputra

Dibrugarh

Xichang

Luzhou

Chang Jiang (Yangtze)

Bhagalpur

Rangpur

Guwahati

Zunyi

Hu

INDIA

Shillong

Panzhihua

Guiyang

Ranchi

Asansol

Rajshahi

Sylhet

Imphal

Dali

Tropic of Cancer

BANGLADESH

Myitkyina

Kunming

Dhaka

Aizawl

Liuzho

Kolkata
(Calcutta)

Khulna

Lashio

Red

Gejiu

Wuz

Chittagong

Monywa

Mandalay

Simao

Nanning

Cuttack

Mouths of the Ganges

▲ Mount Victoria
3,053m
(10,016ft)

Lao Cai

Yul

Bay of Bengal

**BURMA
(MYANMAR)**

Taunggyi

Phongsali

Son La

Thai Nguyen

Hanoi

Sittwe

Irrawaddy

Mekong

Hai Phong

Gulf of Tonkin

Ha

Nay Pyi Taw

**INDIAN
OCEAN**

Sandoway

Pye

Salween

Louangphrabang

Thanh Hoa

Henzada

Chiang Mai

LAOS

VIETNAM

Pathein

Pegu

THAILAND

Vientiane

Vinh

Rangoon

Udon Thani

Sanya

68

C 90°E D Mouths of the Irrawaddy

Moulmein

F 100° G 105° 110°

95°

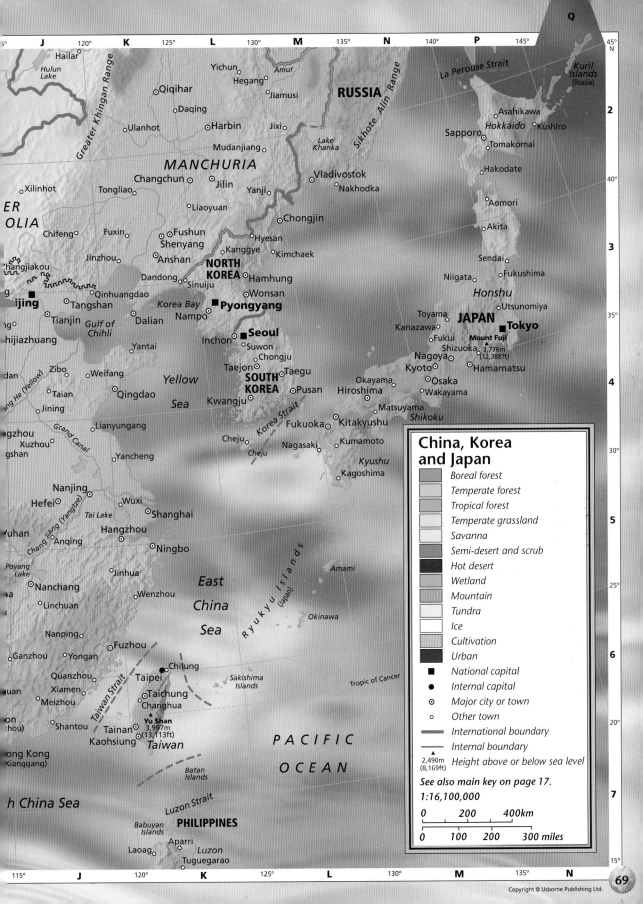

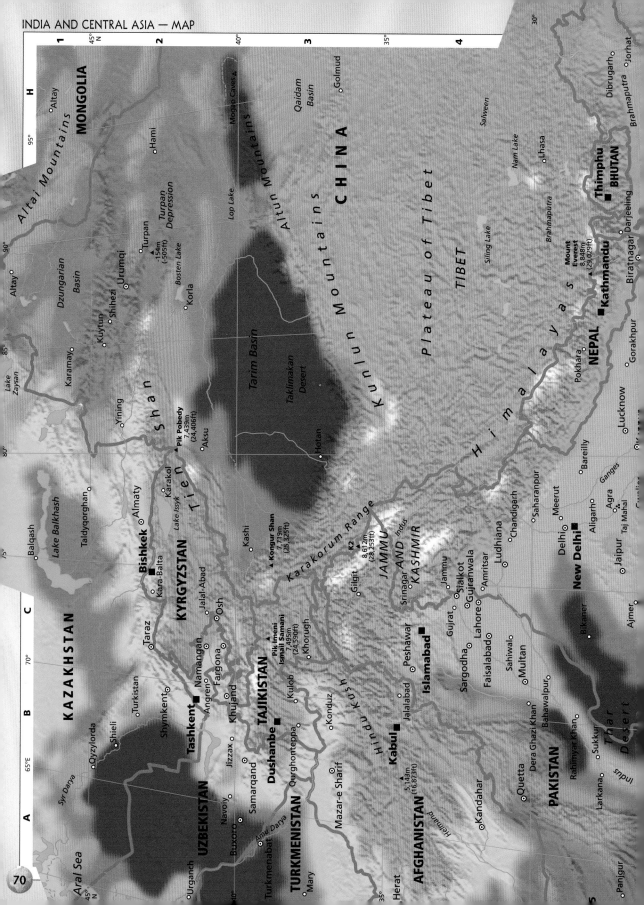

India and
Central Asia

Boreal forest
Temperate forest
Tropical forest
Temperate grassland
Savanna
Semi-desert and scrub
Hot desert
Wetland
Mountain
Tundra
Ice
Cultivation
Urban

■ National capital
● Internal capital
◉ Major city or town
○ Other town
─ International boundary
── Internal boundary
▲ 2,490m (8,169ft) Height above or below sea level

See also main key on page 17.

1:13,800,000

0 100 200 300 400km
0   100   200   300 miles

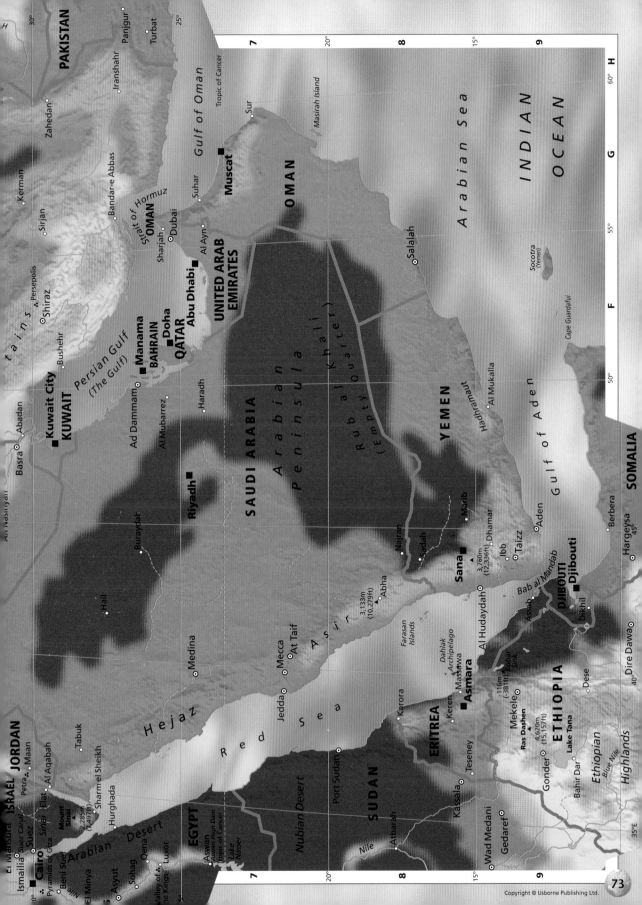

PAKISTAN

Panjgur
Turbat
Iranshahr
Zahedan
Kerman
Sirjan
Shiraz
Persepolis
Bushehr
Bandar-e Abbas

Gulf of Oman
Tropic of Cancer
Masirah Island

Sur
Suhar
Muscat
OMAN
Strait of Hormuz
Dubai
Sharjah
OMAN
Al Ayn

Arabian Sea

INDIAN OCEAN

Salalah
Socotra (Yemen)
Cape Guardafui

ISRAEL
JORDAN
Ismailia
El Mansura
Suez Canal
Suez
Sinai
Eilat
Al Aqabah
Petra
Maan
Tabuk
Sharm el Sheikh
Hurghada
Mount Sinai
2,285m (7,497ft)
Qena
Luxor
Valley of the Kings
Asyut
Sohag
Beni Suef
El Minya
Cairo
Pyramids of Giza
Aswan
Aswan High Dam
Tropic of Cancer
Lake Nasser

EGYPT
Arabian Desert
Nile
Nubian Desert

SUDAN
Port Sudan
Atbarah
Wad Medani
Gedaref
Kassala
Atbarah
Nile

Abadan
Basra
Kuwait City
KUWAIT
Kuwait City
Ad Dammam
Al Mubarrez
Haradh

Persian Gulf (The Gulf)
Manama
BAHRAIN
Doha
QATAR
Abu Dhabi
UNITED ARAB EMIRATES

SAUDI ARABIA
Riyadh
Buraydah
Hail
Medina
Mecca
At Taif
Jedda
3,133m (10,279ft)
Abha

Arabian Peninsula

Rub al Khali (Empty Quarter)

Najran
Sadah
Marib
Sana
3,760m (12,336ft)
Dhamar
Ibb
Taizz
Aden
Al Mukalla
Hadhramaut

YEMEN

Asir
Hejaz
Red Sea
Farasan Islands
Dahlak Archipelago
Al Hudaydah
Bab al Mandab
Assab

Gulf of Aden

Berbera
Hargeysa

SOMALIA

Djibouti
DJIBOUTI
Dikhil
-116m (-381ft) Kobar Sink
Mekele
4,620m (15,157ft)
Ras Dashen
Gonder
Bahir Dar
Lake Tana
Dese
Dire Dawa

ETHIOPIA
Ethiopian Highlands
Blue Nile

ERITREA
Asmara
Keren
Karora
Teseney
Massawa

73

A
B
C
D

1
2

60°
80°
20°
40°
60°

UNITED
KINGDOM
London

*North
Sea*

*Norwegian
Sea*

Arctic Circle

Svalbard
(Norway)

A R

Franz Josef
Land

Paris

NETHERLANDS
BELGIUM
LUXEMBOURG
FRANCE

DENMARK

NORWAY
Oslo

SWEDEN

North Cape

*Barents
Sea*

Novaya
Zemlya

GERMANY
Berlin

Stockholm

FINLAND

Murmansk

*Kola
Peninsula*

*Kara
Sea*

3

*Baltic
Sea*

Helsinki

CZECH
REPUBLIC
AUSTRIA
POLAND
SLOVAKIA
Budapest
HUNGARY

LITHUANIA
Warsaw
LATVIA
Vilnius

ESTONIA

Lake
Ladoga

St. Petersburg

Lake
Onega

Arkhangelsk

Vorkuta

Minsk
BELARUS

Lviv

Cherepovets

Ukhta

ROMANIA
Kiev
MOLDOVA
Chisinau
UKRAINE

Moscow

Ryazan

Nizhniy Novgorod

Volga

Ural Mountains

Ob

Novyy Urengoy

West Siberian

Odesa
Kharkiv

Voronezh

Kazan

Perm

Plain

Dnipropetrovsk

Simferopol

Samara

Yekaterinburg

Surgut

Ob

Yenisey

40°
N

*Black
Sea*

Rostov

Volgograd
Krasnodar

Oral

Orenburg

Chelyabinsk

Irtysh

R U

Tomsk
Kra

Ankara

TURKEY

Mount Elbrus
5,642m
(18,510ft)

Astrakhan

Aqtobe

Omsk

Novosibirsk

Adana

GEORGIA

Atyrau

KAZAKHSTAN

Pavlodar

Barnaul

Tbilisi

Aqtau

Astana

ARMENIA
Yerevan

*Caspian
Sea*

*Aral
Sea*

Qaraghandy

Oskemen

Altay

SYRIA

AZERBAIJAN
Baku

Nukus

Qyzylorda

Balqash

Mosul

Tabriz

Dasoguz

UZBEKISTAN

Lake
Balkhash

4

Baghdad

IRAQ

Tehran

Damavand
5,604m
(18,386ft)

TURKMENISTAN

Shymkent

Almaty

Urumc

Ashgabat
(Ashkhabad)

Tashkent

BISHKEK
KYRGYZSTAN

Tien Shan

Ahvaz

Esfahan

Turkmenabat

Samarqand

Osh

Aksu

Mashhad

Dushanbe

Tarim Basin

Kuwait City
KUWAIT

IRAN

TAJIKISTAN

Teklimakan Desert

SAUDI
ARABIA

Shiraz

Herat

Mazar-e Sharif

Hotan

Riyadh

Manama

AFGHANISTAN

QATAR
Doha

Bandar-e
Abbas

Zahedan

Kabul

Kandahar

Islamabad

K2
8,612m
(28,253ft)

Srinagar

Abu Dhabi

PAKISTAN

Indus

Lahore

INDIA

Plateau of Tibet

C
D
E

60°E
80°

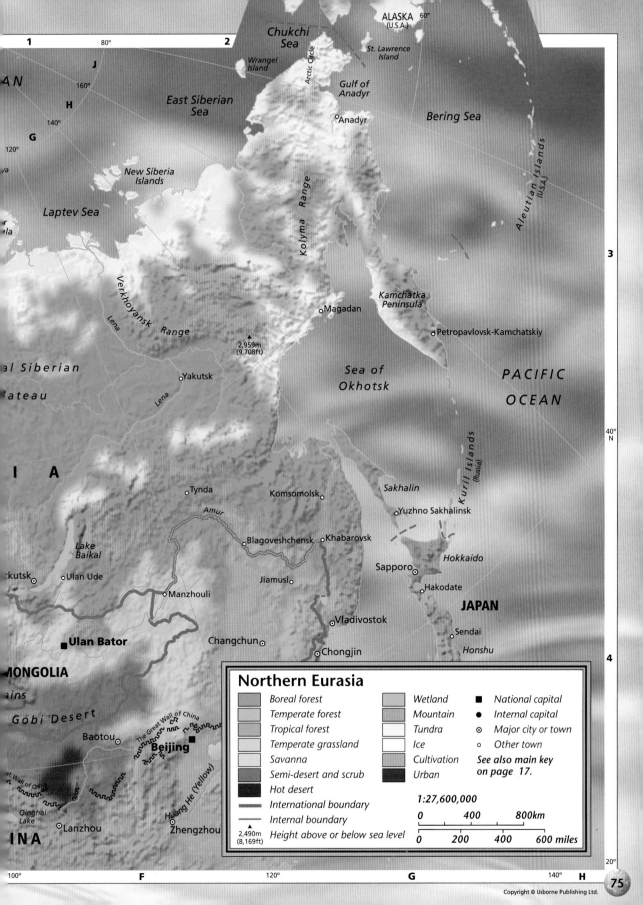

ALASKA 60°
(U.S.A.)

Chukchi Sea

Wrangel Island
St. Lawrence Island

Gulf of Anadyr

East Siberian Sea

Bering Sea

Anadyr

New Siberia Islands

Laptev Sea

Aleutian Islands (U.S.A.)

Kolyma Range

Verkhoyansk Range

Lena

Magadan

Kamchatka Peninsula

2,959m (9,708ft)

Petropavlovsk-Kamchatskiy

al Siberian lateau

Yakutsk

Lena

Sea of Okhotsk

PACIFIC OCEAN

40° N

Kuril Islands (Russia)

I A

Tynda

Komsomolsk

Sakhalin

Amur

Yuzhno Sakhalinsk

Lake Baikal

Blagoveshchensk
Khabarovsk

Hokkaido

Jiamusi

Sapporo

kutsk
Ulan Ude

Manzhouli

Hakodate

JAPAN

Vladivostok

Sendai

Ulan Bator

Changchun

Chongjin

Honshu

MONGOLIA

ins

Gobi Desert

The Great Wall of China

Baotou

Beijing

t Wall of China

Qinghai Lake

Lanzhou

Huang He (Yellow)

Zhengzhou

INA

Northern Eurasia

Boreal forest
Temperate forest
Tropical forest
Temperate grassland
Savanna
Semi-desert and scrub
Hot desert

Wetland
Mountain
Tundra
Ice
Cultivation
Urban

■ National capital
● Internal capital
⊙ Major city or town
○ Other town

See also main key on page 17.

International boundary
Internal boundary
▲ 2,490m (8,169ft) Height above or below sea level

1:27,600,000

0   400   800km

0   200   400   600 miles

20°

1   80°   2

J
H
140°
G
120°

100°   F   120°   G   140°   H   75°

EUROPE

Europe is a small continent, but it holds 50 countries and more than 700 million people. Russia is an enormous country, spanning two continents. Its western part is in Europe, while its eastern part is in Asia. The European part of Russia is larger than any other country in Europe.

The shading on this map is there to help you see clearly the different countries that make up the continent.

Arctic Circle

ARCTIC OCEAN

Reykjavik
■ **ICELAND**

Norwegian
Sea

Faroe Islands
(Denmark)

SW

Shetland
Islands

NORWAY

Oslo ■

Orkney
Islands

Stock▶

North
Sea

DENMARK
Copenhagen ■

IRELAND
Dublin ■

UNITED
KINGDOM

The
Hague ■
London ■

■ **Amsterdam**
NETHERLANDS

Berlin ■

Brussels ■
BELGIUM

GERMANY

LUXEMBOURG
■ **Luxembourg**

Prague ■

CZE
REPU

Paris ■

Rhine

Vienna
Bratisla

ATLANTIC

OCEAN

Bay
of
Biscay

FRANCE

LIECHTENSTEIN
Bern ■ ■**Vaduz** **AUSTRIA** **B**
SWITZERLAND

SLOVENIA
Ljubljana ■

■ **Z**
C

MONACO

ANDORRA ■
Andorra
la Vella

SAN MARINO ■

BOSN
HERZE
Sar.

PORTUGAL

Lisbon ■

■ **Madrid**

SPAIN

Corsica

ITALY

MO

Po
Rome ■ **VATICAN CITY**

Balearic
Islands

Sardinia

Mediterranean Sea

Sicily

■ **MALTA**
Valletta

Barents Sea

Murmansk

Arctic Circle

Arkhangelsk

FINLAND

R U S S I A

St. Petersburg

Tallinn
TONIA

Nizhniy Novgorod   Kazan

LATVIA

Moscow

NIA
ius

Volga

Minsk
BELARUS

Kiev
Dnieper   Volgograd

UKRAINE

MOLDOVA

Chisinau

OMANIA

Bucharest

Black Sea

anube

BULGARIA
Sofia
e
IA   **TURKEY**

Athens

Crete

Facts

Total land area *10,180,000 sq km (3,930,520 sq miles) (including European Russia)*
Total population *742 million (including all of Russia)*
Biggest city Moscow, Russia
Biggest country Russia *Total area: 17,075,200 sq km (6,592,772 sq miles) Area of European Russia: 4,294,400 sq km (1,658,077 sq miles)*
Smallest country Vatican City *0.44 sq km (0.17 sq miles)*

Highest mountain Mount Elbrus, Russia *5,642m (18,510ft)*
Longest river Volga *3,692km (2,294 miles)*
Biggest lake Lake Ladoga, Russia *17,700 sq km (6,834 sq miles)*
Highest waterfall Vinnufossen, Norway *865m (2,837ft)*
Biggest desert No deserts in Europe
Biggest island Great Britain *209,331 sq km (80,823 sq miles)*

Main mineral deposits Bauxite, zinc, iron, potash, fluorspar
Main fuel deposits Oil, coal, natural gas, peat, uranium

A dairy cow in Devon, in the south of England

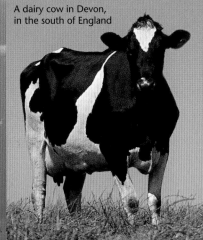

Europe has lots of islands and many of its countries are largely surrounded by sea. The Alps, one of Europe's principal mountain ranges, lies in the west, and is the source of many of its major rivers, including the Rhine and the Rhone.

Europe by night

Satellite pictures taken at night show how much light is being generated in different areas. Highly populated areas, such as Europe, where there are many big cities, light up brightly at night. This is because when many people live in one area, the combined lights of all the buildings at night are so bright they show up as a dot.

This is a satellite image of Mount Vesuvius, a volcano in southern Italy. The black dot in the middle is the crater

Mount Vesuvius

Mount Vesuvius is a volcano near the city of Naples in southern Italy. It is famous for its eruption in AD79, which buried the towns of Pompeii and Herculaneum in around 30m (100ft) of ash, mud and stones. The towns remained buried until the 18th century when they were rediscovered.

Vesuvius is monitored very carefully today, as it is close to the city of Naples and more than four million people live nearby. It has had over 50 minor eruptions since the one in AD79.

This satellite image of Europe was taken at night, but the land and water have been falsely-shaded, so you can see their outlines clearly. Each blue dot represents a highly populated area that is lit up.

Internet links

For links to websites where you can explore Europe's landscapes and find out more about Mount Vesuvius' famous eruption, go to **www.usborne.com/quicklinks**

This area of the Alps is in Switzerland. Over 70% of Switzerland is mountainous.

The Rhine River

The Rhine River carries more traffic than any other river in the world. It is 1,320km (820 miles) long and winds through the west of Europe, flowing from the Alps in Switzerland, along the Swiss-Austrian border, through Germany and France to the Netherlands. Many cities lie along its banks, including Strasbourg, in France, and Cologne, in Germany.

This is a section of the Rhine River running through west Germany. The river is black, vegetation is blue and buildings are brown. The patchwork of rectangles to the east of the river is farmland.

Norwegian fjords

Norway's dramatic coastline is a mixture of steep mountains and long, thin inlets of water, called fjords. The fjords were formed by glaciers. When glacier ice builds up at the top of a mountain, it becomes heavy and starts to slide down the slopes, carving out a deep channel in the rock. When the glacier melts, the water fills the channel, making a fjord.

The satellite image below shows an area of Norway's coastline. The long, thin blue strips are inlets of water, called fjords.

Eastern Europe stretches as far as the Ural Mountains, which separate European Russia from Asian Russia. Northern Europe is made up of Iceland and the Scandinavian countries, including Norway and Sweden.

Onion-shaped domes

Early Russian churches have an easily recognizable style, with high walls, very few doors and windows, and steeply-sloped roofs topped with onion-shaped domes. This style became popular during the 11th century. Many of these early churches were built from wood, as it was a building material widely available from Russia's dense forests.

This is the Church of the Intercession on Kizhi Island in northern Russia. It was built almost entirely from wood in 1764.

This is a Viking helmet. It was discovered in a grave in Uppland, Sweden.

Viking lands

During the 9th to the 11th centuries the Vikings, a group of master ship builders and sea traders from Scandinavia, dominated northern Europe. Viking heritage can still be seen today. The Vikings carved stories and pictures into large stones, called rune stones. Many of these stones have survived and give clues to how they lived. The Viking Ship Museum in Oslo, Norway, has three well-preserved Viking ships, and in Sweden, a Viking festival is held each year in a reconstructed Viking village.

In this dramatic image of Budapest you can see the Chain Bridge, which links Buda and Pest across the Danube River.

Internet links

For links to websites where you can find out about the Vikings, go to **www.usborne.com/quicklinks**

Danube River

The Danube River flows from the west to the east of Europe, through many major cities, including Bratislava, the capital of Slovakia, and Budapest, the capital of Hungary. The river splits Budapest into two parts, Buda and Pest. The Royal Palace, is in Buda, on the west bank, while Hungary's parliament building is in Pest, on the east bank.

Atlantic puffins

One type of bird common throughout northern Europe is the Atlantic puffin. Atlantic puffins are sea birds that live in the cold waters around the coasts of the North Atlantic Ocean.

Atlantic puffins are very skilled at diving underwater to catch fish to eat. They only come ashore once a year to nest on rocky cliff tops and grassy islands. Iceland has the largest puffin population in the world at around nine million.

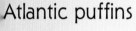

These are Atlantic puffins. They are about 18cm (10in) tall and have yellow, orange and blue beaks, which is why they are also known as sea parrots.

The west of Europe stretches as far as Portugal on the Atlantic coast, while southern Europe reaches down to the many small islands in the Mediterranean Sea, where the climate is famously sunny, warm and dry.

Sights of London

There are many famous sights in London, from the huge clock tower of Big Ben to Buckingham Palace, the official residency of the Queen.

One of the city's most recent additions is the London Eye, the world's largest Ferris wheel, which was constructed to mark the millennium. The top of the wheel is 135m (443ft) high, giving an impressive view of the city.

The London Eye sits on the south bank of the River Thames. Big Ben sits on the opposite bank.

Internet links

For links to websites where you can find sightseeing guides to the countries and famous landmarks of Europe, go to **www.usborne.com/quicklinks**

Eiffel Tower

The Eiffel Tower in Paris, France, was opened in 1889, and has since had over 200 million visitors. It was built for an international exhibition celebrating the scientific and engineering achievements of the time. The iron structure is around 300m (980ft) tall and has three levels with many shops and restaurants.

There are over 350 electric lamps fitted to the outside of the Eiffel Tower, lighting it up dramatically at night.

The Leaning Tower

One of Italy's most famous sights is the Leaning Tower of Pisa. The 55m (180ft) tall bell tower is part of Pisa Cathedral. Building work began on it in 1173, and the tower started to lean while it was being built. It leans because the ground beneath it is a mixture of sand and clay, which are easily compressed. The huge weight of the tower compressed the ground more in some areas than others, so the tower began to lean.

This marble statue of a discus thrower is a copy of a bronze statue from 5th-century Greece. The statue, housed in the National Museum in Rome, Italy, is a symbol of the Olympic games.

Home of the Olympics

Athletes from all over the world compete in the Olympic games every four years. The first Olympic games were held in celebration of the Greek god Zeus in Olympia, Greece, in 776BC. Today, some of the foundations, steps and pillars of the original stadium, which seated around 30,000 spectators, remain. The start and finish lines of the running track, and the judges' seats, have also survived.

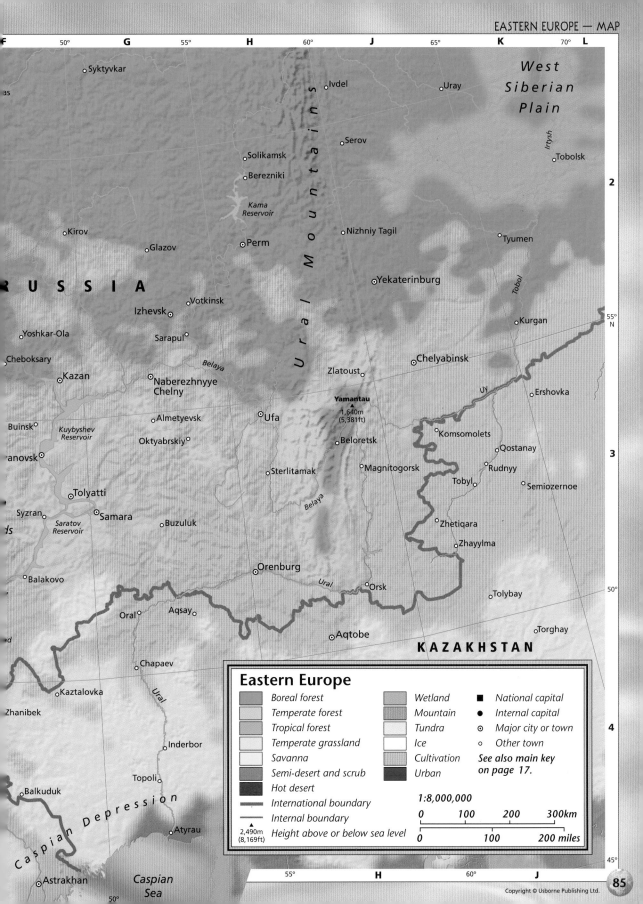

RUSSIA

KAZAKHSTAN

West Siberian Plain

Ural Mountains

Caspian Depression

Caspian Sea

Syktyvkar
Ivdel
Uray
Serov
Solikamsk
Berezniki
Tobolsk
Kama Reservoir
Kirov
Glazov
Perm
Nizhniy Tagil
Tyumen
Yekaterinburg
Votkinsk
Izhevsk
Sarapul
Belaya
Kurgan
Yoshkar-Ola
Cheboksary
Zlatoust
Chelyabinsk
Kazan
Naberezhnyye Chelny
Ershovka
Uy
Tobol
Almetyevsk
Ufa
Yamantau ▲ 1,640m (5,381ft)
Komsomolets
Buinsk
Kuybyshev Reservoir
Oktyabrskiy
Beloretsk
Qostanay
...anovsk
Sterlitamak
Magnitogorsk
Rudnyy
Semiozernoe
Tolyatti
Belaya
Tobyl
Syzran
Saratov Reservoir
Samara
Buzuluk
Zhetiqara
Zhayylma
Orenburg
Ural
Orsk
Tolybay
Balakovo
Oral
Aqsay
Aqtobe
Torghay
Chapaev
Ural
Kaztalovka
Zhanibek
Inderbor
Topoli
Balkuduk
Atyrau
Astrakhan

Eastern Europe

▇ Boreal forest	▇ Wetland
▇ Temperate forest	▇ Mountain
▇ Tropical forest	▇ Tundra
▇ Temperate grassland	▇ Ice
▇ Savanna	▇ Cultivation
▇ Semi-desert and scrub	▇ Urban
▇ Hot desert	

■ National capital
● Internal capital
◉ Major city or town
○ Other town

See also main key on page 17.

━━ International boundary
─── Internal boundary
▲ 2,490m (8,169ft) Height above or below sea level

1:8,000,000

0   100   200   300km

0   100   200 miles

Barents Sea

Kola Peninsula

White Sea

Arctic Circle

North Cape

RUSSIA

Vadso
Severomorsk
Murmansk
Kirkenes
Utsjoki
Sevettijärvi
Kaamanen
Monchegorsk
▲1,191m (3,907ft)
Apatity
Kandalaksha
Belomorsk
Lake Vyg
Lake Onega
Medvezhyegorsk
Petrozavodsk
St. Petersburg
Volkhov
Tikhvin
Kirishi
Pushkin
Gatchina
Zelenogorsk
Vyborg
Kingisepp
Narva
Tallinn

Lake Top
Lake Kuyto
Kostomuksha
Lake Seg
Lake Pya
Lake Ladoga

Hammerfest
Soroya
Alta
Tromso

Lapland

Lokan Reservoir
Lake Inari
Sodankyla
Kuusamo
Kuhmo
Lieksa
Pielis Lake
Kuopio
Hauki Lake
Varkaus
Puula Lake
Saimaa Lake
Pihlaja Lake
Lappeenranta
Kouvola
Kotka
Helsinki
Espoo
Gulf of Finland

Rovaniemi
Kajaani
Oulu Lake
Kiuruvesi
Jyvaskyla
Mikkeli
Pajanne Lake
Lahti

FINLAND

Oulu
Raahe
Kokkola
Saarijarvi
Alavus
Hameenlinna
Tampere
Turku

Tornio
Kurikka
Vaasa
Nasi Lake
Pori
Rauma

Kiruna
Boden
Skelleftea
Umea
Aland Islands
Gulf of Bothnia

Narvik
Kebnekaise ▲2,114m (6,935ft)
Svolvaer
Horn Lake
Storavan Lake
Stora Lule Lake
Lule Lake
Ume
Sundsvall
Hudiksvall
Gavle
Uppsala
Eskilstuna
Stockholm

Vesteralen
Lofoten
Bodo
Moi Rana

Storuman

Ostersund
Indals
Stor Lake
Borlange
Karlstad
Orebro

SWEDEN

Namsos
Steinkjer
Trondheim
Oppdal
Lillehammer
Glama
Dal
Klar

Norwegian Sea

Vikna
Froya
Hitra
Smola
Kristiansund
Alesund
Oppdal
Honefoss
Drammen
Oslo
Fredrikstad

NORWAY
Galdhopiggen ▲2,469m (8,100ft)

Bergen
Odda
Sula
Sotra
Stavanger
Karmoy

ICELAND

Langanes
Seydhisfjordhur
Siglufjordhur
Vatnajokull
Hvannadalshnukur ▲2,119m (6,952ft)
Reykjavik
Faxafloi
Keflavik
Isafjordhur
ATLANTIC OCEAN
Arctic Circle
Same scale as main map

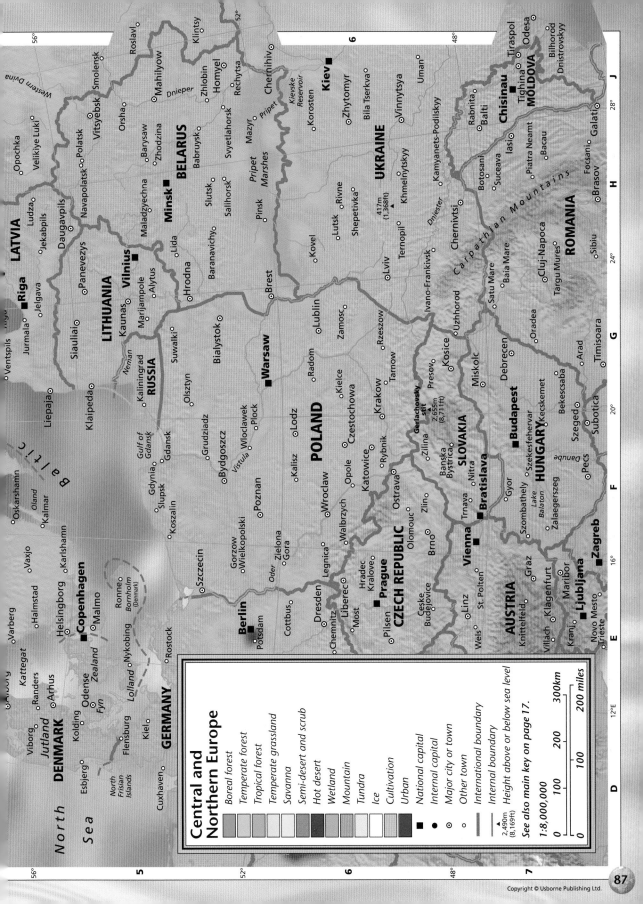

Central and Northern Europe

Legend:
- Boreal forest
- Temperate forest
- Tropical forest
- Temperate grassland
- Savanna
- Semi-desert and scrub
- Hot desert
- Wetland
- Mountain
- Tundra
- Ice
- Cultivation
- Urban
- National capital
- Internal capital
- Major city or town
- Other town
- International boundary
- Internal boundary
- 2,490m (8,165ft) Height above or below sea level

See also main key on page 17.

1:8,000,000

0 100 200 300km
0 100 200 miles

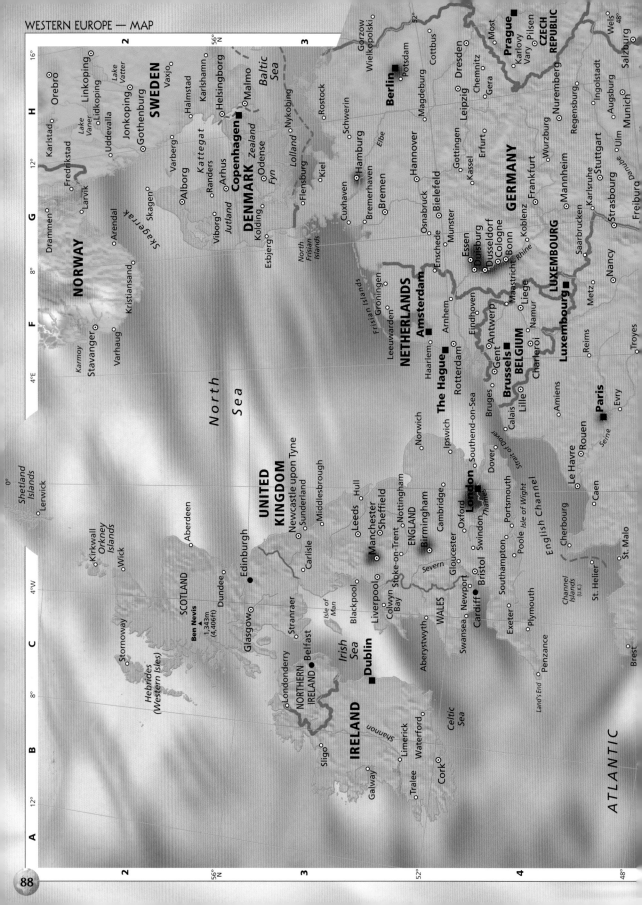

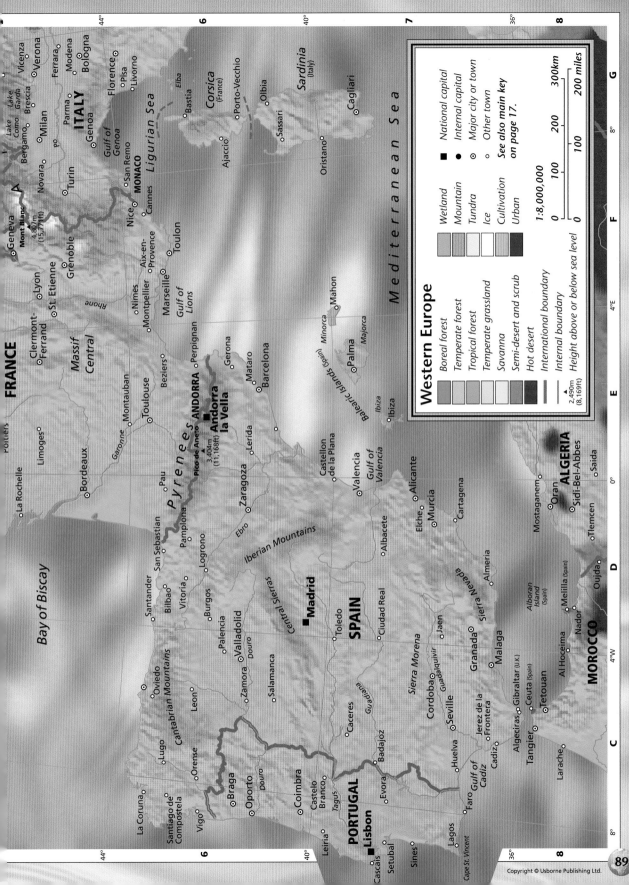

Western Europe

Legend:

- ■ National capital
- ● Internal capital
- ◎ Major city or town
- ○ Other town
- *See also main key on page 17.*

1:8,000,000

Scale:
0 100 200 300km
0 100 200 miles

Land types:
- Boreal forest
- Temperate forest
- Tropical forest
- Temperate grassland
- Savanna
- Semi-desert and scrub
- Hot desert

- Wetland
- Mountain
- Tundra
- Ice
- Cultivation
- Urban

International boundary
Internal boundary

▲ 2,490m (8,169ft) Height above or below sea level

Map labels

FRANCE

Pontivy
La Rochelle
Limoges
Bordeaux
Clermont-Ferrand
Massif Central
Lyon
St-Etienne
Geneva
Mont Blanc 4,807m (15,771ft)
Grenoble
Aix-en-Provence
Nîmes
Montpellier
Marseille
Toulon
Gulf of Lions
Perpignan
Beziers
Toulouse
Montauban
Garonne
Pau
Pamplona
Rhône
Nice
Cannes
San Remo
MONACO
Gulf of Genoa
Ligurian Sea

ITALY

Turin
Novara
Milan
Bergamo
Brescia
Lake Como
Lake Garda
Vicenza
Verona
Ferrara
Modena
Bologna
Parma
Po
Genoa
Pisa
Livorno
Florence
Elba
Bastia
Corsica (France)
Ajaccio
Porto-Vecchio
Olbia
Sassari
Sardinia (Italy)
Oristano
Cagliari

Mediterranean Sea

Pyrenees
Pico de Aneto 3,404m (11,168ft)
ANDORRA
Andorra la Vella
Gerona
Mataro
Barcelona
Lerida
Zaragoza
Ebro
Iberian Mountains
Castellon de la Plana
Valencia
Gulf of Valencia
Balearic Islands (Spain)
Minorca
Mahon
Majorca
Palma
Ibiza
Ibiza

SPAIN

Bay of Biscay
San Sebastian
Bilbao
Santander
Vitoria
Logroño
Burgos
Palencia
Valladolid
Cantabrian Mountains
Oviedo
Leon
Zamora
Salamanca
Douro
Central Sierras
Madrid
Toledo
Ciudad Real
Albacete
Elche
Murcia
Cartagena
Alicante
Almeria
Sierra Nevada
Granada
Malaga
Jaen
Cordoba
Guadalquivir
Seville
Sierra Morena
Guadiana
Caceres
Badajoz
Ciudad Real

PORTUGAL

La Coruña
Santiago de Compostela
Vigo
Lugo
Orense
Braga
Oporto
Douro
Coimbra
Castelo Branco
Evora
Tagus
Lisbon
Cascais
Setubal
Sines
Lagos
Cape St. Vincent
Leiria
Faro
Gulf of Cadiz
Huelva
Cadiz
Jerez de la Frontera
Algeciras
Gibraltar (U.K.)
Ceuta (Spain)
Tangier
Larache

MOROCCO

Tetouan
Al Hoceima
Nador
Oujda
Melilla (Spain)
Alboran Island (Spain)

ALGERIA

Oran
Mostaganem
Sidi-Bel-Abbes
Saida
Tlemcen

Copyright © Usborne Publishing Ltd.

A 0° B 4°E C 8° D 12° E 16°

1

Cherbourg
Le Havre
Caen
Rouen
Amiens
Charleroi
Namur
BELGIUM
Koblenz
Erfurt
Gera
Dresden
Chemnitz
Wrocła
Wa
Liberec
Most
Hradec Kralove
Paris
Reims
LUXEMBOURG
■ **Luxembourg**
Frankfurt
Wurzburg
Karlovy
Vary
Pilsen
Prague ■
CZECH REPUBLIC
Evry
Metz
Mannheim
Saarbrucken
GERMANY
Nuremberg
Olom
48°
N
Le Mans
Nancy
Karlsruhe
Regensburg
Ingolstadt
Ceske
Budejovice
Brno
Angers
Orleans
Troyes
Strasbourg
Rhine
Stuttgart
Danube
Ulm
Augsburg
Linz
Vienna ■
Poitiers
Tours
Nevers
Dijon
Basel
Freiburg
Munich
Wels
St. Polten
Bra
Loire
Besancon
Zurich
Winterthur
Kempten
Salzburg

2

FRANCE
Chalon-
sur-Saone
Biel
Bern ■
Lucerne
■ **Vaduz**
Innsbruck
AUSTRIA
Knittelfeld
Szom
Limoges
Geneva
SWITZERLAND
Lausanne
LIECHTENSTEIN
Grossglockner
3,798m
(12,461ft)
Graz
Zala
Clermont-Ferrand
Lyon
Lake Geneva
Bolzano
Villach
Klagenfurt
Maribor
Mont Blanc
4,807m
(15,771ft)
A   l   p   s
*Lake
Como*
Trento
Kranj
SLOVENIA
■ **Ljubljana**
Zagr
44°
*Massif
Central*
Grenoble
Novara
Bergamo
*Lake
Garda*
Vicenza
Novo
Mesto
CRO
Garonne
Turin
Milan
Brescia
Verona
Trieste
Karlovac
Montauban
Po
Venice
Rijeka
Banja L
Toulouse
Parma
Ferrara
Bologna
Ravenna
Pula
BOS
Montpellier
Nimes
Genoa
Modena
Zadar
AN
Beziers
Aix-en-
Provence
Nice
San Remo
*Gulf of
Genoa*
ITALY
Rimini
HERZE
Andorra la Vella ■
*Gulf of
Lions*
Marseille
Cannes
MONACO
Livorno
Pisa
SAN MARINO
Ancona
Split

3

Toulon
Ligurian Sea
Florence
*A
p
p
e
n
n
i
n
e
s*
Perugia
*A
d
r
i
a
t
i
c
S
e*
Bastia
Elba
Terni
Pescara
Southern Europe

■ Boreal forest
▦ Temperate forest
▦ Tropical forest
▦ Temperate grassland
▦ Savanna
▦ Semi-desert and scrub
▦ Hot desert
▦ Wetland
▦ Mountain
▦ Tundra
▦ Ice
▦ Cultivation
▦ Urban
■ National capital
● Internal capital
⊙ Major city or town
○ Other town
— International boundary
— Internal boundary
▲ 2,490m
(8,169ft) Height above or below sea level

See also main key on page 17.

1:8,000,000

0   100   200   300km

0   100   200 miles

Ajaccio
*Corsica
(France)*
VATICAN CITY
■ **Rome**
Porto-Vecchio
Olbia
Foggia
40°
Sassari
Naples
Pompeii
Salerno
Tarar
*Sardinia
(Italy)*
Tyrrhenian
Sea

4

Oristano
Cosenza
Ca
Cagliari
*Lipari
Islands*
M e d i t e r r a n e a n   S e a
Trapani
Palermo
Messina
36°
Annaba
Menzel
Bourguiba
Bizerte
Carthage
Sicily
Mount Etna
3,323m
(10,902ft)
Catania
Agrigento
Guelma
Souk Ahras
■ **Tunis**
*Pantelleria
(Italy)*
Ragusa
Syracuse
Nabeul
TUNISIA
MALTA

5

Tebessa
Sousse
Valletta ■
Kasserine
Kairouan
Monastir
*Pelagian Islands
(Italy)*
El Jem
Biskra

AFRICA

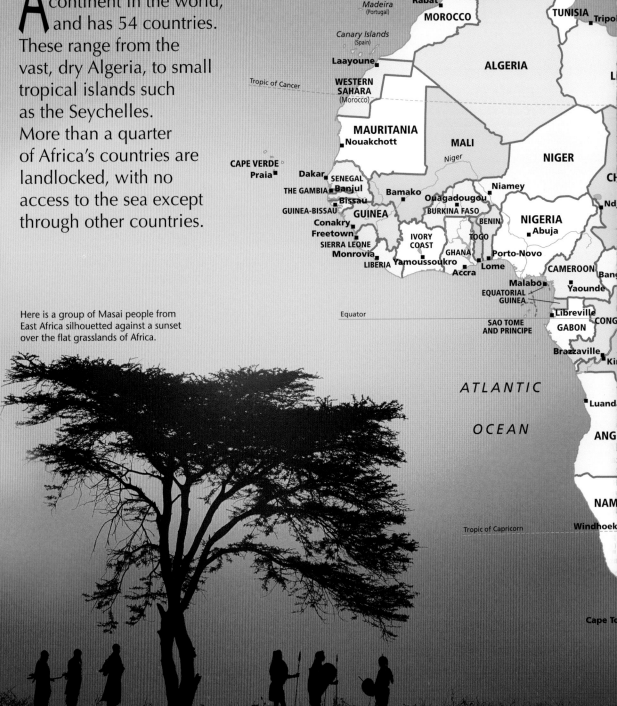

Africa is the second-biggest continent in the world, and has 54 countries. These range from the vast, dry Algeria, to small tropical islands such as the Seychelles. More than a quarter of Africa's countries are landlocked, with no access to the sea except through other countries.

Here is a group of Masai people from East Africa silhouetted against a sunset over the flat grasslands of Africa.

Algiers
Tunis
Madeira
(Portugal)
Rabat
MOROCCO
TUNISIA
Tripol
Canary Islands
(Spain)
Laayoune
ALGERIA
L
Tropic of Cancer
WESTERN
SAHARA
(Morocco)
MAURITANIA
Nouakchott
MALI
NIGER
Niger
CAPE VERDE
Praia
Dakar
SENEGAL
Niamey
CH
THE GAMBIA
Banjul
Bamako
Ouagadougou
GUINEA-BISSAU
Bissau
BURKINA FASO
Nd
Conakry
GUINEA
BENIN
NIGERIA
Freetown
TOGO
Abuja
SIERRA LEONE
IVORY
COAST
Monrovia
GHANA
Porto-Novo
LIBERIA
Yamoussoukro
Lome
CAMEROON
Bang
Accra
Malabo
Yaounde
EQUATORIAL
GUINEA
Libreville
CONG
SAO TOME
AND PRINCIPE
GABON
Equator
Brazzaville
Kin

ATLANTIC

OCEAN

Luanda

ANG

NAM

Tropic of Capricorn
Windhoek

Cape To

The shading on this map is
there to help you see clearly
the different countries that
make up the continent.

Cairo

EGYPT

Tropic of Cancer

Nile

Khartoum

ERITREA
Asmara

SUDAN

DJIBOUTI Djibouti

Addis Ababa SOMALIA

SOUTH
SUDAN ETHIOPIA

Juba

UGANDA
Kampala KENYA Mogadishu

Kigali Nairobi Equator

RWANDA
BURUNDI
Bujumbura

Dodoma Victoria
SEYCHELLES

TANZANIA Dar es Salaam

INDIAN

MALAWI Moroni
Lilongwe COMOROS

OCEAN

A
a

Harare MOZAMBIQUE Antananarivo
IMBABWE MAURITIUS
NA MADAGASCAR Port Louis

Reunion
(France) Tropic of Capricorn

Pretoria
(Tshwane) Maputo
bane SWAZILAND
Lobamba
tein
Maseru
ESOTHO

Facts

Total land area 30,311,690 sq km
(11,703,409 sq miles)
Total population 1.1 billion
Biggest city Cairo, Egypt
Biggest country Algeria 2,381,740
sq km (919,595 sq miles)
Smallest country Seychelles
455 sq km (176 sq miles)

Highest mountain Kilimanjaro,
Tanzania 5,895m (19,341ft)
Longest river Nile, running from to
Burundi to Egypt 6,671km (4,145 miles)
Biggest lake Lake Victoria, between
Tanzania, Kenya and Uganda
69,484 sq km (26,828 sq miles)
Highest waterfall Tugela Falls, on
the Tugela River, South Africa
948m (3,110ft)
Biggest desert Sahara, North Africa
9,100,000 sq km (3,513,530 sq miles)
Biggest island Madagascar 587,713
sq km (226,917 sq miles)

Main mineral deposits Gold, copper,
diamonds, iron ore, manganese, bauxite
Main fuel deposits Coal, uranium,
natural gas

A greater
flamingo in
the Transvaal
National Park

Africa is home to the world's longest river, the Nile, and its largest desert, the Sahara. In southern Africa there are two more large deserts, the Kalahari and the Namib. Africa also has enormous rainforests in central areas, near the Equator.

A convoy of camels moves across the Sahara Desert in North Africa. The strange swirls of sand are formed by strong winds.

Desert weather

Temperatures in the Sahara Desert can rise as high as 55°C (131°F) during the day, but often fall below freezing point at night. Strong winds blow across the desert and whip up mini whirlwinds called dust devils. These suck up sand and hurl it high into the air.

This satellite image clearly shows the vast Sahara Desert in North Africa. It covers an area about the size of the U.S.A.

Moroccan mountain life

The Atlas Mountains dominate the country of Morocco, north of the Sahara Desert. High in the mountains are villages which are home to groups of African people called Berbers. Berbers have lived in Morocco for thousands of years and today still follow their traditional way of life, herding sheep and goats.

This image shows the curves and folds of the Atlas Mountains in Morocco. They were formed by earthquakes and other movements of the Earth.

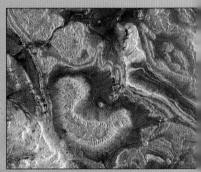

Internet links

For links to websites where you can explore the extreme landscapes of Africa, go to
www.usborne.com/quicklinks

River in the desert

The River Nile winds its way through eastern Africa, from Burundi all the way to the Mediterranean Sea. It is almost the only water source in this dry, arid part of Africa, so major cities, such as Cairo in Egypt, have grown up near it. The soil near the Nile's banks is fertile enough to farm on, especially near the coast where the river splits into many streams.

Wild forests

The large, dense rainforests of central Africa are home to more than half of Africa's wild animals, including chimpanzees, gorillas and elephants. Many of these animals have never come into contact with humans.

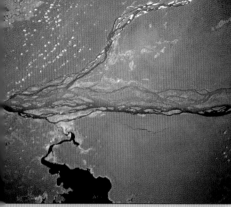

The dense rainforest of central Africa is pink in this satellite image. Running across the middle of the picture is the large Congo River. It splits into many smaller rivers, creating a huge swampy area.

The dark blue water in the lower right of this satellite image is the Red Sea. The triangular piece of land jutting into it is part of Egypt.

This is the River Nile, running through Egypt. As the river reaches the sea, it splits into many streams that create an expanse of fertile, swampy land. This is the large green area at the top of the image.

One of Africa's most populous countries is Egypt, which has busy cities such as its capital, Cairo, as well as the remains of ancient civilizations. Africa also has many areas of natural beauty, such as the vast wildlife parks in the south and east of the continent.

Pyramids and the Sphinx

One of the ancient wonders of the world is found at Giza, in Egypt – the group of three Great Pyramids. These stone structures were built by the ancient Egyptians as tombs for their pharaohs, or kings. The biggest pyramid is about 140m (480ft) high, and probably took 20 years to build. You can see a picture of the pyramids on page 1 of this atlas.

In front of the pyramids stands the Great Sphinx, an enormous statue of a lion with a man's head. It was probably carved as a monument to a pharaoh, though no one is sure which one. Some historians believe there are secret rooms and tunnels underneath the Sphinx.

This is the Great Sphinx of Egypt. It was carved out of soft limestone which has crumbled over the years. Part of the Sphinx's nose is now missing.

Cape Town

At Africa's southern tip, in the country of South Africa, is the city of Cape Town. It is famous for its elegant buildings, sandy beaches and busy waterfront. The city is right next to Table Mountain, which gets its name from its distinctive flat top. Thick clouds often cover the mountain and are nicknamed the Table Cloth.

This is Cape Town, with Table Mountain behind.

A panther chameleon clings to a branch. It can wrap its tail around the branch too, for extra grip. Panther chameleons live only in Madagascar.

On safari

Wild animals such as lions, elephants, buffaloes and zebras live on the grasslands of eastern and southern Africa. The land is divided into many specially protected wildlife parks that tourists can visit on safari trips.

These parks are some of the last remaining places where cheetahs live. These big cats were once found all over Africa but are now endangered. Cheetahs are the world's fastest land animals, able to run at a speed of 115kph (70mph).

Wildlife island

Madagascar is a large island in the Indian Ocean, off Africa's southeastern coast. It has thick, steamy rainforests which are home to many animals not found anywhere else in the world. These include rare chameleons and over 50 species of monkey-like animals called lemurs.

Internet links

For links to websites where you can see inside a pyramid and find about African wildlife, go to **www.usborne.com/quicklinks**

A cheetah in Kenya, eastern Africa, hisses and spits fiercely to scare away enemies.

A 0° **B** 5°E 20°

GREECE

Saida

Djelfa

Batna
Tebessa
Biskra
Annaba
Menzel
Bourguiba
Bizerte
Carthage
Tunis
Kairouan
Sousse
Monastir
El Jem

Sicily
(Italy)
Catania
Syracuse

MALTA
Valletta

Atlas Mountains

El Oued
Touggourt
Gafsa
Sfax
*Kerkenah
Islands*

Ghardaia

Ouargla
Tozeur
Gabes
Jerba
Gulf of Gabes

*Chott
el Jerid*
Tataouine
TUNISIA

*Pantelleria
(Italy)*

*Pelagian
Islands
(Italy)*

Tripoli
Al Khums
Misratah

Leptis Magna
Gharyan

Cyrene
Al Bayda

Mediterran

2

Surt

Benghazi

Ajdabiya

*Gulf of
Sidra*

**30°
N**

*Tademait
Plateau*

Ghadamis

*Great
Eastern Erg*

ALGERIA

3

25°

Illizi

Sabha

Ghat

Murzuq

LIBYA

*Ahaggar
Mountains*

Mount Tahat
2918m
(9,573ft)
▲

Tamanrasset

4

20°

*Djado
Plateau*

*Tibesti
Mountains*

Emi Kousai
▲
3,415m
(11,204ft)

MALI

S

A

H

A

R

A

5

Agadez

NIGER

Faya-Largeau

*Bodele
Depression*

*Ennedi
Plateau*

15°

Tahoua

CHAD

Dosso

Sokoto

Maradi

Zinder

Mao

S

A

H

E

L

Abeche

6

Birnin-Kebbi
Katsina

Gusau
Kano

Lake Chad

Ndjamena

Mongo

Kandi

Zaria

Potiskum
Maiduguri

*Kainji
Reservoir*
Kaduna
NIGERIA

10°

Am Timan

Saki

Minna
Bida
Jos
Kumo

Maroua

7

Niger
Abuja
CAMEROON
Bongor

Birac

B 5°E **C** 10° **D** 15° **E** 20° **F**

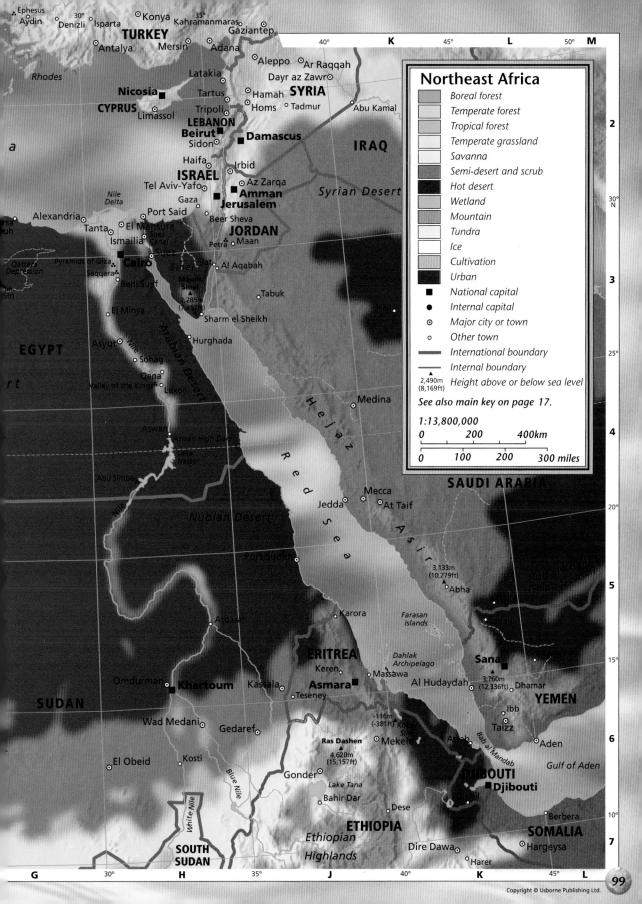

Northeast Africa

Ephesus
Aydin 30° **Denizli** **Isparta** **Konya** 35° **Kahramanmaras**
Gaziantep 40° K 45° L 50° M

TURKEY
Antalya **Mersin** **Adana**

Rhodes **Latakia** **Aleppo** **Ar Raqqah**
Dayr az Zawr
Tartus **Hamah** **SYRIA**
Nicosia **Tripoli** **Homs** **Tadmur** **Abu Kamal** 2
CYPRUS **Limassol**
LEBANON
Beirut **Damascus** **IRAQ**
Sidon
a **Haifa** **Irbid**
ISRAEL **Az Zarqa** *Syrian Desert* 30°N
Tel Aviv-Yafo **Amman**
Gaza **Jerusalem**
Alexandria **Port Said** **Beer Sheva**
Tanta **El Mansura** **JORDAN** **Maan**
Ismailia *Suez Canal* **Petra**
Suez **Eilat** **Al Aqabah** 3
Qattara **Pyramids of Giza** **Cairo** *Sinai*
Depression **Saqqara** **Tabuk**
Beni Suef **Mount Sinai** 25°
2,285m (7,497ft)
EGYPT **El Minya** **Sharm el Sheikh**
Asyut **Hurghada**
Sohag *Arabian Desert*
Qena *Nile*
Valley of the Kings **Luxor** **Medina**
Aswan *Hejaz*
Aswan High Dam 4
Lake Nasser
Abu Simbel *Red Sea*
Mecca 20°
Jedda **At Taif** *Asir* **SAUDI ARABIA**
Nubian Desert
Port Sudan
3,133m (10,279ft) 5
Abha
Karora
Farasan Islands
Atbara
Dahlak Archipelago **Sana** 15°
ERITREA **Keren** **Massawa** **3,760m** (12,336ft) **Dhamar**
Omdurman **Khartoum** **Kassala** **Asmara** **Al Hudaydah** **YEMEN**
Teseney **Ibb**
SUDAN **Taizz** 6
Wad Medani **Gedaref** **-116m** (-381ft)
Aden
Ras Dashen **Mekele** **Asab** *Gulf of Aden*
El Obeid **Kosti** **4,620m** (15,157ft) **Bab al Mandab**
Gonder **DJIBOUTI**
Lake Tana **Djibouti**
Bahir Dar **Dese** **Berbera** 10°
ETHIOPIA **SOMALIA**
White Nile *Blue Nile* *Ethiopian* **Dire Dawa** **Hargeysa** 7
SOUTH SUDAN *Highlands* **Harer**
G 30° H 35° J 40° K 45° L

Legend

	Boreal forest
	Temperate forest
	Tropical forest
	Temperate grassland
	Savanna
	Semi-desert and scrub
	Hot desert
	Wetland
	Mountain
	Tundra
	Ice
	Cultivation
	Urban
■	National capital
●	Internal capital
⊙	Major city or town
○	Other town
—	International boundary
—	Internal boundary
▲ 2,490m (8,169ft)	Height above or below sea level

See also main key on page 17.

1:13,800,000

0   200   400km
0 100 200 300 miles

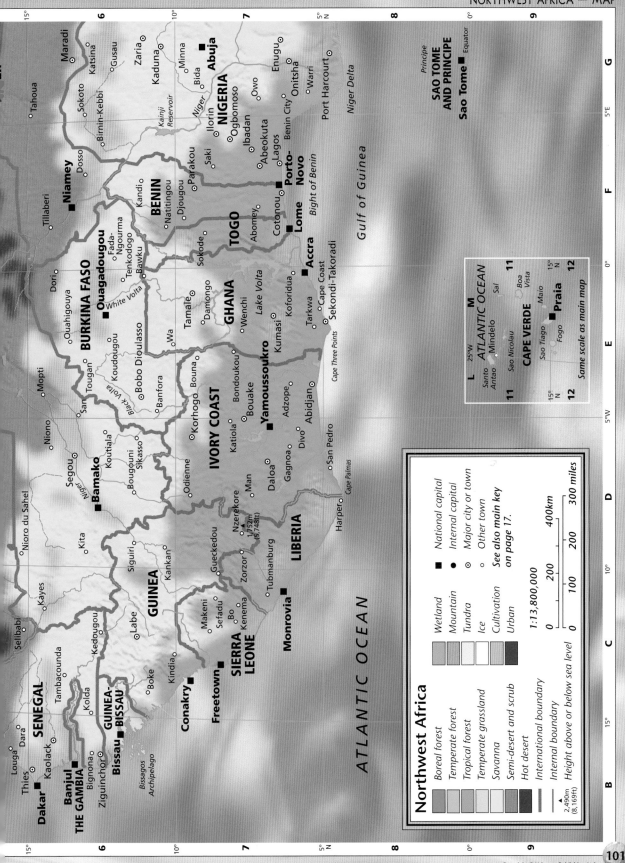

Northwest Africa

Boreal forest
Temperate forest
Tropical forest
Temperate grassland
Savanna
Semi-desert and scrub
Hot desert
International boundary
Internal boundary
▲ 2,490m (8,169ft)
Height above or below sea level

■ National capital
● Internal capital
⊙ Major city or town
○ Other town

See also main key on page 17.

1:13,800,000

0   100   200   300 miles
0   200   400km

Wetland
Mountain
Tundra
Ice
Cultivation
Urban

ATLANTIC OCEAN

SENEGAL
Louga
Thies ■ Dakar
Kaolack
Banjul ■
THE GAMBIA
Bignona
Ziguinchor
Bissau ■
GUINEA-BISSAU
Bissagos Archipelago
Selibabi
Nioro du Sahel
Kayes
Tambacounda
Kolda
Dara
Kedougou
Boke
Kindia
Conakry ■
Freetown ■
SIERRA LEONE
Makeni
Sefadu
Bo
Kenema
Kita
Labe
Siguiri
Kankan
GUINEA
Gueckedou
Nzerekore ▲ 1,752m (5,748ft)
Zorzor
Tubmanburg
Kenieran
LIBERIA
Monrovia ■
Harper
Cape Palmas
San Pedro
Cape Three Points
Sekondi-Takoradi
Tarkwa
Cape Coast
Accra ■
GHANA
Koforidua
Kumasi
Wenchi
Lake Volta
Damongo
Tamale
Wa
Bouna
Bondoukou
Bouake
Yamoussoukro ■
Divo
Gagnoa
Daloa
Man
Adzope
Abidjan
IVORY COAST
Katiola
Odienne
Korhogo
Bobo Dioulasso
Banfora
Sikasso
Bougouni
Koutiala
Bamako ■
Segou
Niono
Nioro du Sahel
Mopti
San
Tougan
Ouahigouya
BURKINA FASO
Ouagadougou ■
Dori
Fada-Ngourma
Tenkodogo
Bawku
White Volta
Black Volta
Koudougou
Sokode
TOGO
Lome ■
Cotonou
Abomey
Natitingou
Djougou
BENIN
Porto-Novo ■
Parakou
Kandi
Saki
Abeokuta
Lagos
Ibadan
Ogbomoso
Ilorin
NIGERIA
Abuja ■
Bida
Minna
Kaduna
Zaria
Gusau
Katsina
Sokoto
Birnin-Kebbi
Dosso
Niamey ■
Tillaberi
Tahoua
Maradi
Kainji Reservoir
Niger
Enugu
Owo
Benin City
Onitsha
Warri
Port Harcourt
Niger Delta
Bight of Benin
Gulf of Guinea

L 25°W
ATLANTIC OCEAN
Santo Antao
Sao Nicolau
Mindelo
Sal
Boa Vista
M 11
CAPE VERDE
Sao Tiago
Maio
Praia ■
Fogo
15°N
12
15°N 11
12
Same scale as main map

Principe
SAO TOME AND PRINCIPE
Sao Tome ■
Equator

Dougou
Tenkodogo

Kainji

Niger

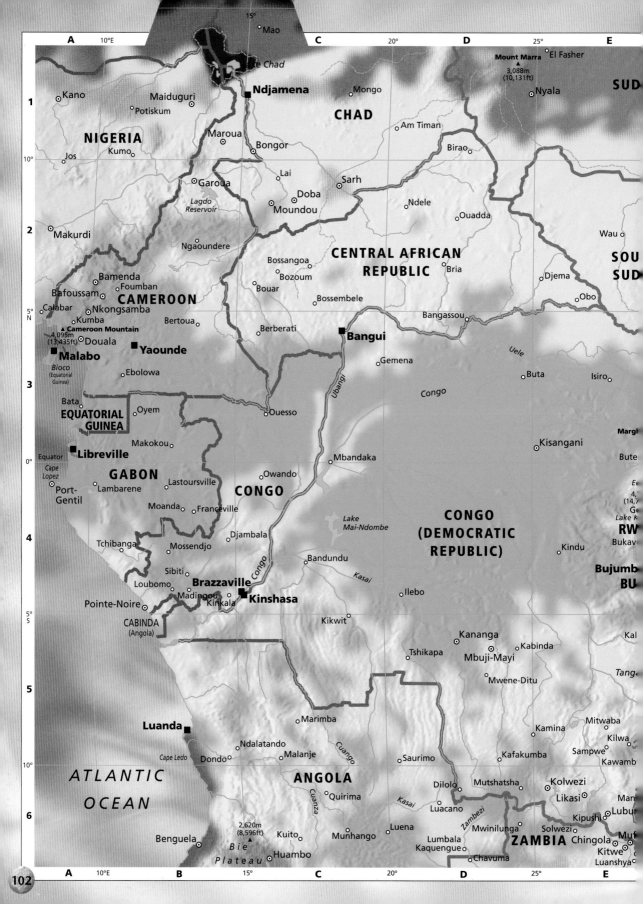

A 10°E **B** 15° **C** 20° **D** 25° **E**

15°

Mao

Lake Chad

■ **Ndjamena**

Mongo

CHAD

Mount Marra
3,088m
(10,131ft)
El Fasher

Nyala

SUD

1

Kano

Maiduguri

Potiskum

NIGERIA

Jos

Kumo

Maroua

Bongor

Am Timan

Birao

10°

Garoua

Lai

Sarh

Ndele

Ouadda

2

Makurdi

Lagdo
Reservoir

Doba

Moundou

Wau

SOU

SUD

Ngaoundere

Bossangoa

CENTRAL AFRICAN
REPUBLIC

Bria

Djema

Bamenda

Foumban

Bozoum

Bouar

Bossembele

Obo

Bafoussam

CAMEROON

Calabar

Nkongsamba

Bertoua

Berberati

Bangassou

5°N

Kumba

Cameroon Mountain
4,095m
(13,435ft)

Douala

■ **Malabo**

■ **Yaounde**

■ **Bangui**

Gemena

Buta

Isiro

Margl

3

Bioco
(Equatorial
Guinea)

Ebolowa

Ubangi

Congo

Kisangani

Bute

Bata

EQUATORIAL
GUINEA

Oyem

Ouesso

Uele

Makokou

Mbandaka

E
4,
(14,
G

Equator

Cape
Lopez

■ **Libreville**

GABON

Lastoursville

Owando

CONGO (DEMOCRATIC
REPUBLIC)

Lake k

RW

0°

Port-
Gentil

Lambarene

Moanda

Franceville

CONGO

Lake
Mai-Ndombe

Kindu

Bukav

4

Tchibanga

Mossendjo

Djambala

Bandundu

Kasai

Bujumb

BU

Sibiti

Congo

Ilebo

Loubomo

Brazzaville

Kikwit

Madingou

■ **Kinshasa**

Kinkala

Kananga

Kabinda

Kal

5°S

Pointe-Noire

CABINDA
(Angola)

Tshikapa

Mbuji-Mayi

Mwene-Ditu

Tang

5

Kamina

Mitwaba

■ **Luanda**

Marimba

Kilwa

Sampwe

Kawamb

Cape Ledo

Ndalandato

Malanje

Cuango

Saurimo

Kafakumba

Dondo

ANGOLA

Quirima

Kamina

10°

Cuanza

Kasai

Dilolo

Mutshatsha

Kolwezi

Likasi

Man

ATLANTIC

Luacano

Zambezi

Kipushi

Lubur

6

OCEAN

2,620m
(8,596ft)

Kuito

Munhango

Luena

Lumbala
Kaquengue

Mwinilunga

Solwezi

ZAMBIA

Chingola

Mu

Benguela

Bie
Plateau

Huambo

Chavuma

Kitwe

Luanshya

A 10°E **B** 15° **C** 20° **D** 25° **E**

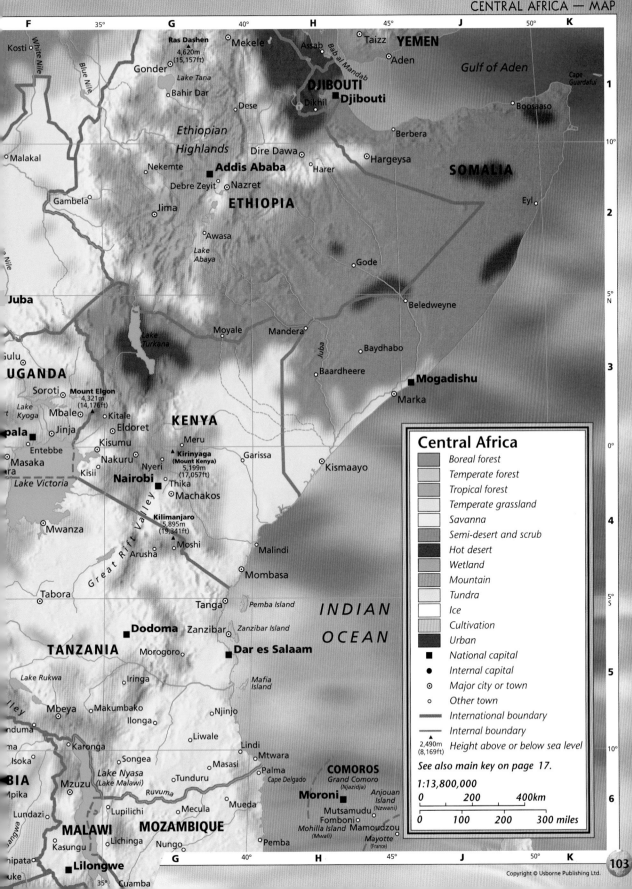

F 35° **G** 40° **H** 45° **J** 50° **K**

Kosti

White Nile

Blue Nile

Ras Dashen
4,620m
(15,157ft)

Gonder

Mekele

Assab

Bab al Mandab

Taizz

YEMEN

Aden

Gulf of Aden

Cape
Guardafui

1

Lake Tana

Bahir Dar

Ethiopian
Highlands

DJIBOUTI

Dikhil

Djibouti

Berbera

Boosaaso

Malakal

Dese

Nekemte

Dire Dawa

Addis Ababa

Harer

Hargeysa

SOMALIA

10°

Gambela

Debre Zeyit

Nazret

Eyl

2

Nile

Jima

ETHIOPIA

Awasa

Lake
Abaya

Gode

5°
N

Juba

Moyale

Mandera

Juba

Baydhabo

Beledweyne

3

Gulu

UGANDA

Lake
Turkana

Baardheere

Mogadishu

Soroti

Mount Elgon
4,321m
(14,176ft)

Marka

0°

Lake
Kyoga

Mbale

Kitale

KENYA

Meru

Garissa

Jinja

Eldoret

pala

Entebbe

Kisumu

Nakuru

Nyeri

▲ Kirinyaga
(Mount Kenya)
5,199m
(17,057ft)

Kismaayo

Masaka

Kisii

Nairobi

Thika

Lake Victoria

Machakos

5°
S

Mwanza

Great Rift Valley

Kilimanjaro
5,895m
(19,341ft)

Moshi

Malindi

4

Arusha

Mombasa

Tabora

Tanga

Pemba Island

INDIAN

OCEAN

Dodoma

Zanzibar

Zanzibar Island

TANZANIA

Morogoro

Dar es Salaam

5

Lake Rukwa

Iringa

Mafia
Island

Mbeya

Makumbako

Njinjo

nduma

Ilonga

Liwale

10°

Isoka

Karonga

Songea

Masasi

Lindi

Mtwara

COMOROS

BIA

Mzuzu

Lake Nyasa
(Lake Malawi)

Tunduru

Palma

Cape Delgado

Grand Comoro
(Njazidja)

Mpika

Lupilichi

Ruvuma

Mecula

Mueda

Moroni

Anjouan
Island
(Nzwani)

6

Lundazi

MALAWI

Lichinga

Nungo

Mutsamudu

Fomboni

Mamoudzou

ngwa

Kasungu

MOZAMBIQUE

Pemba

Mohilla Island
(Mwali)

Mayotte
(France)

ipata

uke

Lilongwe

Cuamba

G 40° **H** 45° **J** 50° **K**

Central Africa

	Boreal forest
	Temperate forest
	Tropical forest
	Temperate grassland
	Savanna
	Semi-desert and scrub
	Hot desert
	Wetland
	Mountain
	Tundra
	Ice
	Cultivation
	Urban
■	National capital
●	Internal capital
⊙	Major city or town
○	Other town
—	International boundary
—	Internal boundary
▲ 2,490m (8,169ft)	Height above or below sea level

See also main key on page 17.

1:13,800,000

0   200   400km

0   100   200   300 miles

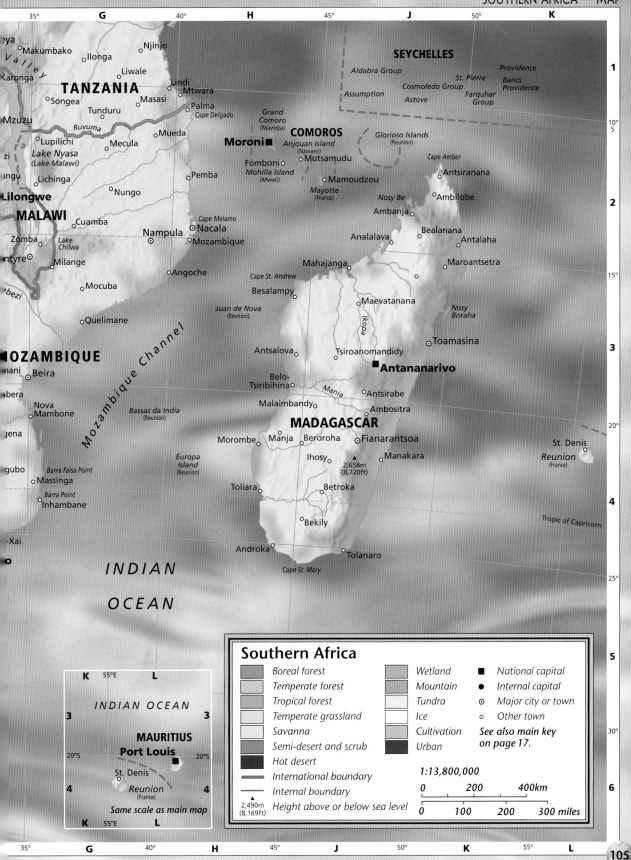

Southern Africa

- Boreal forest
- Temperate forest
- Tropical forest
- Temperate grassland
- Savanna
- Semi-desert and scrub
- Hot desert
- Wetland
- Mountain
- Tundra
- Ice
- Cultivation
- Urban
- International boundary
- Internal boundary
- ▲ 2,490m (8,169ft) Height above or below sea level
- ■ National capital
- ● Internal capital
- ⊙ Major city or town
- ○ Other town

See also main key on page 17.

1:13,800,000

0   200   400km

0   100   200   300 miles

SEYCHELLES
Aldabra Group
Assumption
Cosmoledo Group
Astove
St. Pierre
Farquhar Group
Providence
Bancs
Providence

TANZANIA
Makumbako
Ilonga
Njinjo
Liwale
Karonga
Songea
Tunduru
Lindi
Mtwara
Masasi
Palma
Cape Delgado
Mueda
Mecula
Ruvuma
Lupilichi
Lake Nyasa
(Lake Malawi)
Mzuzu
Lichinga
Nungo

Grand Comoro
(Njazidja)
COMOROS
Moroni ■
Fomboni
Mohilla Island
(Mwali)
Anjouan Island
(Nzwani)
Mutsamudu
Mamoudzou
Mayotte
(France)

Glorioso Islands
(Reunion)
Cape Amber
Antsiranana
Ambilobe
Nosy Be
Ambanja
Analalava
Bealanana
Antalaha
Maroantsetra

MALAWI
Lilongwe
Cuamba
Zomba
Lake Chilwa
ntyre
Milange
Nampula
Cape Melamo
Nacala
Mozambique
Pemba
Angoche
Mocuba

MOZAMBIQUE
Quelimane
zezi
Mahajanga
Cape St. Andrew
Besalampy
Juan de Nova
(Reunion)
Maevatanana
Ikopa
Nosy Boraha
Toamasina
Antsalova
Tsiroanomandidy
Antananarivo ■
Mania
Antsirabe
Ambositra

Beira
Nova Mambone
Bassas da India
(Reunion)
Belo-Tsiribihina
Malaimbandy

MADAGASCAR
Morombe
Manja
Beroroha
Fianarantsoa
Ihosy
▲ 2,658m (8,720ft)
Manakara
St. Denis
Reunion
(France)

Massinga
Barra Falsa Point
Barra Point
Inhambane
Europa Island
(Reunion)
Toliara
Betroka
Bekily
Androka
Cape St. Mary
Tolanaro
Tropic of Capricorn

Xai

INDIAN OCEAN

Inset (Mauritius)
K 55°E L
INDIAN OCEAN
MAURITIUS
Port Louis
20°S
St. Denis
Reunion
(France)
Same scale as main map

Copyright © Usborne Publishing Ltd.

THE ARCTIC AND ANTARCTICA

The Arctic and Antarctica are the world's coldest places. The Arctic is the area around the North Pole, including the Arctic Ocean and the most northerly parts of Europe, North America and Asia. Antarctica is a huge continent at the South Pole.

Frozen island

Within the Arctic is Greenland, the world's largest island. Most Greenlanders live along the rocky coast, as the main body of land is covered in thick ice for most of the year.

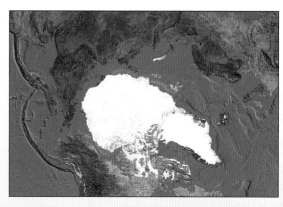

The large white area in this satellite image is ice, covering the Arctic Ocean and Greenland. At the top left of the image is the edge of Russia and at the top right is part of Europe.

This is the entrance to Sweden's Arctic ice hotel. The hotel is open in winter then melts in the spring when the weather gets milder. The next winter, it is built all over again.

Internet links

For links to websites where you can see maps, photos and video clips of the Arctic and Antarctic, and find out about the animals that live at the opposite ends of the Earth, go to **www.usborne.com/quicklinks**

A hotel of ice

Every winter, a hotel made entirely of ice is built in the far north of Sweden. Each piece of furniture is sculpted from ice, and even the beds are made of ice blocks. Guests sleep in special thermal sleeping bags with animal skins piled on top for extra warmth.

Icy continent

A huge, jagged sheet of ice
permanently covers almost
all of Antarctica, and spreads
out over nearby seas as well.
Scientists think that the area
in the far west of the continent
may be made up of many islands,
but it is hard to tell because they
are so far beneath the ice.

Mountains run down the middle of Antarctica,
and in the west there are volcanoes.
Amazingly, one volcano heats the sea near it
so much that it is warm enough to swim in.

The darkest shading on
this satellite image of
Antarctica indicates ice
that is over 3km
(2 miles) deep.

Life in Antarctica

The temperature in Antarctica can fall as low
as -80°C (-112°F) in winter. It is too cold for
people to live there, though scientists visit
to study the area. No plants grow in the
ice, and the only land animals are
tiny mites. But many animals live
in the seas around Antarctica,
including penguins, seals,
whales and fish.

These penguins are on
the coast of Antarctica.
They live in the
ocean but come
onto land
to breed.

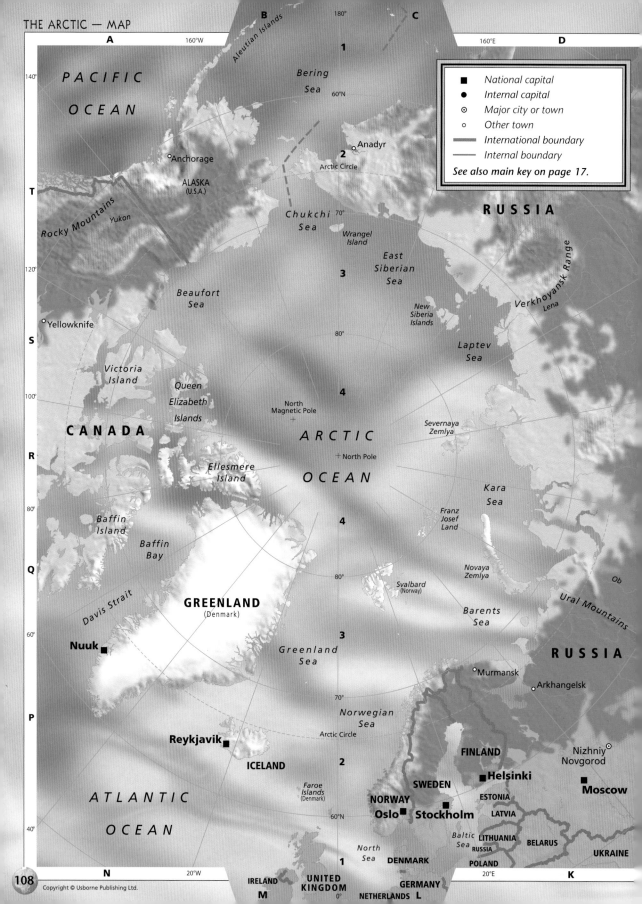

A 160°W B 180° C 160°E D

1

Bering Sea
60°N

2 ○ Anadyr
Arctic Circle

PACIFIC OCEAN
140°

○ Anchorage

ALASKA (U.S.A.)
T
120°

Rocky Mountains Yukon

Chukchi Sea 70°

Wrangel Island

3 *East Siberian Sea*

RUSSIA

Verkhoyansk Range
Lena

Beaufort Sea

New Siberia Islands

Laptev Sea

S 80°

○ Yellowknife

Victoria Island

4

North Magnetic Pole +

ARCTIC

Severnaya Zemlya

Kara Sea

Queen Elizabeth Islands

CANADA

R *OCEAN*

+ North Pole

Franz Josef Land

80°

Baffin Island

Ellesmere Island

4

Novaya Zemlya

Ob

Q 80°

Baffin Bay

80°

Svalbard (Norway)

Barents Sea

Ural Mountains

Davis Strait

GREENLAND (Denmark)

RUSSIA

60°

■ **Nuuk**

3

Greenland Sea

70°

○ Murmansk

○ Arkhangelsk

P

Norwegian Sea
70°
Arctic Circle

2

FINLAND

Nizhniy Novgorod ⊙

■ **Reykjavik**

ICELAND

■ **Helsinki**

SWEDEN

40°

ATLANTIC OCEAN

Faroe Islands (Denmark)

NORWAY
Oslo ■ ■ **Stockholm**

ESTONIA

■ **Moscow**

LATVIA

60°N

1

Baltic Sea

LITHUANIA

RUSSIA

BELARUS

North Sea

DENMARK

POLAND

UKRAINE

N 20°W

IRELAND

UNITED KINGDOM

GERMANY

20°E K

M 0° L

NETHERLANDS

Key:

■ National capital
● Internal capital
⊙ Major city or town
○ Other town
━━ International boundary
── Internal boundary

See also main key on page 17.

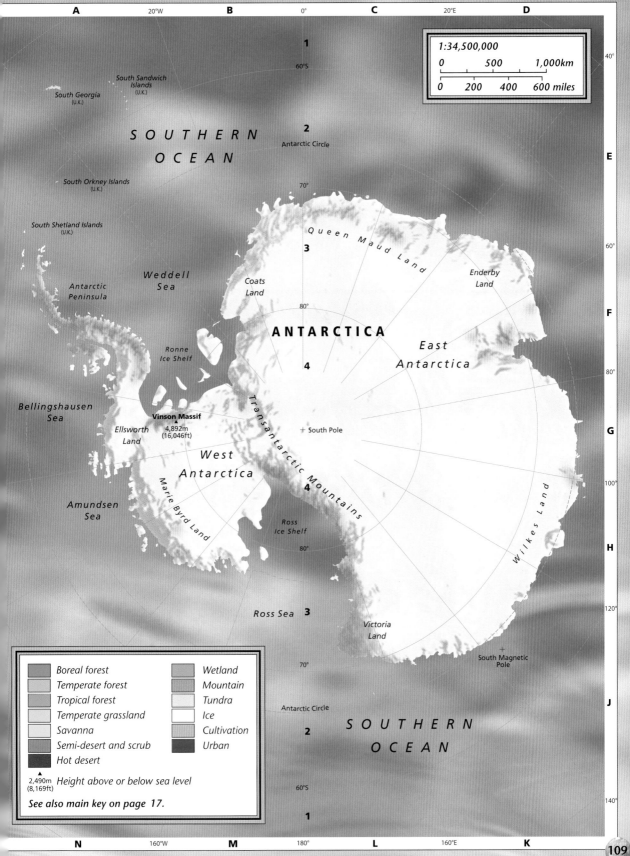

A   20°W   **B**   0°   **C**   20°E   **D**

1

60°S

1:34,500,000

0	500	1,000km

0	200	400	600 miles

40°

E

South Sandwich
Islands
(U.K.)

South Georgia
(U.K.)

2

Antarctic Circle

S O U T H E R N

O C E A N

South Orkney Islands
(U.K.)

70°

60°

South Shetland Islands
(U.K.)

3

Queen Maud Land

Enderby
Land

Coats
Land

Antarctic
Peninsula

Weddell
Sea

ANTARCTICA

F

80°

East
Antarctica

Ronne
Ice Shelf

4

80°

Bellingshausen
Sea

Vinson Massif
▲
4,892m
(16,046ft)

Transantarctic Mountains

+ South Pole

G

Ellsworth
Land

West
Antarctica

4

Amundsen
Sea

Marie Byrd Land

Ross
Ice Shelf

Wilkes Land

100°

80°

H

120°

Ross Sea **3**

Victoria
Land

South Magnetic
Pole

70°

J

Antarctic Circle

S O U T H E R N

O C E A N

2

60°S

140°

1

	Boreal forest		Wetland
	Temperate forest		Mountain
	Tropical forest		Tundra
	Temperate grassland		Ice
	Savanna		Cultivation
	Semi-desert and scrub		Urban
	Hot desert		

▲ 2,490m
(8,169ft) Height above or below sea level

See also main key on page 17.

N   160°W   **M**   180°   **L**   160°E   **K**

GEOGRAPHY QUIZ

est your knowledge of the world's countries, cities, sights and animals with these quiz questions. The answers are on page 129.

The enormous, elaborate church above was designed by a famous Spanish architect named Antonio Gaudi.

Mystery places

Which famous sights are shown in the photographs on this page? Each has clues to help you.

The marble building on the left is one of the Seven Wonders of the Modern World. It was built by an Indian emperor.

This famous steel bridge crosses the bay of a large North American city. It opened in 1937 and for many years was the longest suspension bridge in the world.

This city skyline is dominated by the tallest freestanding structure in the world. Visitors can eat in a restaurant on the 122nd level, or admire the view from Level 124. Can you name the tower and the city?

The ruins above are the remains of some of Europe's most important ancient temples and other public buildings.

Quick quiz

1. Which country's flag consists of a red circle on a white background?

2. When it is noon in Britain, what time is it in Mexico?

3. In which country is the Great Victoria Desert?

4. Which continent is the third-largest in the world?

5. In which country is Brno?

6. What is the world's deepest lake?

7. Name the smallest country in Europe.

8. Which country lies between Nicaragua and Panama?

9. In which country would you pay using naira and kobo as currency?

10. What is Turkey's capital city?

Internet links

For links to websites where you can try test-yourself quizzes and brush up your knowledge of world geography, go to **www.usborne.com/quicklinks**

Survival challenge

Could you survive in the world's toughest terrains? Take this test to find out.

1. Which of the following would not be very useful on a trip to Antarctica?
a) A warm hat and gloves
b) An umbrella
c) Sunglasses and sunscreen

2. You are in the Sahara Desert and are short of drinking water. What should you do?
a) Stay active, so you produce sweat to cool yourself down.
b) Put on extra clothes and rest as much as possible.
c) Talk and sing songs to keep yourself alert.

3. When on safari in Africa, which of these spiders should you avoid?
a) Six-eyed crab spiders
b) Button spiders
c) Violin spiders

4. You are walking in the Rocky Mountains and meet a grizzly bear. What should you do?
a) Lie on the ground and play dead.
b) Turn and run away as fast as possible.
c) Back away slowly and calmly.

This grizzly bear is in the Rocky Mountains in Utah, U.S.A. Grizzly bears like to keep well away from humans, but will occasionally attack if they feel threatened.

GAZETTEER OF STATES

Afghanistan

Albania

Algeria

Andorra

Angola

Antigua and Barbuda

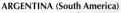

• Argentina

This gazetteer lists the world's 195 independent states, along with key facts about each one. In the lists of languages, the language that is most widely spoken is given first, even if it is not the official language. In the lists of religions, the one followed by the most people is also placed first. Every state has a national flag, which is usually used to represent the country abroad. A few states also have a state flag which they prefer to use instead. The state flags appear here with a dot beside them.

AFGHANISTAN (Asia)
Area: 647,500 sq km (250,001 sq miles)
Population: 30,551,674
Capital city: Kabul
Main languages: Dari, Pashto
Main religion: Muslim
Government: Islamic republic
Currency: 1 afghani = 100 puls

ALBANIA (Europe)
Area: 28,748 sq km (11,100 sq miles)
Population: 3,173,271
Capital city: Tirana
Main language: Albanian
Main religions: Muslim, Albanian Orthodox
Government: democratic republic
Currency: 1 lek = 100 qintars

ALGERIA (Africa)
Area: 2,381,740 sq km (919,595 sq miles)
Population: 39,208,194
Capital city: Algiers
Main languages: Arabic, French, Berber dialects
Main religion: Sunni Muslim
Government: republic
Currency: 1 Algerian dinar = 100 centimes

ANDORRA (Europe)
Area: 468 sq km (181 sq miles)
Population: 79,218
Capital city: Andorra la Vella
Main languages: Catalan, Spanish
Main religion: Roman Catholic
Government: parliamentary democracy
Currency: 1 euro = 100 cents

ANGOLA (Africa)
Area: 1,246,700 sq km (481,354 sq miles)
Population: 21,471,618
Capital city: Luanda
Main languages: Kilongo, Kimbundu, other Bantu languages, Portuguese
Main religions: indigenous, Roman Catholic, Protestant
Government: presidential republic
Currency: 1 kwanza = 100 centimos

ANTIGUA AND BARBUDA (North America)
Area: 443 sq km (171 sq miles)
Population: 89,985
Capital city: Saint John's
Main languages: Caribbean Creole, English
Main religion: Protestant
Government: constitutional monarchy
Currency: 1 East Caribbean dollar = 100 cents

ARGENTINA (South America)
Area: 2,766,890 sq km (1,068,302 sq miles)
Population: 41,446,246
Capital city: Buenos Aires
Main language: Spanish
Main religion: Roman Catholic
Government: republic
Currency: 1 peso = 100 centavos

ARMENIA (Asia)
Area: 29,743 sq km (11,484 sq miles)
Population: 2,976,566
Capital city: Yerevan
Main language: Armenian
Main religion: Armenian Orthodox
Government: republic
Currency: 1 dram = 100 luma

AUSTRALIA (Australasia/Oceania)
Area: 7,741,220 sq km (2,988,902 sq miles)
Population: 23,342,553
Capital city: Canberra
Main language: English
Main religion: Christian
Government: federal democratic monarchy
Currency: 1 Australian dollar = 100 cents

AUSTRIA (Europe)
Area: 83,870 sq km (32,382 sq miles)
Population: 8,495,145
Capital city: Vienna
Main language: German
Main religion: Roman Catholic
Government: federal republic
Currency: 1 euro = 100 cents

Armenia

Australia

Austria

Azerbaijan

Bahamas, The

Bahrain

Bangladesh

Barbados

AZERBAIJAN (Asia)
Area: 86,600 sq km (33,436 sq miles)
Population: 9,413,420
Capital city: Baku
Main language: Azeri
Main religion: Muslim
Government: republic
Currency: 1 manat = 100 gopiks

Belarus

BAHAMAS, THE (North America)
Area: 13,940 sq km (5,382 sq miles)
Population: 377,374
Capital city: Nassau
Main languages: Bahamian Creole, English
Main religion: Christian
Government: parliamentary democracy
Currency: 1 Bahamian dollar = 100 cents

Belgium

BAHRAIN (Asia)
Area: 665 sq km (257 sq miles)
Population: 1,332,171
Capital city: Manama
Main languages: Arabic, English
Main religion: Muslim
Government: constitutional monarchy
Currency: 1 Bahraini dinar = 1,000 fils

BANGLADESH (Asia)
Area: 144,000 sq km (55,599 sq miles)
Population: 156,594,962
Capital city: Dhaka
Main languages: Bengali, English
Main religions: Muslim, Hindu
Government: parliamentary democracy
Currency: 1 taka = 100 poisha

Belize

BARBADOS (North America)
Area: 431 sq km (166 sq miles)
Population: 284,644
Capital city: Bridgetown
Main languages: Bajan, English
Main religion: Christian
Government: parliamentary democracy
Currency: 1 Barbadian dollar = 100 cents

BELARUS (Europe)
Area: 207,600 sq km (80,155 sq miles)
Population: 9,356,678
Capital city: Minsk
Main language: Belarusian
Main religion: Eastern Orthodox
Government: republic
Currency: 1 Belarusian ruble = 100 kopecks

Benin

BELGIUM (Europe)
Area: 30,528 sq km (11,787 sq miles)
Population: 11,104,476
Capital city: Brussels
Main languages: Dutch, French, German
Main religions: Roman Catholic, Protestant
Government: constitutional monarchy
Currency: 1 euro = 100 cents

Bhutan

BELIZE (North America)
Area: 22,966 sq km (8,867 sq miles)
Population: 331,900
Capital city: Belmopan
Main languages: Spanish, Belize
Creole, English, Garifuna, Maya

Bolivia

Main religions: Roman Catholic, Protestant
Government: parliamentary democracy
Currency: 1 Belizean dollar = 100 cents

BENIN (Africa)
Area: 112,620 sq km (43,483 sq miles)
Population: 10,323,474
Capital city: Porto-Novo
Main languages: Fon, French, Yoruba, Adja
Main religions: indigenous, Christian, Muslim
Government: republic
Currency: 1 CFA* franc = 100 centimes

BHUTAN (Asia)
Area: 47,000 sq km (18,147 sq miles)
Population: 753,947
Capital city: Thimphu
Main languages: Dzongkha, Nepali
Main religions: Buddhist, Hindu
Government: constitutional monarchy
Currency: 1 ngultrum = 100 chetrum

BOLIVIA (South America)
Area: 1,098,580 sq km (424,164 sq miles)
Population: 10,671,200
Capital cities: La Paz/Sucre
Main languages: Spanish, Quechua, Aymara
Main religion: Roman Catholic
Government: republic
Currency: 1 boliviano = 100 centavos

BOSNIA AND HERZEGOVINA (Europe)
Area: 51,209 sq km (19,772 sq miles)
Population: 3,829,307
Capital city: Sarajevo
Main languages: Bosnian, Serbian, Croatian
Main religions: Muslim, Orthodox, Roman Catholic
Government: democratic federal republic
Currency: 1 marka = 100 feninga

BOTSWANA (Africa)
Area: 600,370 sq km (231,804 sq miles)
Population: 2,021,144
Capital city: Gaborone
Main languages: Setswana, Kalanga, English
Main religions: indigenous, Christian
Government: parliamentary republic
Currency: 1 pula = 100 thebe

BRAZIL (South America)
Area: 8,511,965 sq km (3,286,488 sq miles)
Population: 200,361,925
Capital city: Brasilia
Main language: Portuguese
Main religion: Roman Catholic
Government: federal republic
Currency: 1 real = 100 centavos

BRUNEI (Asia)
Area: 5,770 sq km (2,228 sq miles)
Population: 417,784
Capital city: Bandar Seri Begawan
Main languages: Malay, English, Chinese
Main religions: Muslim, Buddhist
Government: constitutional sultanate (a type of monarchy)
Currency: 1 Bruneian dollar = 100 cents

Bosnia and Herzegovina

Botswana

Brazil

Brunei

Bulgaria

Burkina Faso

Burma (Myanmar)

*CFA = Communaute Financiere Africaine

GAZETTEER OF STATES CONTINUED:

Burundi

BULGARIA (Europe)
Area: 110,910 sq km (42,823 sq miles)
Population: 7,222,943
Capital city: Sofia
Main language: Bulgarian
Main religions: Bulgarian Orthodox, Muslim
Government: parliamentary democracy
Currency: 1 lev = 100 stotinki

BURKINA FASO (Africa)
Area: 274,200 sq km (105,869 sq miles)
Population: 16,934,839
Capital city: Ouagadougou
Main languages: Moore, Jula, French
Main religions: Muslim, indigenous
Government: parliamentary republic
Currency: 1 CFA* franc = 100 centimes

BURMA (MYANMAR) (Asia)
Area: 678,500 sq km (261,970 sq miles)
Population: 53,259,018
Capital city: Nay Pyi Taw
Main language: Burmese
Main religion: Buddhist
Government: military dictatorship
Currency: 1 kyat = 100 pyas

Cambodia

BURUNDI (Africa)
Area: 27,830 sq km (10,745 sq miles)
Population: 10,162,532
Capital city: Bujumbura
Main languages: Kirundi, French, Swahili
Main religions: Christian, indigenous
Government: republic
Currency: 1 Burundi franc = 100 centimes

CAMBODIA (Asia)
Area: 181,040 sq km (69,900 sq miles)
Population: 15,135,169
Capital city: Phnom Penh
Main language: Khmer, French
Main religion: Buddhist
Government: constitutional monarchy
Currency: 1 new riel = 100 sen

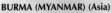

Cameroon

CAMEROON (Africa)
Area: 475,440 sq km (183,568 sq miles)
Population: 22,253,959
Capital city: Yaounde
Main languages: Cameroon Pidgin English,
Ewondo, Fula, French, English
Main religions: indigenous, Christian, Muslim
Government: republic
Currency: 1 CFA* franc = 100 centimes

CANADA (North America)
Area: 9,984,670 sq km (3,855,103 sq miles)
Population: 35,181,704
Capital city: Ottawa
Main languages: English, French
Main religions: Roman Catholic, Protestant
Government: federal democracy
Currency: 1 Canadian dollar = 100 cents

Canada

CAPE VERDE (Africa)
Area: 4,033 sq km (1,557 sq miles)
Population: 498,897
Capital city: Praia
Main languages: Crioulo*, Portuguese

Cape Verde

Central African Republic

Chad

(Cape Verde continued)
Main religions: Roman Catholic, Protestant
Government: republic
Currency: 1 Cape Verdean escudo = 100
centavos

CENTRAL AFRICAN REPUBLIC (Africa)
Area: 622,984 sq km (240,535 sq miles)
Population: 4,616,417
Capital city: Bangui
Main languages: Sangho, French
Main religions: indigenous, Christian, Muslim
Government: republic
Currency: 1 CFA* franc = 100 centimes

CHAD (Africa)
Area: 1,284,000 sq km (495,755 sq miles)
Population: 12,825,314
Capital city: N'Djamena
Main languages: Arabic, Sara, French
Main religions: Muslim, Christian,
indigenous
Government: republic
Currency: 1 CFA* franc = 100 centimes

CHILE (South America)
Area: 756,950 sq km (292,260 sq miles)
Population: 17,619,708
Capital city: Santiago
Main language: Spanish
Main religions: Roman Catholic, Protestant
Government: republic
Currency: 1 Chilean peso = 100 centavos

CHINA (Asia)
Area: 9,596,960 sq km (3,705,407 sq miles)
Population: 1,385,566,537
Capital city: Beijing
Main languages: Mandarin Chinese, Yue, Wu
Main religions: Taoist, Buddhist
Government: communist republic
Currency: 1 yuan = 10 jiao

COLOMBIA (South America)
Area: 1,138,910 sq km (439,736 sq miles)
Population: 48,321,405
Capital city: Bogota
Main language: Spanish
Main religion: Roman Catholic
Government: republic
Currency: 1 Colombian peso = 100 centavos

COMOROS (Africa)
Area: 2,170 sq km (838 sq miles)
Population: 734,917
Capital city: Moroni
Main languages: Comorian*, French, Arabic
Main religion: Sunni Muslim
Government: republic
Currency: 1 Comoran franc = 100 centimes

CONGO (Africa)
Area: 342,000 sq km (132,047 sq miles)
Population: 4,447,632
Capital city: Brazzaville
Main languages: Munukutuba, Lingala,
French
Main religions: Christian, animist
Government: republic
Currency: 1 CFA* franc = 100 centimes

Chile

China

Colombia

Comoros

Congo

Congo (Democratic Republic)

Costa Rica

*CFA = Communaute Financiere Africaine; Comorian = a blend of Swahili
and Arabic; Crioulo = a blend of Portuguese and West African

Croatia

Cuba

Cyprus

Czech Republic

Denmark

Djibouti

Dominica

CONGO (DEMOCRATIC REPUBLIC) (Africa)
Area: 2,345,410 sq km (905,568 sq miles)
Population: 67,513,677
Capital city: Kinshasa
Main languages: Lingala, Swahili, Kikongo, Tshiluba, French, Kingwana
Main religions: Roman Catholic, Protestant, Kimbanguist, Muslim
Government: republic
Currency: 1 Congolese franc = 100 centimes

COSTA RICA (North America)
Area: 51,100 sq km (19,730 sq miles)
Population: 4,872,166
Capital city: San Jose
Main language: Spanish
Main religions: Roman Catholic, Evangelical
Government: democratic republic
Currency: 1 Costa Rican colon = 100 centimos

CROATIA (Europe)
Area: 56,542 sq km (21,831 sq miles)
Population: 4,289,714
Capital city: Zagreb
Main language: Croatian
Main religions: Roman Catholic, Orthodox
Government: republic
Currency: 1 kuna = 100 lipas

CUBA (North America)
Area: 110,860 sq km (42,803 sq miles)
Population: 11,265,629
Capital city: Havana
Main language: Spanish
Main religion: Roman Catholic
Government: communist republic
Currency: 1 Cuban peso = 100 centavos

CYPRUS (Europe)
Area: 9,250 sq km (3,571 sq miles)
Population: 1,141,166
Capital city: Nicosia
Main languages: Greek, Turkish, English
Main religions: Greek Orthodox, Muslim
Government: republic with a self-proclaimed independent Turkish area
Currency: Greek Cypriot area: 1 euro = 100 cents; Turkish Cypriot area: 1 Turkish lira = 100 kurus

CZECH REPUBLIC (Europe)
Area: 78,866 sq km (30,450 sq miles)
Population: 10,702,197
Capital city: Prague
Main language: Czech
Main religion: Roman Catholic
Government: republic
Currency: 1 koruna = 100 haleru

DENMARK (Europe)
Area: 43,094 sq km (16,639 sq miles)
Population: 5,619,096
Capital city: Copenhagen
Main language: Danish
Main religion: Evangelical Lutheran
Government: constitutional monarchy
Currency: 1 Danish krone = 100 oere

DJIBOUTI (Africa)
Area: 23,000 sq km (8,880 sq miles)
Population: 872,932
Capital city: Djibouti
Main languages: Afar, Somali, Arabic, French
Main religion: Muslim
Government: republic
Currency: 1 Djiboutian franc = 100 centimes

DOMINICA (North America)
Area: 754 sq km (291 sq miles)
Population: 72,003
Capital city: Roseau
Main languages: English, French patois
Main religions: Roman Catholic, Protestant
Government: democratic republic
Currency: 1 East Caribbean dollar = 100 cents

DOMINICAN REPUBLIC (North America)
Area: 48,380 sq km (18,680 sq miles)
Population: 10,219,630
Capital city: Santo Domingo
Main language: Spanish
Main religion: Roman Catholic
Government: democratic republic
Currency: 1 Dominican peso = 100 centavos

EAST TIMOR (Asia)
Area: 15,007 sq km (5,794 sq miles)
Population: 1,132,879
Capital city: Dili
Main languages: Tetun (Tetum), Bahasa Indonesia, Portuguese
Main religions: Roman Catholic, animist
Government: republic
Currency: 1 U.S. dollar = 100 cents

ECUADOR (South America)
Area: 283,560 sq km (109,483 sq miles)
Population: 15,737,878
Capital city: Quito
Main languages: Spanish, Quechua
Main religion: Roman Catholic
Government: republic
Currency: 1 U.S. dollar = 100 cents

EGYPT (Africa)
Area: 1,001,450 sq km (386,662 sq miles)
Population: 82,056,378
Capital city: Cairo
Main language: Arabic
Main religion: Sunni Muslim
Government: transitional
Currency: 1 Egyptian pound = 100 piasters

EL SALVADOR (North America)
Area: 21,040 sq km (8,124 sq miles)
Population: 6,340,454
Capital city: San Salvador
Main language: Spanish
Main religion: Roman Catholic
Government: republic
Currency: 1 U.S. dollar = 100 cents

EQUATORIAL GUINEA (Africa)
Area: 28,050 sq km (10,830 sq miles)
Population: 757,014
Capital city: Malabo
Main languages: Fang, Bubi, other Bantu

• **Dominican Republic**

East Timor

• **Ecuador**

Egypt

• **El Salvador**

Equatorial Guinea

Eritrea

*CFA = Communaute Financiere Africaine

GAZETTEER OF STATES CONTINUED:

Estonia

Ethiopia

Federated States of Micronesia

Fiji

Finland

France

Gabon

languages, Spanish, French, Pidgin English
Main religion: Christian
Government: republic
Currency: 1 CFA* franc = 100 centimes

ERITREA (Africa)
Area: 121,320 sq km (46,842 sq miles)
Population: 6,333,135
Capital city: Asmara
Main languages: Tigrinya, Afar, Arabic
Main religions: Muslim, Coptic Christian, Roman Catholic, Protestant
Government: republic
Currency: 1 nafka = 100 cents

ESTONIA (Europe)
Area: 45,226 sq km (17,462 sq miles)
Population: 1,287,251
Capital city: Tallinn
Main languages: Estonian, Russian
Main religions: Evangelical Lutheran, Russian and Estonian Orthodox, other Christian
Government: parliamentary democracy
Currency: 1 Euro = 100 cents

ETHIOPIA (Africa)
Area: 1,127,127 sq km (435,186 sq miles)
Population: 94,100,756
Capital city: Addis Ababa
Main languages: Amharic, Tigrinya, Arabic
Main religions: Muslim, Ethiopian Orthodox, animist
Government: federal republic
Currency: 1 birr = 100 santim

FEDERATED STATES OF MICRONESIA (Australasia/Oceania)
Area: 702 sq km (271 sq miles)
Population: 103,549
Capital city: Palikir
Main languages: Chuuk, Ponapean, English
Main religions: Roman Catholic, Protestant
Government: federal republic
Currency: 1 U.S. dollar = 100 cents

FIJI (Australasia/Oceania)
Area: 18,270 sq km (7,054 sq miles)
Population: 881,065
Capital city: Suva
Main languages: Fijian, Hindustani, English
Main religions: Christian, Hindu
Government: republic
Currency: 1 Fijian dollar = 100 cents

FINLAND (Europe)
Area: 338,145 sq km (130,559 sq miles)
Population: 5,426,323
Capital city: Helsinki
Main language: Finnish, Swedish
Main religion: Evangelical Lutheran
Government: republic
Currency: 1 euro = 100 cents

FRANCE (Europe)
Area: 547,030 sq km (211,209 sq miles)
Population: 64,291,280
Capital city: Paris
Main language: French

Main religion: Roman Catholic
Government: republic
Currency: 1 euro = 100 cents

GABON (Africa)
Area: 267,667 sq km (103,347 sq miles)
Population: 1,671,711
Capital city: Libreville
Main languages: Fang, Myene, French
Main religions: Christian, animist
Government: republic
Currency: 1 CFA* franc = 100 centimes

GAMBIA, THE (Africa)
Area: 11,300 sq km (4,363 sq miles)
Population: 1,849,285
Capital city: Banjul
Main languages: Mandinka, Fula, Wolof, English
Main religion: Muslim
Government: democratic republic
Currency: 1 dalasi = 100 butut

GEORGIA (Asia)
Area: 69,700 sq km (26,911 sq miles)
Population: 4,340,895
Capital city: Tbilisi
Main languages: Georgian, Russian
Main religions: Georgian Orthodox, Muslim, Russian Orthodox
Government: republic
Currency: 1 lari = 100 tetri

GERMANY (Europe)
Area: 357,021 sq km (137,847 sq miles)
Population: 82,726,626
Capital city: Berlin
Main language: German
Main religions: Protestant, Roman Catholic
Government: federal republic
Currency: 1 euro = 100 cents

GHANA (Africa)
Area: 239,460 sq km (92,456 sq miles)
Population: 25,904,598
Capital city: Accra
Main languages: Twi, Fante, Ga, Hausa, Dagbani, Ewe, Nzemi, English
Main religions: indigenous, Muslim, Christian
Government: republic
Currency: 1 new cedi = 100 pesewas

GREECE (Europe)
Area: 131,940 sq km (50,942 sq miles)
Population: 11,127,990
Capital city: Athens
Main language: Greek
Main religion: Greek Orthodox
Government: parliamentary republic
Currency: 1 euro = 100 cents

GRENADA (North America)
Area: 344 sq km (133 sq miles)
Population: 105,897
Capital city: Saint George's
Main languages: English, French patois
Main religions: Roman Catholic, Protestant
Government: parliamentary democracy
Currency: 1 East Caribbean dollar = 100 cents

Gambia, The

Georgia

Germany

Ghana

Greece

Grenada

Guatemala

Guinea

GUATEMALA (North America)
Area: 108,890 sq km (42,043 sq miles)
Population: 15,468,203
Capital city: Guatemala City
Main languages: Spanish, Amerindian languages including Quiche, Kekchi, Cakchiquel, Mam
Main religions: Roman Catholic, Protestant, indigenous Mayan beliefs
Government: democratic republic
Currency: 1 quetzal = 100 centavos

Guinea-Bissau

GUINEA (Africa)
Area: 245,857 sq km (94,926 sq miles)
Population: 11,745,189
Capital city: Conakry
Main languages: Fuuta Jalon, Mallinke, Susu, French
Main religion: Muslim
Government: republic
Currency: 1 Guinean franc = 100 centimes

Guyana

GUINEA-BISSAU (Africa)
Area: 36,120 sq km (13,946 sq miles)
Population: 1,704,255
Capital city: Bissau
Main languages: Crioulo*, Balante, Pulaar, Mandjak, Mandinka, Portuguese
Main religions: indigenous, Muslim
Government: republic
Currency: 1 CFA* franc = 100 centimes

Haiti

GUYANA (South America)
Area: 214,970 sq km (83,000 sq miles)
Population: 799,613
Capital city: Georgetown
Main languages: Guyanese Creole, English, Amerindian languages, Caribbean Hindi
Main religions: Christian, Hindu
Government: republic
Currency: 1 Guyanese dollar = 100 cents

Honduras

HAITI (North America)
Area: 27,750 sq km (10,714 sq miles)
Population: 10,317,461
Capital city: Port-au-Prince
Main languages: Haitian Creole, French
Main religions: Roman Catholic, Protestant, Voodoo
Government: republic
Currency: 1 gourde = 100 centimes

Hungary

HONDURAS (North America)
Area: 112,090 sq km (43,278 sq miles)
Population: 8,097,688
Capital city: Tegucigalpa
Main language: Spanish
Main religion: Roman Catholic
Government: republic
Currency: 1 lempira = 100 centavos

Iceland

HUNGARY (Europe)
Area: 93,030 sq km (35,919 sq miles)
Population: 9,954,941
Capital city: Budapest
Main language: Hungarian
Main religions: Roman Catholic, Calvinist
Government: republic
Currency: 1 forint = 100 filler

ICELAND (Europe)
Area: 103,000 sq km (39,769 sq miles)
Population: 329,535
Capital city: Reykjavik
Main language: Icelandic
Main religion: Evangelical Lutheran
Government: constitutional republic
Currency: Icelandic krona (plural: kronur)

India

INDIA (Asia)
Area: 3,287,590 sq km (1,269,346 sq miles)
Population: 1,252,139,596
Capital city: New Delhi
Main languages: Hindi, English, Bengali, Urdu, over 1,600 other languages and dialects
Main religions: Hindu, Muslim
Government: federal republic
Currency: 1 Indian rupee = 100 paise

Indonesia

INDONESIA (Asia)
Area: 1,919,440 sq km (741,100 sq miles)
Population: 249,865,631
Capital city: Jakarta
Main languages: Bahasa Indonesia, English, Dutch, Javanese
Main religion: Muslim
Government: republic
Currency: 1 Indonesian rupiah = 100 sen

Iran

IRAN (Asia)
Area: 1,648,000 sq km (636,296 sq miles)
Population: 77,447,168
Capital city: Tehran
Main languages: Farsi and other Persian dialects, Azeri
Main religions: Shi'a Muslim, Sunni Muslim
Government: Islamic republic
Currency: 10 Iranian rials = 1 toman

Iraq

IRAQ (Asia)
Area: 437,072 sq km (168,754 sq miles)
Population: 33,765,232
Capital city: Baghdad
Main languages: Arabic, Kurdish
Main religion: Muslim
Government: democratic federal republic
Currency: 1 Iraqi dinar = 1,000 fulus

Ireland

IRELAND (Europe)
Area: 70,280 sq km (27,135 sq miles)
Population: 4,627,173
Capital city: Dublin
Main languages: English, Irish (Gaelic)
Main religion: Roman Catholic
Government: republic
Currency: 1 euro = 100 cents

Israel

ISRAEL (Asia)
Area: 20,770 sq km (8,019 sq miles)
Population: 7,733,144
Capital city: Jerusalem
Main languages: Hebrew, Arabic
Main religions: Jewish, Muslim
Government: republic
Currency: 1 Israeli shekel = 100 agorot

Italy

ITALY (Europe)
Area: 301,230 sq km (116,306 sq miles)

*CFA = Communaute Financiere Africaine;
Crioulo = a blend of Portuguese and West African

GAZETTEER OF STATES CONTINUED:

Ivory Coast

Population: 60,990,277
Capital city: Rome
Main language: Italian, French, German
Main religion: Roman Catholic
Government: republic
Currency: 1 euro = 100 cents

IVORY COAST (Africa)
Area: 322,460 sq km (124,503 sq miles)
Population: 20,316,086
Capital city: Yamoussoukro
Main languages: Baoule, Dioula, French
Main religions: Christian, Muslim, animist
Government: republic
Currency: 1 CFA* = 100 centimes

Jamaica

JAMAICA (North America)
Area: 10,991 sq km (4,244 sq miles)
Population: 2,783,888
Capital city: Kingston
Main languages: Southwestern Caribbean Creole, English
Main religion: Protestant
Government: parliamentary democracy
Currency: 1 Jamaican dollar = 100 cents

Japan

JAPAN (Asia)
Area: 377,835 sq km (145,883 sq miles)
Population: 127,143,577
Capital city: Tokyo
Main language: Japanese
Main religions: Shinto, Buddhist
Government: parliamentary monarchy
Currency: 1 yen = 100 sen

Jordan

JORDAN (Asia)
Area: 92,300 sq km (35,637 sq miles)
Population: 7,273,799
Capital city: Amman
Main languages: Arabic, English
Main religion: Sunni Muslim
Government: constitutional monarchy
Currency: 1 Jordanian dinar = 1,000 fulus

Kazakhstan

KAZAKHSTAN (Asia)
Area: 2,717,300 sq km (1,049,155 sq miles)
Population: 16,440,586
Capital city: Astana
Main languages: Kazakh, Russian
Main religions: Muslim, Russian Orthodox
Government: republic
Currency: 1 Kazakhstani tenge = 100 tiyin

Kenya

KENYA (Africa)
Area: 582,650 sq km (224,962 sq miles)
Population: 44,353,691
Capital city: Nairobi
Main languages: Swahili, English, Kiswahili, Bantu languages
Main religions: Christian, indigenous
Government: republic
Currency: 1 Kenyan shilling = 100 cents

Kiribati

KIRIBATI (Australasia/Oceania)
Area: 811 sq km (313 sq miles)
Population: 102,351
Capital city: Bairiki
Main languages: Gilbertese, i-Kiribati, English
Main religions: Roman Catholic, Protestant

Government: republic
Currency: 1 Australian dollar = 100 cents

KOSOVO (Europe)
Area: 10,887 sq km (4,203 sq miles)
Population: 1,815,606
Capital city: Pristina
Main languages: Albanian, Serbian, Bosnian, Turkish
Main religion: Muslim, Serbian Orthodox, Roman Catholic
Government: republic
Currency: 1 euro = 100 cents

KUWAIT (Asia)
Area: 17,820 sq km (6,880 sq miles)
Population: 3,368,572
Capital city: Kuwait City
Main languages: Arabic, English
Main religion: Muslim
Government: constitutional monarchy
Currency: 1 Kuwaiti dinar = 1,000 fulus

KYRGYZSTAN (Asia)
Area: 198,500 sq km (76,641 sq miles)
Population: 5,547,548
Capital city: Bishkek
Main languages: Kyrgyz, Russian, Uzbek
Main religions: Muslim, Russian Orthodox
Government: republic
Currency: 1 Kyrgyzstani som = 100 tyiyn

LAOS (Asia)
Area: 236,800 sq km (91,429 sq miles)
Population: 6,769,727
Capital city: Vientiane
Main languages: Lao, French, English
Main religions: Buddhist, animist
Government: communist republic
Currency: 1 new kip = 100 at

LATVIA (Europe)
Area: 64,589 sq km (24,938 sq miles)
Population: 2,050,317
Capital city: Riga
Main languages: Latvian, Russian
Main religions: Lutheran, Roman Catholic, Russian Orthodox
Government: republic
Currency: 1 euro = 100 cents**

LEBANON (Asia)
Area: 10,400 sq km (4,015 sq miles)
Population: 4,821,971
Capital city: Beirut
Main languages: Arabic, French, English
Main religions: Muslim, Christian
Government: republic
Currency: 1 Lebanese pound = 100 piasters

LESOTHO (Africa)
Area: 30,355 sq km (11,720 sq miles)
Population: 2,074,465
Capital city: Maseru
Main languages: Sesotho, English, Zulu, Xhosa
Main religions: Christian, indigenous
Government: constitutional monarchy
Currency: 1 loti = 100 lisente

LIBERIA (Africa)
Area: 111,370 sq km (43,000 sq miles)

Kosovo

Kuwait

Kyrgyzstan

Laos

Latvia

Lebanon

Lesotho

*CFA = Communaute Financiere Africaine; **From 2014, replacing Latvian lats and santims

Liberia

Population: 4,294,077
Capital city: Monrovia
Main languages: Kpelle, English, Bassa
Main religions: indigenous, Christian, Muslim
Government: republic
Currency: 1 Liberian dollar = 100 cents

LIBYA (Africa)
Area: 1,759,540 sq km (679,362 sq miles)
Population: 6,201,521
Capital city: Tripoli
Main languages: Arabic, Italian, English
Main religion: Sunni Muslim
Government: emerging democratic republic
Currency: 1 Libyan dinar = 1,000 dirhams

Libya

LIECHTENSTEIN (Europe)
Area: 160 sq km (62 sq miles)
Population: 36,925
Capital city: Vaduz
Main languages: German
Main religion: Roman Catholic
Government: constitutional monarchy
Currency: 1 Swiss franc = 100 centimes

Liechtenstein

LITHUANIA (Europe)
Area: 65,300 sq km (25,212 sq miles)
Population: 3,016,933
Capital city: Vilnius
Main languages: Lithuanian, Polish, Russian
Main religions: Roman Catholic, Lutheran, Russian Orthodox
Government: parliamentary democracy
Currency: 1 Lithuanian litas = 100 centas

Lithuania

LUXEMBOURG (Europe)
Area: 2,586 sq km (998 sq miles)
Population: 530,380
Capital city: Luxembourg
Main languages: Luxembourgish, German, French
Main religion: Roman Catholic
Government: constitutional monarchy
Currency: 1 euro = 100 cents

Luxembourg

MACEDONIA (Europe)
Area: 25,333 sq km (9,781 sq miles)
Population: 2,107,158
Capital city: Skopje
Main languages: Macedonian, Albanian
Main religions: Macedonian Orthodox, Muslim
Government: republic
Currency: 1 Macedonian denar = 100 deni

Macedonia

MADAGASCAR (Africa)
Area: 587,040 sq km (226,657 sq miles)
Population: 22,924,851
Capital city: Antananarivo
Main languages: Malagasy, French, Cotiers
Main religions: indigenous beliefs, Christian
Government: republic
Currency: 1 ariary = 5 iraimbilanja

Madagascar

MALAWI (Africa)
Area: 118,480 sq km (45,745 sq miles)
Population: 16,362,567
Capital city: Lilongwe
Main languages: Chichewa, English, Chinyanja

Main religions: Protestant, Roman Catholic, Muslim
Government: republic
Currency: 1 Malawian kwacha = 100 tambala

Malawi

MALAYSIA (Asia)
Area: 329,750 sq km (127,317 sq miles)
Population: 29,716,965
Capital city: Kuala Lumpur
Main languages: Bahasa Melayu, English, Chinese dialects, Tamil
Main religions: Muslim, Buddhist, Daoist
Government: constitutional monarchy
Currency: 1 ringgit = 100 sen

Malaysia

MALDIVES (Asia)
Area: 300 sq km (116 sq miles)
Population: 345,023
Capital city: Male
Main languages: Maldivian, English
Main religion: Sunni Muslim
Government: republic
Currency: 1 rufiyaa = 100 laari

Maldives

MALI (Africa)
Area: 1,240,000 sq km (478,767 sq miles)
Population: 15,301,650
Capital city: Bamako
Main languages: Bambara, Fulani, Songhai, French
Main religion: Muslim
Government: republic
Currency: 1 CFA* franc = 100 centimes

Mali

MALTA (Europe)
Area: 316 sq km (122 sq miles)
Population: 429,004
Capital city: Valletta
Main languages: Maltese, English
Main religion: Roman Catholic
Government: democratic republic
Currency: 1 euro = 100 cents

Malta

MARSHALL ISLANDS (Australasia/Oceania)
Area: 181 sq km (70 sq miles)
Population: 52,634
Capital city: Majuro
Main languages: Marshallese, English
Main religion: Protestant
Government: republic
Currency: 1 U.S. dollar = 100 cents

Marshall Islands

MAURITANIA (Africa)
Area: 1,030,700 sq km (397,955 sq miles)
Population: 3,889,880
Capital city: Nouakchott
Main languages: Arabic, Wolof, French
Main religion: Muslim
Government: Islamic republic
Currency: 1 ouguiya = 5 khoums

MAURITIUS (Africa)
Area: 2,040 sq km (788 sq miles)
Population: 1,244,403
Capital city: Port Louis
Main languages: Mauritius Creole French, French, Hindi, Bhojpuri, Urdu, Tamil, English
Main religion: Hindu, Christian, English
Government: parliamentary democracy
Currency: 1 Mauritian rupee = 100 cents

Mauritania

GAZETTEER OF STATES CONTINUED:

Mauritius

MEXICO (North America)
Nationality: Mexican
Area: 1,972,550 sq km (761,606 sq miles)
Population: 122,332,399
Capital city: Mexico City
Main languages: Spanish, Mayan, Nahuatl
Main religion: Roman Catholic, Protestant
Government: federal republic
Currency: 1 new Mexican peso = 100 centavos

Mexico

MOLDOVA (Europe)
Area: 33,843 sq km (13,067 sq miles)
Population: 3,487,204
Capital city: Chisinau
Main languages: Moldovan, Russian, Gagauz
Main religion: Eastern Orthodox
Government: republic
Currency: 1 Moldovan leu = 100 bani

Moldova

MONACO (Europe)
Area: 1.95 sq km (0.75 sq miles)
Population: 37,831
Capital city: Monaco
Main languages: French, Monegasque, Italian
Main religion: Roman Catholic
Government: constitutional monarchy
Currency: 1 euro = 100 cents

MONGOLIA (Asia)
Area: 1,564,116 sq km (603,909 sq miles)
Population: 2,839,073
Capital city: Ulan Bator
Main language: Khalkha Mongol
Main religion: Tibetan Buddhist Lamaist
Government: republic
Currency: Mongolian tugrik

Monaco

MONTENEGRO (Europe)
Area: 14,026 sq km (5,415 sq miles)
Population: 621,383
Capital city: Podgorica
Main language: Serbian, Montenegrin
Main religion: Orthodox Christian, Muslim
Government: republic
Currency: 1 euro = 100 cents

Mongolia

MOROCCO (Africa)
Area: 446,550 sq km (172,414 sq miles)
Population: 33,008,150
Capital city: Rabat
Main languages: Arabic, Berber, French
Main religion: Muslim
Government: constitutional monarchy
Currency: 1 Moroccan dirham = 100 centimes

Montenegro

MOZAMBIQUE (Africa)
Area: 801,590 sq km (309,496 sq miles)
Population: 25,833,752
Capital city: Maputo
Main languages: Makua, Tsonga, Portuguese,
Emskhuwa, Xichangana
Main religions: indigenous, Christian, Muslim
Government: republic
Currency: 1 metical = 100 centavos

NAMIBIA (Africa)
Area: 825,418 sq km (318,696 sq miles)
Population: 2,303,315
Capital city: Windhoek

Morocco

Main languages: Afrikaans, German, English
Main religions: Christian, indigenous
Government: republic
Currency: 1 Namibian dollar = 100 cents

NAURU (Australasia/Oceania)
Area: 21 sq km (8 sq miles)
Population: 10,051
Capital: Yaren
Main languages: Nauruan, English
Main religion: Christian
Government: republic
Currency: 1 Australian dollar = 100 cents

NEPAL (Asia)
Area: 147,181 sq km (56,827 sq miles)
Population: 27,797,457
Capital city: Kathmandu
Main languages: Nepali, Maithili
Main religions: Hindu, Buddhist
Government: federal republic
Currency: 1 Nepalese rupee = 100 paisa

NETHERLANDS (Europe)
Area: 41,526 sq km (16,033 sq miles)
Population: 16,759,229
Capital cities: Amsterdam, The Hague
Main language: Dutch
Main religion: Protestant, Roman Catholic
Government: constitutional monarchy
Currency: 1 euro = 100 cents

NEW ZEALAND (Australasia/Oceania)
Area: 268,680 sq km (103,738 sq miles)
Population: 4,505,761
Capital city: Wellington
Main languages: English, Maori
Main religion: Christian
Government: parliamentary democracy
Currency: 1 New Zealand dollar = 100 cents

NICARAGUA (North America)
Area: 129,494 sq km (49,998 sq miles)
Population: 6,080,478
Capital city: Managua
Main language: Spanish
Main religion: Roman Catholic, Protestant
Government: republic
Currency: 1 gold cordoba = 100 centavos

NIGER (Africa)
Area: 1,267,000 sq km (489,191 sq miles)
Population: 17,831,270
Capital city: Niamey
Main languages: Hausa, Djerma, French
Main religion: Muslim
Government: republic
Currency: 1 CFA* franc = 100 centimes

NIGERIA (Africa)
Area: 923,768 sq km (356,669 sq miles)
Population: 173,615,345
Capital city: Abuja
Main languages: Hausa, Yoruba, Igbo,
English, Fulani
Main religions: Muslim, Christian, indigenous
Government: federal republic
Currency: 1 naira = 100 kobo

Mozambique

Namibia

Nauru

Nepal

Netherlands

New Zealand

Nicaragua

*CFA = Communaute Financiere Africaine

Niger

NORTH KOREA (Asia)
Area: 120,540 sq km (46,541 sq miles)
Population: 24,895,480
Capital city: Pyongyang
Main language: Korean
Main religions: Buddhist, Confucian
Government: authoritarian socialist
Currency: 1 North Korean won = 100 chon

NORWAY (Europe)
Area: 323,802 sq km (125,021 sq miles)
Population: 5,042,671
Capital city: Oslo
Main language: Norwegian
Main religion: Evangelical Lutheran
Government: constitutional monarchy
Currency: 1 Norwegian krone = 100 oere

OMAN (Asia)
Area: 212,460 sq km (82,031 sq miles)
Population: 3,632,444
Capital city: Muscat
Main languages: Arabic, English, Baluchi
Main religion: Muslim
Government: monarchy
Currency: 1 Omani rial = 1,000 baiza

PAKISTAN (Asia)
Area: 803,940 sq km (310,403 sq miles)
Population: 182,142,594
Capital city: Islamabad
Main languages: Punjabi, Sindhi, Urdu, English
Main religion: Muslim
Government: federal republic
Currency: 1 Pakistani rupee = 100 paisa

PALAU (Australasia/Oceania)
Area: 458 sq km (177 sq miles)
Population: 20,918
Capital city: Melekeok
Main languages: Palauan, English, Philipino
Main religions: Christian, Modekngei
Government: democratic republic
Currency: 1 U.S. dollar = 100 cents

PANAMA (North America)
Area: 78,200 sq km (30,193 sq miles)
Population: 3,864,170
Capital city: Panama City
Main languages: Spanish, English
Main religions: Roman Catholic, Protestant
Government: democracy
Currency: 1 balboa = 100 centesimos

PAPUA NEW GUINEA
(Australasia/Oceania)
Area: 462,840 sq km (178,704 sq miles)
Population: 7,321,262
Capital city: Port Moresby
Main languages: Tok Pisin, Hiri Motu, English
Main religions: Christian, indigenous
Government: parliamentary democracy
Currency: 1 kina = 100 toea

PARAGUAY (South America)
Area: 406,750 sq km (157,047 sq miles)
Population: 6,802,295

Nigeria

North Korea

Norway

Oman

Pakistan

Palau

Capital city: Asuncion
Main languages: Guarani, Spanish
Main religion: Roman Catholic
Government: republic
Currency: 1 guarani = 100 centimos

PERU (South America)
Area: 1,285,220 sq km (496,226 sq miles)
Population: 30,375,603
Capital city: Lima
Main languages: Spanish, Quechua, Aymara
Main religion: Roman Catholic
Government: republic
Currency: 1 nuevo sol = 100 centimos

PHILIPPINES (Asia)
Area: 300,000 sq km (115,831 sq miles)
Population: 98,393,574
Capital city: Manila
Main languages: Tagalog, English, Ilocano, Cebuano
Main religion: Roman Catholic
Government: republic
Currency: 1 Philippine peso = 100 centavos

POLAND (Europe)
Area: 312,679 sq km (120,726 sq miles)
Population: 38,216,635
Capital city: Warsaw
Main language: Polish
Main religion: Roman Catholic
Government: democratic republic
Currency: 1 zloty = 100 groszy

PORTUGAL (Europe)
Area: 92,391 sq km (35,672 sq miles)
Population: 10,608,156
Capital city: Lisbon
Main language: Portuguese
Main religion: Roman Catholic
Government: democratic republic
Currency: 1 euro = 100 cents

QATAR (Asia)
Area: 11,437 sq km (4,416 sq miles)
Population: 2,168,673
Capital city: Doha
Main languages: Arabic, English
Main religion: Muslim
Government: monarchy
Currency: 1 Qatari riyal = 100 dirhams

ROMANIA (Europe)
Area: 237,500 sq km (91,699 sq miles)
Population: 21,698,585
Capital city: Bucharest
Main languages: Romanian, Hungarian, German
Main religion: Romanian Orthodox
Government: republic
Currency: 1 leu = 100 bani

RUSSIA (Europe and Asia)
Area: 17,075,200 sq km (6,592,772 sq miles)
Population: 142,833,689
Capital city: Moscow
Main language: Russian
Main religions: Russian Orthodox, Muslim
Government: federal government
Currency: 1 ruble = 100 kopeks

Panama

**Papua
New Guinea**

Paraguay

• Peru

Philippines

Poland

Portugal

GAZETTEER OF STATES CONTINUED:

Qatar

Romania

Russia

Rwanda

Saint Kitts and Nevis

Saint Lucia

Saint Vincent and the Grenadines

Samoa

San Marino

Sao Tome and Principe

Saudi Arabia

Senegal

Serbia

Seychelles

RWANDA (Africa)
Area: 26,338 sq km (10,169 sq miles)
Population: 11,776,522
Capital city: Kigali
Main languages: Kinyarwanda, French, English, Swahili
Main religions: Roman Catholic, Protestant, Adventist
Government: republic
Currency: 1 Rwandan franc = 100 centimes

SAINT KITTS AND NEVIS (North America)
Area: 261 sq km (101 sq miles)
Population: 54,191
Capital city: Basseterre
Main language: English
Main religions: Protestant, Roman Catholic
Government: constitutional monarchy
Currency: 1 East Caribbean dollar = 100 cents

SAINT LUCIA (North America)
Area: 616 sq km (238 sq miles)
Population: 182,273
Capital city: Castries
Main languages: French patois, English
Main religion: Roman Catholic, Protestant
Government: parliamentary democracy
Currency: 1 East Caribbean dollar = 100 cents

SAINT VINCENT AND THE GRENADINES (North America)
Area: 389 sq km (150 sq miles)
Population: 109,373
Capital city: Kingstown
Main languages: English, French patois
Main religions: Protestant, Roman Catholic
Government: parliamentary democracy
Currency: 1 East Caribbean dollar = 100 cents

SAMOA (Australasia/Oceania)
Area: 2,944 sq km (1,137 sq miles)
Population: 190,372
Capital city: Apia
Main languages: Samoan, English
Main religion: Christian
Government: constitutional monarchy
Currency: 1 tala = 100 sene

SAN MARINO (Europe)
Area: 61 sq km (24 sq miles)
Population: 31,448
Capital city: San Marino
Main language: Italian
Main religion: Roman Catholic
Government: republic
Currency: 1 euro = 100 cents

SAO TOME AND PRINCIPE (Africa)
Area: 1,001 sq km (386 sq miles)
Population: 192,993
Capital city: Sao Tome
Main languages: Crioulo* dialects, Portuguese
Main religion: Christian
Government: republic
Currency: 1 dobra = 100 centimos

SAUDI ARABIA (Asia)
Area: 2,149,690 sq km (830,000 sq miles)

Population: 28,828,870
Capital city: Riyadh
Main language: Arabic
Main religion: Muslim
Government: monarchy
Currency: 1 Saudi riyal = 100 halalah

SENEGAL (Africa)
Area: 196,190 sq km (75,749 sq miles)
Population: 14,133,280
Capital city: Dakar
Main languages: Wolof, French, Pulaar
Main religion: Muslim
Government: democratic republic
Currency: 1 CFA* franc = 100 centimes

SERBIA (Europe)
Area: 77,474 sq km (29,913 sq miles)
Population: 9,510,506
Capital city: Belgrade
Main language: Serbian, Hungarian
Main religion: Serbian Orthodox, Roman Catholic, Muslim
Government: republic
Currency: 1 Serbian dinar = 100 para

SEYCHELLES (Africa)
Area: 455 sq km (176 sq miles)
Population: 92,838
Capital city: Victoria
Main language: Seselwa, English
Main religion: Roman Catholic
Government: republic
Currency: 1 Seychellois rupee = 100 cents

SIERRA LEONE (Africa)
Area: 71,740 sq km (27,699 sq miles)
Population: 6,092,075
Capital city: Freetown
Main languages: Mende, Temne, Krio, English
Main religions: Muslim, indigenous, Christian
Government: republic
Currency: 1 leone = 100 cents

SINGAPORE (Asia)
Area: 693 sq km (268 sq miles)
Population: 5,411,737
Capital city: Singapore
Main languages: Chinese, Malay, English, Tamil
Main religions: Buddhist, Muslim
Government: parliamentary republic
Currency: 1 Singapore dollar = 100 cents

SLOVAKIA (Europe)
Area: 48,845 sq km (18,859 sq miles)
Population: 5,450,223
Capital city: Bratislava
Main languages: Slovak, Hungarian
Main religion: Roman Catholic, Protestant
Government: parliamentary democracy
Currency: 1 euro = 100 cents

SLOVENIA (Europe)
Area: 20,273 sq km (7,827 sq miles)
Population: 2,071,997
Capital city: Ljubljana

*CFA = Communaute Financiere Africaine; Crioulo = a blend of Portuguese and West African

Sierra Leone

Main language: Slovenian
Main religion: Roman Catholic
Government: democratic republic
Currency: 1 euro = 100 cents

**SOLOMON ISLANDS
(Australasia/Oceania)**
Area: 28,450 sq km (10,985 sq miles)
Population: 561,231
Capital city: Honiara
Main languages: Solomon pidgin, Kwara'ae,
To'abaita, English
Main religion: Christian
Government: parliamentary democracy
Currency: 1 Solomon Islands dollar =
100 cents

Singapore

SOMALIA (Africa)
Area: 637,657 sq km (246,201 sq miles)
Population: 10,495,583
Capital city: Mogadishu
Main languages: Somali, Arabic, Oromo
Main religion: Sunni Muslim
Government: federal parliamentary republic
Currency: 1 Somali shilling = 100 cents

SOUTH AFRICA (Africa)
Area: 1,219,912 sq km (471,011 sq miles)
Population: 52,776,130
Capital cities: Pretoria, Cape Town, Bloemfontein
Main languages: Zulu, Xhosa, Afrikaans, Pedi,
English, Tswana, Sotho, Tsonga, Swati, Venda,
Ndebele, Isi Zulu, Isi Xhosa
Main religions: Christian, indigenous
Government: republic
Currency: 1 rand = 100 cents

Slovakia

SOUTH KOREA (Asia)
Area: 98,480 sq km (38,023 sq miles)
Population: 48,508,972
Capital city: Seoul
Main language: Korean
Main religions: Christian, Buddhist
Government: republic
Currency: 1 South Korean won = 100 jeon

• Slovenia

SOUTH SUDAN (Africa)
Area: 619,745 sq km (239,285 sq miles)
Population: 11,296,173
Capital city: Juba
Main languages: English, Arabic, Dinka,
Nuer, Bari, Zande, Shilluk
Main religions: indigenous, Christian, Islam
Government: federal democratic republic
Currency: 1 South Sudanese pound =
100 piastres

Solomon Islands

SPAIN (Europe)
Area: 504,750 sq km (194,885 sq miles)
Population: 46,926,963
Capital city: Madrid
Main languages: Castilian Spanish, Catalan
Main religion: Roman Catholic
Government: constitutional monarchy
Currency: 1 euro = 100 cents

SRI LANKA (Asia)
Area: 65,610 sq km (25,332 sq miles)
Population: 46,926,963

Somalia

South Africa

Capital cities: Colombo, Sri Jayewardenepura
Kotte
Main languages: Sinhala, Tamil, English
Main religions: Buddhist, Hindu, Muslim
Government: republic
Currency: 1 Sri Lankan rupee = 100 cents

SUDAN (Africa)
Area: 1,844,797 sq km (712,280 sq miles)
Population: 37,964,306
Capital city: Khartoum
Main languages: Arabic (official), English
(official), Nubian, Ta Bedawie, Fur
Main religions: Sunni Muslim
Government: federal republic
Currency: 1 Sudanese pound = 100 piastres

SURINAME (South America)
Area: 163,270 sq km (63,039 sq miles)
Population: 539,276
Capital city: Paramaribo
Main languages: Sranang Tongo, Dutch,
English
Main religions: Hindu, Christian, Muslim
Government: republic
Currency: 1 Surinamese dollar = 100 cents

SWAZILAND (Africa)
Area: 17,363 sq km (6,704 sq miles)
Population: 1,249,514
Capital cities: Mbabane, Lobamba
Main languages: Swati, English
Main religions: Christian, indigenous, Muslim
Government: monarchy
Currency: 1 lilangeni = 100 cents

SWEDEN (Europe)
Area: 449,964 sq km (173,732 sq miles)
Population: 9,571,105
Capital city: Stockholm
Main language: Swedish
Main religion: Lutheran
Government: constitutional monarchy
Currency: 1 Swedish krona = 100 oere

SWITZERLAND (Europe)
Area: 41,290 sq km (15,942 sq miles)
Population: 8,077,833
Capital city: Bern
Main languages: German, French, Italian
Main religions: Roman Catholic, Protestant
Government: federal republic
Currency: 1 Swiss franc, franken or frano =
100 centimes, rappen or centesimi

SYRIA (Asia)
Area: 185,180 sq km (71,498 sq miles)
Population: 21,898,061
Capital city: Damascus
Main languages: Arabic, Kurdish
Main religions: Muslim, Christian
Government: republic
Currency: 1 Syrian pound = 100 piastres

TAJIKISTAN (Asia)
Area: 143,100 sq km (55,251 sq miles)
Population: 8,207,834
Capital city: Dushanbe
Main languages: Tajik, Russian

South Korea

South Sudan

• Spain

Sri Lanka

Sudan

Suriname

Swaziland

Sweden

Switzerland

Syria

Tajikistan

Tanzania

Thailand

Togo

Main religion: Sunni Muslim
Government: republic
Currency: 1 somoni = 100 dirams

TANZANIA (Africa)
Area: 945,087 sq km (364,900 sq miles)
Population: 49,253,126
Capital cities: Dar es Salaam, Dodoma
Main languages: Swahili, English, Sukuma
Main religions: Christian, Muslim, indigenous
Government: republic
Currency: 1 Tanzanian shilling = 100 cents

THAILAND (Asia)
Area: 514,000 sq km (198,457 sq miles)
Population: 67,010,502
Capital city: Bangkok
Main languages: Thai, English, Chaochow
Main religion: Buddhist
Government: constitutional monarchy
Currency: 1 baht = 100 satang

TOGO (Africa)
Area: 56,785 sq km (21,925 sq miles)
Population: 6,816,982
Capital city: Lome
Main languages: Mina, Ewe, Kabye, French
Main religions: indigenous, Christian, Muslim
Government: republic
Currency: 1 CFA* franc = 100 centimes

TONGA (Australasia/Oceania)
Area: 748 sq km (289 sq miles)
Population: 105,323
Capital city: Nukualofa
Main languages: Tongan, English
Main religion: Christian
Government: constitutional monarchy
Currency: 1 pa'anga = 100 seniti

TRINIDAD AND TOBAGO (North America)
Area: 5,128 sq km (1,980 sq miles)
Population: 1,341,151
Capital city: Port-of-Spain
Main languages: English, French, Spanish, Hindi
Main religions: Christian, Hindu
Government: parliamentary democracy
Currency: 1 Trinidad and Tobago dollar = 100 cents

TUNISIA (Africa)
Area: 163,610 sq km (63,170 sq miles)
Population: 10,996,515
Capital city: Tunis
Main languages: Arabic, French
Main religion: Muslim
Government: republic
Currency: 1 Tunisian dinar = 1,000 millimes

TURKEY (Europe and Asia)
Area: 780,580 sq km (301,384 sq miles)
Population: 74,932,641
Capital city: Ankara
Main language: Turkish
Main religion: Muslim
Government: democratic republic
Currency: 1 Turkish lira = 100 kurus

TURKMENISTAN (Asia)
Area: 488,100 sq km (188,456 sq miles)
Population: 5,240,072

Capital city: Ashgabat (Ashkhabad)
Main languages: Turkmen, Russian
Main religion: Muslim
Government: republic
Currency: 1 Turkmen new manat = 100 tenge

TUVALU (Australasia/Oceania)
Area: 26 sq km (10 sq miles)
Population: 9,876
Capital city: Funafuti
Main languages: Tuvaluan, English
Main religion: Congregationalist
Government: constitutional monarchy
Currency: 1 Tuvaluan dollar or 1 Australian dollar = 100 cents

UGANDA (Africa)
Area: 236,040 sq km (91,136 sq miles)
Population: 37,578,876
Capital city: Kampala
Main languages: Luganda, English, Swahili
Main religion: Christian, Muslim, indigenous
Government: republic
Currency: 1 Ugandan shilling = 100 cents

UKRAINE (Europe)
Area: 603,700 sq km (233,090 sq miles)
Population: 45,238,805
Capital city: Kiev
Main languages: Ukrainian, Russian
Main religion: Ukrainian Orthodox
Government: republic
Currency: 1 hryvnia = 100 kopiykas

UNITED ARAB EMIRATES (Asia)
Area: 83,600 sq km (32,278 sq miles)
Population: 9,346,129
Capital city: Abu Dhabi
Main languages: Arabic, English
Main religion: Muslim
Government: federation
Currency: 1 Emirati dirham = 100 fulus

UNITED KINGDOM (Europe)
Area: 244,820 sq km (94,526 sq miles)
Population: 63,136,265
Capital city: London
Main language: English
Main religions: Anglican, Roman Catholic
Government: constitutional monarchy
Currency: 1 British pound = 100 pence

UNITED STATES OF AMERICA (North America)
Area: 9,826,630 sq km (3,794,083 sq miles)
Population: 320,050,716
Capital city: Washington D.C.
Main language: English
Main religions: Protestant, Roman Catholic
Government: federal republic
Currency: 1 U.S. dollar = 100 cents

URUGUAY (South America)
Area: 176,220 sq km (68,039 sq miles)
Population: 3,407,062
Capital city: Montevideo
Main language: Spanish
Main religion: Roman Catholic
Government: republic
Currency: 1 Uruguayan peso = 100 centesimos

Tonga

Trinidad and Tobago

Tunisia

Turkey

Turkmenistan

Tuvalu

Uganda

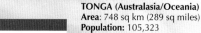

UZBEKISTAN (Asia)
Area: 447,400 sq km (172,742 sq miles)
Population: 28,934,102
Capital city: Tashkent
Main languages: Uzbek, Russian
Main religions: Muslim, Eastern Orthodox
Government: republic
Currency: 1 Uzbekistani sum = 100 tiyin

VANUATU (Australasia/Oceania)
Area: 12,200 sq km (4,710 sq miles)
Population: 252,763
Capital city: Port Vila
Main languages: Bislama, French, English
Main religion: Christian
Government: republic
Currency: 1 vatu = 100 centimes

VATICAN CITY (Europe)
Area: 0.44 sq km (0.17 sq miles)
Population: 799
Capital city: Vatican City
Main languages: Italian, Latin
Main religion: Roman Catholic
Government: led by the Pope
Currency: 1 euro = 100 cents

VENEZUELA (South America)
Area: 912,050 sq km (352,144 sq miles)
Population: 30,405,207
Capital city: Caracas
Main language: Spanish
Main religion: Roman Catholic
Government: federal republic
Currency: 1 bolivar = 100 centimos

VIETNAM (Asia)
Area: 329,560 sq km (127,244 sq miles)
Population: 91,679,733
Capital city: Hanoi
Main languages: Vietnamese, French, English, Khmer, Chinese
Main religion: Buddhist
Government: communist state
Currency: Vietnamese dong

YEMEN (Asia)
Area: 527,970 sq km (203,850 sq miles)
Population: 24,407,381
Capital city: Sana
Main language: Arabic
Main religion: Muslim
Government: republic
Currency: 1 Yemeni rial = 100 fulus

ZAMBIA (Africa)
Area: 752,614 sq km (290,586 sq miles)
Population: 14,538,640
Capital city: Lusaka
Main languages: Bemba, Tonga, Nyanja, English, Kaonda, Lozi, Lunda, Luvale
Main religions: Christian, Muslim, Hindu
Government: republic
Currency: 1 Zambian kwacha = 100 ngwee

ZIMBABWE (Africa)
Area: 390,580 sq km (150,804 sq miles)
Population: 14,149,648
Capital city: Harare
Main languages: Shona, Ndebele, English
Main religions: Christian, indigenous
Government: republic
Currency: 1 Zimbabwean dollar = 100 cents

Ukraine

United Arab Emirates

United Kingdom

United States of America

Uruguay

Uzbekistan

Vanuatu

Vatican City

Venezuela

Vietnam

Yemen

Zambia

Zimbabwe

The United Nations

The United Nations (U.N.) is an organization which aims to bring countries together to work for peace and development. Of the world's 195 states, 193 are members of the U.N. Those that don't belong are Kosovo and the Vatican City.

Internet links

For links to websites with flags, facts, maps, quizzes, and more information about the U.N., go to www.usborne.com/quicklinks

Ban Ki-moon, the Secretary-General of the U.N., shakes hands with Hillary Clinton, the Secretary of State of the U.S.A.

TIME ZONES

When it's midday in Rio de Janeiro, it's midnight in Tokyo. This is because we divide the Earth into different time zones. Within each zone, people usually set their clocks to the same time. If you fly between two zones, you change your watch to the time of the new zone.

Dividing up time

There are 25 different time zones. They are separated by one-hour intervals and there is a new time zone roughly every 15 degrees of longitude*. The zones are measured in hours ahead of or behind Greenwich Mean Time, or GMT, which is the time at the Prime Meridian Line*.

Governments can change their countries' time zones. So, for convenience, whole countries usually keep the same local time instead of sticking to the zones exactly. For example, China could be divided into several time zones, but instead the whole country keeps the same time. A few areas, such as India, Iran and parts of Australia, use non-standard half-hour deviations.

Summer time

Some countries adjust their clocks in summer. For example, in the U.K. everybody's clocks go forward one hour. This is known as Daylight Saving Time or Summer Time. It is a way of getting more out of the days by giving people an extra hour of daylight in the evening. It reduces energy use because people don't use as much electricity for lights.

Changing dates

On the opposite side of the world from the Prime Meridian Line is the International Date Line, which runs mostly through the Pacific Ocean and bends to avoid land. Places to the west of it are 24 hours ahead of places to the east. This means that if you travel east across it you lose a day and if you travel west across you gain a day.

This map shows the different time zones. The times at the top of the map tell you the time it is in the different zones when it is noon at the Prime Meridian Line. The numbers in circles tell you how many hours ahead of or behind Greenwich Mean Time an area is.

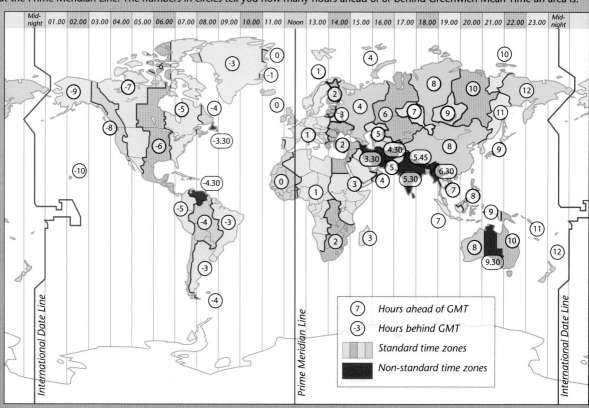

*Longitude, 6; Prime Meridian Line, 6

GENERAL INDEX

Places featured in the maps in this atlas are listed in a separate index on pages 130–143.

Answers to geography quiz (pages 110–111)

Mystery places

Top left: La Sagrada Familia church in Barcelona, Spain
Top right: The Taj Mahal near Agra, India
Middle left: The Golden Gate Bridge in San Francisco, U.S.A.
Middle right: The Acropolis in Athens, Greece
Bottom: The Burj Khalifa in Dubai, United Arab Emirates

Quick quiz

1. Japan
2. 6 a.m.
3. Australia
4. North America
5. Czech Republic
6. Lake Baikal, Russia
7. Vatican City
8. Costa Rica
9. Nigeria
10. Ankara

Survival challenge

1. b. An umbrella would not be useful as it doesn't rain in Antarctica. It's also the world's windiest continent, so an umbrella wouldn't last long! You would need sunglasses and sunscreen, however, as the reflection of the sun off snow is dazzling and can cause sunburn.

2. b. Extra clothes would help to conserve your sweat, which cools down your skin, and resting in the shade (if there is any) would help your body stay as cool as possible. Being active, talking or singing would cause your body to lose moisture and your mouth to dry out – which would make you even thirstier.

3. All of them. Six-eyed crab spiders are one of the most venomous types of spiders in the world. Their bites are so severe that they can cause death. Button spiders have a bite which is very painful, though not lethal, while a bite from a violin spider causes painful swelling.

4. c. A bear will only attack if it thinks you are a threat to it. If you moved away slowly, not making any sudden movements, it would probably leave you alone. You should only lie down (preferably curled into a ball) and play dead if the bear actually takes a swipe at you.

MAP INDEX

This is an index of the places and features named on the maps. Each entry consists of the following parts: the name (given in bold type), the country or region within which it is located (given in italics), the page on which the name can be found (given in bold type), and the grid reference (also given in bold type). For some names, there is also a description explaining what kind of place it is – for example a country, internal administrative area (state or province), national capital or internal capital. To find a place on a map, first find the map indicated by the page reference. Then use the grid reference to find the square containing the name or town symbol. See page 11 for help with using the grid.

Atar, *Mauritania*, 100 C4
Atbarah, *Sudan*, 99 H5
Atbasar, *Kazakhstan*, 72 J1
Athabasca, *Canada*, 30 H3
Athabasca, Lake, *Canada*, 30 J3
Athens, *Greece, national capital*, 91 G4
Atka Island, *U.S.A.*, 31 B3
Atlanta, *U.S.A., internal capital*, 33 K4
Atlantic City, *U.S.A.*, 33 M3
Atlantic Ocean, 20
Atlas Mountains, *Africa*, 100 D2
At Taif, *Saudi Arabia*, 73 D7
Attapu, *Laos*, 66 E5
Attu Island, *U.S.A.*, 31 A3
Atyrau, *Kazakhstan*, 85 G4
Auckland, *New Zealand*, 55 P7
Augsburg, *Germany*, 88 G4
Augusta, *U.S.A., internal capital*, 33 N2
Aurangabad, *India*, 71 D7
Austin, *U.S.A., internal capital*, 32 G4
Australasia and Oceania, 21
Australia, *Australasia, country*, 54 E4
Australian Capital Territory, *Australia, internal admin. area*, 55 J6
Austria, *Europe, country*, 90 E2
Awasa, *Ethiopia*, 103 G2
Ayacucho, *Peru*, 42 D6
Aydin, *Turkey*, 91 H4
Ayers Rock, *Australia*, 54 F5
Ayoun el Atrous, *Mauritania*, 101 D5
Azerbaijan, *Asia, country*, 72 E3
Azores, *Atlantic Ocean*, 100 K10
Azov, Sea of, *Europe*, 91 K2
Az Zarqa, *Jordan*, 73 C5

b

Baardheere, *Somalia*, 103 H3
Babahoyo, *Ecuador*, 42 C4
Bab al Mandab, *Africa/Asia*, 99 K6
Babruysk, *Belarus*, 87 J5
Babuyan Islands, *Philippines*, 67 H4
Babylon, *Iraq*, 72 D5
Bacabal, *Brazil*, 43 K4
Bacau, *Romania*, 91 H2
Bac Lieu, *Vietnam*, 66 E6
Bacolod, *Philippines*, 67 H5
Badajoz, *Spain*, 89 C7
Baffin Bay, *Canada*, 31 N1
Baffin Island, *Canada*, 31 M2
Bafoussam, *Cameroon*, 102 B2
Bage, *Brazil*, 44 H6
Baghdad, *Iraq, national capital*, 72 D5
Bahamas, The, *North America, country*, 33 L5
Bahawalpur, *Pakistan*, 70 C5
Bahia, *Brazil*, 43 L6
Bahia Blanca, *Argentina*, 45 F7
Bahir Dar, *Ethiopia*, 103 G1
Bahrain, *Asia, country*, 73 F6
Baia Mare, *Romania*, 91 G2
Baie-Comeau, *Canada*, 31 N4
Baikal, Lake, *Russia*, 75 F3
Bairiki, *Kiribati, national capital*, 52 E4
Bakersfield, *U.S.A.*, 32 C3
Baku, *Azerbaijan, national capital*, 72 E3
Balakovo, *Russia*, 85 F3
Balaton, Lake, *Hungary*, 87 F7
Balbina Reservoir, *Brazil*, 43 G4
Baldy Peak, *U.S.A.*, 32 E4
Balearic Islands, *Spain*, 89 E7
Bali, *Indonesia*, 64 E5
Balikesir, *Turkey*, 91 H4
Balikpapan, *Indonesia*, 64 E4
Balkanabat, *Turkmenistan*, 72 F4
Balkan Mountains, *Europe*, 91 G3
Balkhash, Lake, *Kazakhstan*, 70 D1
Balkuduk, *Kazakhstan*, 85 F4
Balqash, *Kazakhstan*, 70 D1
Balti, *Moldova*, 91 H2
Baltic Sea, *Europe*, 87 F4
Baltimore, *U.S.A.*, 33 L3
Bamako, *Mali, national capital*, 101 D6
Bamenda, *Cameroon*, 102 B2
Bancs Providence, *Seychelles*, 105 K1
Banda Aceh, *Indonesia*, 64 A2
Bandar-e Abbas, *Iran*, 73 G6

Bandar Seri Begawan, *Brunei, national capital*, 64 D2
Banda Sea, *Indonesia*, 65 G5
Bandundu, *Democratic Republic of Congo*, 102 C4
Bandung, *Indonesia*, 64 C5
Banfora, *Burkina Faso*, 101 E6
Bangalore, *India*, 71 D8
Bangassou, *Central African Republic*, 102 D3
Bangka, *Indonesia*, 64 C4
Bangkok, *Thailand, national capital*, 66 D5
Bangladesh, *Asia, country*, 71 F6
Bangor, *U.S.A.*, 33 N2
Bangui, *Central African Republic, national capital*, 102 C3
Bangweulu, Lake, *Zambia*, 104 E2
Banja Luka, *Bosnia and Herzegovina*, 90 F2
Banjarmasin, *Indonesia*, 64 D4
Banjul, *The Gambia, national capital*, 101 B6
Banks Island, *Canada*, 30 G1
Banks Islands, *Vanuatu*, 55 N2
Banska Bystrica, *Slovakia*, 87 F6
Baoding, *China*, 69 J3
Baoji, *China*, 68 G4
Baotou, *China*, 68 G2
Baqubah, *Iraq*, 72 D5
Baranavichy, *Belarus*, 87 H5
Barbacena, *Brazil*, 44 K4
Barbados, *North America, country*, 34 N5
Barcelona, *Spain*, 89 E6
Barcelona, *Venezuela*, 42 F1
Bareilly, *India*, 70 D5
Barents Sea, *Europe*, 74 B2
Bari, *Italy*, 90 F3
Barinas, *Venezuela*, 42 D2
Barkly Tableland, *Australia*, 54 G3
Barnaul, *Russia*, 74 E3
Barquisimeto, *Venezuela*, 42 E1
Barra Falsa Point, *Mozambique*, 105 G4
Barranquilla, *Colombia*, 42 D1
Barra Point, *Mozambique*, 105 G4
Barreiras, *Brazil*, 44 J2
Barrow, Point, *U.S.A.*, 30 D1
Barysaw, *Belarus*, 87 J5
Basel, *Switzerland*, 90 C2
Basra, *Iraq*, 73 E5
Bassas da India, *Africa*, 105 G4
Basse-Terre, *Guadeloupe*, 34 M4
Basseterre, *St. Kitts and Nevis, national capital*, 34 M4
Bass Strait, *Australia*, 54 J7
Bastia, *France*, 89 G4
Bata, *Equatorial Guinea*, 102 A3
Batan Islands, *Philippines*, 67 H3
Batdambang, *Cambodia*, 66 D5
Bathurst, *Canada*, 31 N4
Bathurst, *U.S.A.*, 33 N1
Bathurst Island, *Canada*, 31 K1
Batna, *Algeria*, 100 G1
Baton Rouge, *U.S.A., internal capital*, 33 H4
Batumi, *Georgia*, 72 D3
Baturaja, *Indonesia*, 64 B4
Bawku, *Ghana*, 101 E6
Bayamo, *Cuba*, 35 J3
Baydhabo, *Somalia*, 103 H3
Bealanana, *Madagascar*, 105 J2
Beaufort Sea, *North America*, 30 F1
Beaufort West, *South Africa*, 104 D6
Beaumont, *U.S.A.*, 33 H4
Bechar, *Algeria*, 100 E2
Beer Sheva, *Israel*, 73 B5
Beijing, *China, national capital*, 69 J3
Beira, *Mozambique*, 105 G3
Beirut, *Lebanon, national capital*, 72 C5
Bejaia, *Algeria*, 100 F1
Bekescsaba, *Hungary*, 87 G7
Bekily, *Madagascar*, 105 J4
Belarus, *Europe, country*, 87 J5
Belaya, *Russia*, 85 G2
Belcher Islands, *Canada*, 31 L3
Beledweyne, *Somalia*, 103 J3
Belem, *Brazil*, 43 J4

Belfast, *United Kingdom, internal capital*, 88 C3
Belgaum, *India*, 71 C7
Belgium, *Europe, country*, 88 E4
Belgrade, *Serbia, national capital* 91 G2
Belitung, *Indonesia*, 64 C4
Belize, *North America, country*, 34 G4
Bellingham, *U.S.A.*, 32 B1
Bellingshausen Sea, *Antarctica*, 109 R2
Belmopan, *Belize, national capital*, 34 G4
Belo Horizonte, *Brazil*, 44 K3
Belomorsk, *Russia*, 86 K2
Beloretsk, *Russia*, 85 H3
Belo-Tsiribihina, *Madagascar*, 105 H3
Bendigo, *Australia*, 54 H7
Bengal, Bay of, *Asia*, 71 F7
Benghazi, *Libya*, 98 F2
Bengkulu, *Indonesia*, 64 B4
Benguela, *Angola*, 104 B2
Beni Mellal, *Morocco*, 100 D2
Benin, *Africa, country*, 101 F6
Benin, Bight of, *Africa*, 101 F7
Benin City, *Nigeria*, 101 G7
Beni Suef, *Egypt*, 99 H3
Ben Nevis, *United Kingdom*, 88 C2
Benoni, *South Africa*, 104 E5
Berbera, *Somalia*, 103 J1
Berberati, *Central African Republic*, 102 C3
Berdyansk, *Ukraine*, 84 D4
Berezniki, *Russia*, 85 H2
Bergamo, *Italy*, 90 D2
Bergen, *Norway*, 86 C3
Bering Sea, *North America*, 30 C2
Bering Strait, *U.S.A.*, 30 B2
Berlin, *Germany, national capital*, 88 H3
Bern, *Switzerland, national capital*, 90 C2
Beroroha, *Madagascar*, 105 J4
Bertoua, *Cameroon*, 102 B3
Besalampy, *Madagascar*, 105 H3
Besancon, *France*, 89 F5
Bethel, *U.S.A.*, 30 C2
Bethlehem, *South Africa*, 104 E5
Betroka, *Madagascar*, 105 J4
Beyneu, *Kazakhstan*, 72 F4
Beysehir Lake, *Turkey*, 91 J4
Beziers, *France*, 89 E6
Bhagalpur, *India*, 70 F5
Bhavnagar, *India*, 71 C6
Bhopal, *India*, 71 D6
Bhutan, *Asia, country*, 70 G5
Biak, *Indonesia*, 65 J4
Bialystok, *Poland*, 87 G5
Bida, *Nigeria*, 101 G7
Biel, *Switzerland*, 90 C2
Bielefeld, *Germany*, 88 G3
Bien Hoa, *Vietnam*, 66 E5
Bie Plateau, *Angola*, 104 B2
Bignona, *Senegal*, 101 B6
Bikaner, *India*, 70 C5
Bila Tserkva, *Ukraine*, 87 J6
Bilbao, *Spain*, 89 D6
Bilhorod Dnistrovskyy, *Ukraine*, 84 C4
Billings, *U.S.A.*, 32 E1
Bindura, *Zimbabwe*, 104 F3
Binga, *Zimbabwe*, 104 E3
Bintulu, *Malaysia*, 64 D3
Bioco, *Equatorial Guinea*, 102 A3
Birao, *Central African Republic*, 102 D1
Biratnagar, *Nepal*, 70 F5
Birjand, *Iran*, 72 G5
Birmingham, *United Kingdom*, 88 D3
Birmingham, *U.S.A.*, 33 J4
Birnin-Kebbi, *Nigeria*, 101 F6
Biscay, Bay of, *Europe*, 89 C5
Bishkek, *Kyrgyzstan, national capital*, 70 C2
Bisho, *South Africa*, 104 E6
Biskra, *Algeria*, 100 G2
Bismarck, *U.S.A., internal capital*, 32 F1
Bismarck Sea, *Papua New Guinea*, 65 L4
Bissagos Archipelago, *Guinea-Bissau*, 101 B6
Bissau, *Guinea-Bissau, national capital*, 101 B6
Bitola, *Macedonia*, 91 G3
Bitterfontein, *South Africa*, 104 C6

Bizerte, *Tunisia*, 98 C1
Blackpool, *United Kingdom*, 88 D3
Black Volta, *Africa*, 101 E6
Black Sea, *Asia/Europe*, 74 B3
Blagoevgrad, *Bulgaria*, 91 G3
Blagoveshchensk, *Russia*, 75 G3
Blanca Bay, *Argentina*, 45 F7
Blanc, Cape, *Africa*, 100 B4
Blanc, Mont, *Europe*, 89 F5
Blantyre, *Malawi*, 105 F3
Blida, *Algeria*, 100 F1
Bloemfontein, *South Africa, national capital*, 104 E5
Blue Nile, *Africa*, 99 H6
Bo, *Sierra Leone*, 101 C7
Boa Vista, *Brazil*, 42 F3
Boa Vista, *Cape Verde*, 101 M11
Bobo Dioulasso, *Burkina Faso*, 101 E6
Bodele Depression, *Africa*, 98 E5
Boden, *Sweden*, 86 G2
Bodo, *Norway*, 86 E2
Bogor, *Indonesia*, 64 C5
Bogota, *Colombia, national capital*, 42 D3
Bohol, *Philippines*, 67 H6
Boise, *U.S.A., internal capital*, 32 C2
Bojnurd, *Iran*, 72 F3
Boke, *Guinea*, 101 C6
Bolivar Peak, *Venezuela*, 42 D2
Bolivia, *South America, country*, 44 E3
Bologna, *Italy*, 90 D2
Bolzano, *Italy*, 90 D2
Bombay, *India*, 71 C7
Bondoukou, *Ivory Coast*, 101 E7
Bongor, *Chad*, 102 C1
Bonin Islands, *Japan*, 52 E2
Bonn, *Germany*, 88 F4
Boosaaso, *Somalia*, 103 J1
Boothia, Gulf of, *Canada*, 31 K1
Boothia Peninsula, *Canada*, 31 K1
Bordeaux, *France*, 89 D5
Bordj Bou Arreridj, *Algeria*, 100 F1
Borlange, *Sweden*, 86 E3
Borneo, *Asia*, 64 D4
Bornholm, *Denmark*, 87 E5
Borovichi, *Russia*, 86 K4
Bosnia and Herzegovina, *Europe, country*, 90 F2
Bosporus, *Turkey*, 91 J3
Bossangoa, *Central African Republic*, 102 C2
Bossembele, *Central African Republic*, 102 C2
Bosten Lake, *China*, 70 F2
Boston, *U.S.A., internal capital*, 33 M2
Bothnia, Gulf of, *Europe*, 86 F3
Botosani, *Romania*, 91 H2
Botswana, *Africa, country*, 104 D4
Bouake, *Ivory Coast*, 101 E7
Bouar, *Central African Republic*, 102 C2
Bougouni, *Mali*, 101 D6
Boujdour, *Western Sahara*, 100 C3
Bouna, *Ivory Coast*, 101 E7
Bozoum, *Central African Republic*, 102 C2
Braga, *Portugal*, 89 B6
Braganca, *Brazil*, 43 J4
Brahmapur, *India*, 71 E7
Brahmaputra, *Asia*, 70 G5
Braila, *Romania*, 91 H2
Brandon, *Canada*, 31 K4
Brandon, *U.S.A.*, 32 G1
Brasilia, *Brazil, national capital*, 44 J3
Brasov, *Romania*, 91 H2
Bratislava, *Slovakia, national capital*, 87 F6
Brazil, *South America, country*, 43 H5
Brazilian Highlands, *Brazil*, 44 K2
Brazzaville, *Congo, national capital*, 102 C4
Bremen, *Germany*, 88 G3
Bremerhaven, *Germany*, 88 G3
Brescia, *Italy*, 90 D2
Brest, *Belarus*, 87 G5
Brest, *France*, 88 C4
Bria, *Central African Republic*, 102 D2
Bridgetown, *Barbados, national capital*, 34 N5
Brisbane, *Australia, internal capital*, 55 K5
Bristol, *United Kingdom*, 88 D4

Bristol Bay, *U.S.A.*, 30 C3
British Columbia, *Canada,*
internal admin. area, 30 G3
Brno, *Czech Republic*, 90 F1
Broken Hill, *Australia*, 54 H6
Brokopondo, *Suriname*, 43 G2
Brooks Range, *U.S.A.*, 30 D2
Brownsville, *U.S.A.*, 32 G5
Bruges, *Belgium*, 88 E4
Brunei, *Asia, country*, 64 E5
Brussels, *Belgium, national capital*, 88 F4
Bryansk, *Russia*, 84 C3
Bucaramanga, *Colombia*, 42 D2
Bucharest, *Romania, national capital,*
91 H2
Budapest, *Hungary, national capital,*
87 F7
Buenaventura, *Colombia*, 42 C3
Buenos Aires, *Argentina, national capital,*
44 G6
Buenos Aires, Lake, *South America,*
45 D9
Buffalo, *U.S.A.*, 33 L2
Buga, *Colombia*, 42 C3
Buinsk, *Russia*, 85 F3
Bujumbura, *Burundi, national capital,*
102 E4
Bukavu, *Democratic Republic of Congo,*
102 E4
Bulawayo, *Zimbabwe*, 104 E4
Bulgan, *Mongolia*, 68 F1
Bulgaria, *Europe, country*, 91 H3
Bunbury, *Australia*, 54 C6
Bundaberg, *Australia*, 55 K4
Buon Me Thuot, *Vietnam*, 66 E5
Buraydah, *Saudi Arabia*, 73 D6
Burgas, *Bulgaria*, 91 H3
Burgos, *Spain*, 89 D6
Burkina Faso, *Africa, country*, 101 E6
Burma, *Asia, country*, 66 C3
Bursa, *Turkey*, 91 J3
Buru, *Indonesia*, 65 G4
Burundi, *Africa, country*, 102 E4
Bushehr, *Iran*, 73 F6
Buta, *Democratic Republic of Congo,*
102 D3
Butare, *Rwanda*, 102 E4
Butembo, *Democratic Republic of Congo,*
102 E3
Buton, *Indonesia*, 65 F4
Butuan, *Philippines*, 67 J6
Buxoro, *Uzbekistan*, 70 A3
Buzau, *Romania*, 91 H2
Buzuluk, *Russia*, 85 G3
Bydgoszcz, *Poland*, 87 F5

C
Cabanatuan, *Philippines*, 67 H4
Cabinda, *Angola, enclave*, 102 B5
Cabonga Reservoir, *Canada*, 33 L1
Cabora Bassa Reservoir, *Mozambique,*
104 F3
Caceres, *Brazil*, 44 G3
Caceres, *Colombia*, 42 C2
Caceres, *Spain*, 89 C7
Cachoeiro de Itapemirim, *Brazil*, 44 K4
Cadiz, *Spain*, 89 C7
Cadiz, Gulf of, *Europe*, 89 C7
Caen, *France*, 88 D4
Cagayan de Oro, *Philippines*, 67 H6
Cagliari, *Italy*, 90 D4
Caicara, *Venezuela*, 42 E2
Cairns, *Australia*, 54 J3
Cairo, *Egypt, national capital*, 99 H3
Caiundo, *Angola*, 104 C3
Cajamarca, *Peru*, 42 C5
Calabar, *Nigeria*, 102 A2
Calais, *France*, 88 E4
Calama, *Chile*, 44 E4
Calamian Group, *Philippines*, 67 G5
Calapan, *Philippines*, 67 H5
Calbayog, *Philippines*, 67 H5
Calcutta, *India*, 71 F6
Calgary, *Canada*, 30 H3
Cali, *Colombia*, 42 C3
Calicut, *India*, 71 D8
California, *U.S.A., internal admin. area,*

32 C3
California, Gulf of, *Mexico*, 34 B2
Camaguey, *Cuba*, 35 J3
Cambodia, *Asia, country*, 66 E5
Cambridge, *United Kingdom*, 88 E3
Cameroon, *Africa, country*, 102 B2
Cameroon Mountain, *Cameroon*, 102 A3
Cameta, *Brazil*, 43 J4
Camiri, *Bolivia*, 44 F4
Campeche, *Mexico*, 34 F4
Campeche, Bay of, *Mexico*, 34 F3
Campina Grande, *Brazil*, 43 L5
Campinas, *Brazil*, 44 J4
Campo Grande, *Brazil*, 44 H4
Campos, *Brazil*, 44 K4
Canada, *North America, country*, 30 J3
Canadian, *U.S.A.*, 32 F3
Canakkale, *Turkey*, 91 H3
Canary Islands, *Atlantic Ocean*, 100 B3
Canaveral, Cape, *U.S.A.*, 33 K5
Canberra, *Australia, national capital,*
55 J7
Cancun, *Mexico*, 35 G3
Cangombe, *Angola*, 104 D2
Cannes, *France*, 89 F6
Cantabrian Mountains, *Spain*, 89 C6
Can Tho, *Vietnam*, 66 E6
Canton, *China*, 69 H6
Cape Coast, *Ghana*, 101 E7
Cape Town, *South Africa, national capital,*
104 C6
Cape Verde, *Atlantic Ocean, country,*
101 L11
Cape York Peninsula, *Australia*, 54 H2
Cap-Haitien, *Haiti*, 35 K4
Caprivi Strip, *Namibia*, 104 D3
Caracas, *Venezuela, national capital,*
42 E1
Cardiff, *United Kingdom, internal capital,*
88 D4
Caribbean Sea, *North/South America,*
35 J4
Carlisle, *United Kingdom*, 88 D3
Carnarvon, *Australia*, 54 B4
Carnarvon, *South Africa*, 104 D6
Carnot, Cape, *Australia*, 54 F6
Caroline Islands, *Federated States of*
Micronesia, 52 B4
Carpathian Mountains, *Europe*, 87 H7
Carpentaria, Gulf of, *Australia*, 54 G2
Carson City, *U.S.A., internal capital,*
32 C3
Cartagena, *Colombia*, 42 C1
Cartagena, *Spain*, 89 D7
Carthage, *Tunisia*, 98 C1
Cartwright, *Canada*, 31 P3
Caruaru, *Brazil*, 43 L5
Casablanca, *Morocco*, 100 D2
Cascade Range, *U.S.A.*, 32 B2
Cascais, *Portugal*, 89 B7
Cascavel, *Brazil*, 44 H4
Casper, *U.S.A.*, 32 E2
Caspian Depression, *Asia*, 72 F2
Caspian Sea, *Asia*, 85 G4
Castellon de la Plana, *Spain*, 89 D7
Castelo Branco, *Portugal*, 89 C7
Castries, *St. Lucia, national capital*, 34 M5
Catamarca, *Argentina*, 44 E5
Catania, *Italy*, 90 E4
Catanzaro, *Italy*, 90 F4
Cat Island, *The Bahamas*, 33 L6
Caucasus Mountains, *Asia/Europe*, 72 D3
Caxias do Sul, *Brazil*, 44 H5
Cayenne, *French Guiana, national capital,*
43 H3
Cayman Islands, *North America*, 35 H4
Cebu, *Philippines*, 67 H5
Cedar Lake *Canada*, 30 J3
Cedar Rapids, *U.S.A.*, 33 H2
Cedros Island, *Mexico*, 34 A2
Ceduna, *Australia*, 54 F6
Celaya, *Mexico*, 34 D3
Celebes, *Indonesia*, 65 F4
Celebes Sea, *Asia*, 67 H7
Celtic Sea, *Europe*, 88 C4
Central African Republic, *Africa, country,*
102 C2

Central Cordillera, *Peru*, 42 C5
Central Russian Uplands, *Russia*, 84 D3
Central Siberian Plateau, *Russia*, 75 F2
Central Sierras, *Spain*, 89 D6
Ceram, *Indonesia*, 65 G4
Ceram Sea, *Indonesia*, 65 G4
Cerro de Pasco, *Peru*, 42 C6
Cesis, *Latvia*, 87 H4
Ceske Budejovice, *Czech Republic*, 90 E1
Ceuta, *Africa*, 89 C8
Chacabuco, *Argentina*, 44 F6
Chad, *Africa, country*, 98 E5
Chad, Lake, *Africa*, 98 D6
Chala, *Peru*, 42 D7
Chalan Kanoa, *Northern Marianas*, 52 B3
Chalkida, *Greece*, 91 H4
Challapata, *Bolivia*, 44 E3
Chalon-sur-Saone, *France*, 89 F5
Chanaral, *Chile*, 44 D5
Chandigarh, *India*, 70 D4
Chandrapur, *India*, 71 D7
Changchun, *China*, 69 L2
Changde, *China*, 68 H5
Changhua, *China*, 69 K6
Chang Jiang, *China*, 69 J4
Changsha, *China*, 69 H5
Changzhi, *China*, 69 H3
Chania, *Greece*, 91 G5
Channel Islands, *Europe*, 88 D4
Channel Islands, *U.S.A.*, 32 C4
Chapaev, *Kazakhstan*, 85 G3
Charagua, *Bolivia*, 44 F3
Charleroi, *Belgium*, 88 F4
Charleston, *South Carolina, U.S.A.*, 33 L4
Charleston, *West Virginia, U.S.A.,*
internal capital, 33 K3
Charlotte, *U.S.A.*, 33 K3
Charlottesville, *U.S.A.*, 33 L3
Charlottetown, *Canada, internal capital,*
31 N4
Chatham Islands, *New Zealand*, 55 R8
Chattanooga, *U.S.A.*, 33 J3
Chavuma, *Zambia*, 104 D2
Cheboksary, *Russia*, 85 F2
Chech Erg, *Africa*, 100 E3
Cheju, *South Korea*, 69 L4
Chelyabinsk, *Russia*, 85 J2
Chemnitz, *Germany*, 88 H4
Chengdu, *China*, 68 F4
Chennai, *India*, 71 E8
Chenzhou, *China*, 69 H5
Cherbourg, *France*, 88 D4
Cherepovets, *Russia*, 84 D2
Cherkasy, *Ukraine*, 84 C4
Chernihiv, *Ukraine*, 84 C3
Chernivtsi, *Ukraine*, 87 H6
Chesterfield Islands, *New Caledonia,*
55 M3
Cheyenne, *U.S.A., internal capital*, 32 F2
Chiang Mai, *Thailand*, 66 C4
Chicago, *U.S.A.*, 33 J2
Chiclayo, *Peru*, 42 C5
Chico, *U.S.A.*, 32 B3
Chicoutimi, *Canada*, 31 M4
Chidley, Cape, *Canada*, 31 N2
Chifeng, *China*, 69 J2
Chigubo, *Mozambique*, 105 F4
Chihli, Gulf of, *China*, 69 J3
Chihuahua, *Mexico*, 34 C2
Chile, *South America, country*, 44 D6
Chillan, *Chile*, 45 D7
Chiloe Island, *Chile*, 45 C8
Chilung, *China*, 69 K6
Chilwa, Lake, *Africa*, 105 G3
Chimanimani, *Zimbabwe*, 105 F3
Chimbote, *Peru*, 42 C5
China, *Asia, country*, 68 G5
Chincha Alta, *Peru*, 42 C6
Chingola, *Zambia*, 104 E2
Chinhoyi, *Zimbabwe*, 104 F3
Chios, *Greece*, 91 H4
Chipata, *Zambia*, 105 F2
Chiredzi, *Zimbabwe*, 104 F4
Chisinau, *Moldova, national capital*, 87 J2
Chittagong, *Bangladesh*, 71 G6
Chongjin, *North Korea*, 69 L2
Chongju, *South Korea*, 69 L3

Chongqing, *China*, 68 G5
Chonos Archipelago, *Chile*, 45 C8
Chott el Jerid, *Tunisia*, 98 C2
Christchurch, *New Zealand*, 55 P8
Christmas Island, *Asia*, 64 C6
Chukchi Sea, *Arctic Ocean*, 108 B2
Chulucanas, *Peru*, 42 B5
Chumphon, *Thailand*, 66 C5
Churchill, *Canada*, 31 K3
Churchill Falls, *Canada*, 31 N3
Cienfuegos, *Cuba*, 35 H3
Cilacap, *Indonesia*, 64 C5
Cincinnati, *U.S.A.*, 33 K3
Ciudad Bolivar, *Venezuela*, 42 F2
Ciudad del Carmen, *Mexico*, 34 F4
Ciudad del Este, *Paraguay*, 44 H5
Ciudad Guayana, *Venezuela*, 42 F2
Ciudad Juarez, *Mexico*, 34 C1
Ciudad Obregon, *Mexico*, 34 C2
Ciudad Real, *Spain*, 89 D7
Ciudad Victoria, *Mexico*, 34 E3
Clark Hill Lake, *U.S.A.*, 33 K4
Clermont-Ferrand, *France*, 89 E5
Cleveland, *U.S.A.*, 33 K2
Cluj-Napoca, *Romania*, 91 G2
Coast Mountains, *Canada*, 30 F3
Coast Ranges, *U.S.A.*, 32 B2
Coats Land, *Antarctica*, 109 A3
Coatzacoalcos, *Mexico*, 34 F4
Cobija, *Bolivia*, 44 E2
Cochabamba, *Bolivia*, 44 E3
Cochin, *India*, 71 D9
Cocos Island, *Costa Rica*, 35 G6
Cod, Cape, *U.S.A.*, 33 N2
Coeur d'Alene, *U.S.A.*, 32 C1
Coiba Island, *Panama*, 35 H6
Coihaique, *Chile*, 45 D9
Coimbatore, *India*, 71 D8
Coimbra, *Portugal*, 89 B6
Colima, *Mexico*, 34 D4
Cologne, *Germany*, 88 F4
Colombia, *South America, country*, 42 D3
Colombo, *Sri Lanka, national capital,*
71 D9
Colon, *Panama*, 35 J6
Colorado, *Argentina*, 45 F7
Colorado, *U.S.A.*, 32 D4
Colorado, *U.S.A., internal admin. area,*
32 E3
Colorado Plateau, *U.S.A.*, 32 D3
Colorado Springs, *U.S.A.*, 32 F3
Columbia, *U.S.A.*, 32 C1
Columbia, *U.S.A., internal capital*, 33 K4
Columbine, Cape, *South Africa*, 104 C6
Columbus, *U.S.A., internal capital*, 33 K3
Colwyn Bay, *United Kingdom*, 88 D3
Como, Lake, *Italy*, 90 D2
Comodoro Rivadavia, *Argentina*, 45 E9
Comoros, *Africa, country*, 105 H2
Conakry, *Guinea, national capital*, 101 C7
Concepcion, *Bolivia*, 44 F3
Concepcion, *Chile*, 45 D7
Concepcion, *Paraguay*, 44 G4
Concord, *U.S.A., internal capital*, 33 M2
Concordia, *Argentina*, 44 G6
Congo, *Africa*, 102 C4
Congo, *Africa, country*, 102 C4
Congo, Democratic Republic of, *Africa,*
country, 102 D4
Connecticut, *U.S.A., internal admin. area,*
33 M2
Con Son, *Vietnam*, 66 E6
Constanta, *Romania*, 91 J2
Constantine, *Algeria*, 100 G1
Cook Islands, *Oceania*, 52 G7
Cook, Mount, *New Zealand*, 55 P8
Cook Strait, *New Zealand*, 55 P8
Copenhagen, *Denmark, national capital,*
87 E5
Copiapo, *Chile*, 44 D5
Coquimbo, *Chile*, 44 D5
Coral Sea, *Oceania*, 55 K2
Coral Sea Islands Territory, *Oceania,*
dependency, 55 K2
Cordoba, *Argentina*, 44 F6
Cordoba, *Spain*, 89 C7
Corfu, *Greece*, 91 F4

Cork, *Ireland*, 88 B4
Corner Brook, *Canada*, 31 P4
Coro, *Venezuela*, 42 E1
Coropuna, Mount, *Peru*, 42 D6
Corpus Christi, *U.S.A.*, 32 G5
Corrientes, *Argentina*, 44 G5
Corsica, *France*, 89 G6
Corum, *Turkey*, 91 K3
Corumba, *Brazil*, 44 G3
Cosenza, *Italy*, 90 F4
Cosmoledo Group, *Seychelles*, 105 J1
Costa Rica, *North America, country*, 35 G6
Cotonou, *Benin*, 101 F7
Cottbus, *Germany*, 88 H4
Cradock, *South Africa*, 104 E6
Craiova, *Romania*, 91 G2
Cravo Norte, *Colombia*, 42 D2
Crete, *Greece*, 91 H5
Criciuma, *Brazil*, 44 J5
Crimea, *Ukraine*, 91 K2
Cristobal Colon, *Colombia*, 42 D1
Croatia, *Europe, country*, 90 F2
Cruzeiro do Sul, *Brazil*, 42 D5
Cuamba, *Mozambique*, 105 G2
Cuangar, *Angola*, 104 C3
Cuango, *Africa*, 104 C1
Cuanza, *Angola*, 104 C2
Cuba, *North America, country*, 35 J3
Cucuta, *Colombia*, 42 D2
Cuenca, *Ecuador*, 42 C4
Cuiaba, *Brazil*, 44 G3
Culiacan, *Mexico*, 34 C3
Cumana, *Venezuela*, 42 F1
Cumberland Peninsula, *Canada*, 31 N2
Cunene, *Africa*, 104 C3
Curitiba, *Brazil*, 44 J5
Cusco, *Peru*, 42 D6
Cuttack, *India*, 71 F6
Cuxhaven, *Germany*, 88 G3
Cyclades, *Greece*, 91 H4
Cyprus, *Asia, country*, 91 J5
Cyrene, *Libya*, 98 F2
Czech Republic, *Europe, country*, 90 E1
Czestochowa, *Poland*, 87 F6

d

Dabeiba, *Colombia*, 42 C2
Dagupan, *Philippines*, 67 H4
Dahlak Archipelago, *Eritrea*, 99 K5
Dakar, *Senegal, national capital*, 101 B6
Dal, *Sweden*, 86 F3
Da Lat, *Vietnam*, 66 E5
Dali, *China*, 68 F5
Dalian, *China*, 69 K3
Dallas, *U.S.A.*, 33 G4
Daloa, *Ivory Coast*, 101 D7
Damascus, *Syria, national capital*, 72 C5
Damavand, *Iran*, 72 F4
Damongo, *Ghana*, 101 E7
Da Nang, *Vietnam*, 66 E4
Dandong, *China*, 69 K2
Danube, *Europe*, 87 F7
Danube, Mouths of the, *Europe*, 91 J2
Daqing, *China*, 69 L1
Dara, *Senegal*, 101 B6
Darbhanga, *India*, 70 F5
Dar es Salaam, *Tanzania, national capital*, 103 G5
Darien, Gulf of, *Colombia*, 42 C2
Darjeeling, *India*, 70 F5
Darling, *Australia*, 54 H6
Darnah, *Libya*, 98 F2
Darwin, *Australia, internal capital*, 54 F2
Darwin, Mount, *Zimbabwe*, 104 F3
Dasht-e Kavir, *Iran*, 72 F5
Dasoguz, *Turkmenistan*, 72 G3
Datong, *China*, 69 H2
Daugavpils, *Latvia*, 87 H5
Davangere, *India*, 71 D8
Davao, *Philippines*, 67 J6
David, *Panama*, 35 H6
Davis Strait, *Canada*, 31 P2
Dawson, *Canada*, 30 F2
Dayr az Zawr, *Syria*, 72 D4
Daytona Beach, *U.S.A.*, 33 K5

De Aar, *South Africa*, 104 D6
Dease Lake, *Canada*, 30 G3
Death Valley, *U.S.A.*, 32 C3
Debrecen, *Hungary*, 87 G7
Debre Zeyit, *Ethiopia*, 103 G2
Deccan Plateau, *India*, 71 D7
Delaware, *U.S.A., internal admin. area*, 33 L3
Delgado, Cape, *Mozambique*, 105 H2
Delhi, *India*, 70 D5
Del Rio, *U.S.A.*, 32 F5
Democratic Republic of Congo, *Africa, country*, 102 D4
Denizli, *Turkey*, 91 J4
Denmark, *Europe, country*, 87 D5
Denpasar, *Indonesia*, 64 E5
D'Entrecasteaux Islands, *Papua New Guinea*, 65 M5
Denver, *U.S.A., internal capital*, 32 E3
Dera Ghazi Khan, *Pakistan*, 70 C4
Derbent, *Russia*, 72 E3
Derby, *U.S.A.*, 33 K2
Dese, *Ethiopia*, 103 G1
Des Moines, *U.S.A., internal capital*, 33 H2
Desna, *Europe*, 84 C3
Detroit, *U.S.A.*, 33 K2
Devon Island, *Canada*, 31 L1
Devonport, *Australia*, 54 J8
Dhaka, *Bangladesh, national capital*, 71 G6
Dhamar, *Yemen*, 73 D9
Dhule, *India*, 71 C6
Dibrugarh, *India*, 70 G5
Dijon, *France*, 89 F5
Dikhil, *Djibouti*, 99 K6
Dili, *East Timor, national capital*, 65 G5
Dilolo, *Democratic Republic of Congo*, 102 D6
Dinaric Alps, *Europe*, 90 E2
Dire Dawa, *Ethiopia*, 103 H2
Divo, *Ivory Coast*, 101 D7
Diyarbakir, *Turkey*, 72 D4
Djado Plateau, *Africa*, 98 D4
Djambala, *Congo*, 102 B4
Djelfa, *Algeria*, 100 F2
Djema, *Central African Republic*, 102 E2
Djemila, *Algeria*, 100 G1
Djibouti, *Africa, country*, 99 K6
Djibouti, *Djibouti, national capital*, 99 K6
Djougou, *Benin*, 101 F7
Dnieper, *Europe*, 84 C4
Dniester, *Europe*, 87 H6
Dniprodzerzhynsk, *Ukraine*, 84 C4
Dnipropetrovsk, *Ukraine*, 84 D4
Doba, *Chad*, 102 C2
Dobrich, *Bulgaria*, 91 H3
Dodecanese, *Greece*, 91 H4
Dodoma, *Tanzania, national capital*, 103 G5
Doha, *Qatar, national capital*, 73 F6
Dolak, *Indonesia*, 65 J5
Dolores, *Argentina*, 45 G7
Dominica, *North America, country*, 34 M4
Dominican Republic, *North America, country*, 35 L3
Don, *Russia*, 84 E4
Dondo, *Angola*, 104 B1
Donets, *Europe*, 84 D4
Donetsk, *Ukraine*, 84 D4
Dongting Lake, *China*, 69 H5
Dori, *Burkina Faso*, 101 E6
Dosso, *Niger*, 101 F6
Douala, *Cameroon*, 102 A3
Douglas, *South Africa*, 104 D5
Dourados, *Brazil*, 44 H4
Douro, *Europe*, 89 C6
Dover, *United Kingdom*, 88 E4
Dover, *U.S.A., internal capital*, 33 L3
Dover, Strait of, *Europe*, 88 E4
Drakensberg, *South Africa*, 104 E6
Drake Passage, *South America*, 45 E11
Drammen, *Norway*, 86 D4
Dresden, *Germany*, 88 H4
Drobeta-Turnu Severin, *Romania*, 91 G2

Dryden, *Canada*, 31 K4
Dubai, *United Arab Emirates*, 73 G6
Dubawnt Lake, *Canada*, 30 J2
Dubbo, *Australia*, 55 J6
Dublin, *Ireland, national capital*, 88 C3
Dubrovnik, *Croatia*, 91 F3
Duisburg, *Germany*, 88 F4
Duitama, *Colombia*, 42 D2
Duluth, *U.S.A.*, 33 H1
Dumaguete, *Philippines*, 67 H6
Dundee, *United Kingdom*, 88 D2
Dunedin, *New Zealand*, 55 P9
Durango, *Mexico*, 34 D3
Durazno, *Uruguay*, 44 G6
Durban, *South Africa*, 104 F5
Durres, *Albania*, 91 F3
Dushanbe, *Tajikistan, national capital*, 70 B3
Dusseldorf, *Germany*, 88 F4
Dzhankoy, *Ukraine*, 91 K2
Dzungarian Basin, *China*, 70 F1

e

East Antarctica, *Antarctica*, 109 E3
East Cape, *New Zealand*, 55 Q7
East China Sea, *Asia*, 69 K5
Easter Island, *Pacific Ocean*, 53 N7
Eastern Cordillera, *Colombia*, 42 D3
Eastern Cordillera, *Peru*, 42 D6
Eastern Ghats, *India*, 71 D8
Eastern Sierra Madre, *Mexico*, 34 D2
East Falkland, *Falkland Islands*, 45 G10
East London, *South Africa*, 104 E6
East Siberian Sea, *Russia*, 75 J2
East Timor, *Asia, country*, 65 G5
Ebolowa, *Cameroon*, 102 B3
Ebro, *Spain*, 89 D6
Ecuador, *South America, country*, 42 B4
Edinburgh, *United Kingdom, internal capital*, 88 D2
Edirne, *Turkey*, 91 H3
Edmonton, *Canada, internal capital*, 30 H3
Edmundston, *Canada*, 31 N4
Edward, Lake, *Africa*, 102 E4
Edwards Plateau, *U.S.A.*, 32 F4
Efate, *Vanuatu*, 55 N3
Egypt, *Africa, country*, 99 G3
Eindhoven, *Netherlands*, 88 F4
Elat, *Israel*, 73 B6
Elazig, *Turkey*, 72 C4
Elba, *Italy*, 90 D3
Elbasan, *Albania*, 91 G3
Elbe, *Europe*, 88 G3
Elbrus, Mount, *Russia*, 72 D3
Elche, *Spain*, 89 D7
Eldorado, *Argentina*, 44 H5
Eldoret, *Kenya*, 103 G3
Elephant Island, *Atlantic Ocean*, 45 H12
Eleuthera, *The Bahamas*, 33 L5
Elgon, Mount, *Uganda*, 103 F3
El Hierro, *Canary Islands*, 100 B3
Elista, *Russia*, 72 E2
El Jadida, *Morocco*, 100 D2
El Jem, *Tunisia*, 98 D1
Ellesmere Island, *Canada*, 108 R3
Ellsworth Land, *Antarctica*, 109 R3
El Mansura, *Egypt*, 99 H2
El Minya, *Egypt*, 99 H3
El Obeid, *Sudan*, 99 H6
El Oued, *Algeria*, 100 G2
El Paso, *U.S.A.*, 32 E4
El Salvador, *North America, country*, 34 G5
Embi, *Kazakhstan*, 72 G2
Emi Koussi, *Chad*, 98 E4
Empty Quarter, *Asia*, 73 E8
Encarnacion, *Paraguay*, 44 G5
Ende, *Indonesia*, 65 F5
Enderby Land, *Antarctica*, 109 E3
Engels, *Russia*, 85 F3
England, *United Kingdom, internal admin. area*, 88 D3
English Channel, *Europe*, 88 D4
Ennedi Plateau, *Africa*, 98 F5

Enschede, *Netherlands*, 88 F3
Entebbe, *Uganda*, 103 F3
Enugu, *Nigeria*, 101 G7
Ephesus, *Turkey*, 91 H4
Equatorial Guinea, *Africa, country*, 102 A3
Erenhot, *China*, 68 H2
Erfurt, *Germany*, 88 G4
Erie, *U.S.A.*, 33 K2
Erie, Lake, *U.S.A.*, 33 K2
Eritrea, *Africa, country*, 99 J5
Er Rachidia, *Morocco*, 100 E2
Ershovka, *Kazakhstan*, 85 K3
Erzurum, *Turkey*, 72 D4
Esbjerg, *Denmark*, 87 D5
Esfahan, *Iran*, 72 F5
Eskilstuna, *Sweden*, 86 F4
Eskisehir, *Turkey*, 91 J4
Esmeraldas, *Ecuador*, 42 C3
Esperance, *Australia*, 54 D6
Espinosa, *Brazil*, 44 K2
Espiritu Santo, *Vanuatu*, 55 N3
Espoo, *Finland*, 86 H3
Espungabera, *Mozambique*, 105 F4
Esquel, *Argentina*, 45 D8
Essaouira, *Morocco*, 100 D2
Es Semara, *Western Sahara*, 100 C3
Essen, *Germany*, 88 F4
Estevan, *Canada*, 30 J4
Estonia, *Europe, country*, 86 H4
Ethiopia, *Africa, country*, 103 G2
Ethiopian Highlands, *Ethiopia*, 103 G1
Etna, Mount, *Italy*, 90 E4
Etosha Pan, *Namibia*, 104 C3
Euboea, *Greece*, 91 G4
Eugene, *U.S.A.*, 32 B2
Eugenia, Point, *Mexico*, 34 A2
Euphrates, *Asia*, 73 E5
Europa Island, *Africa*, 105 H4
Europe, 20–21
Evansville, *U.S.A.*, 33 J3
Everest, Mount, *Asia*, 70 F5
Everglades, The, *U.S.A.*, 33 K5
Evora, *Portugal*, 89 C7
Evry, *France*, 88 E4
Exeter, *United Kingdom*, 88 D4
Eyl, *Somalia*, 103 J2
Eyre, Lake, *Australia*, 54 G5

f

Fada-Ngourma, *Burkina Faso*, 101 F6
Fairbanks, *U.S.A.*, 30 E2
Faisalabad, *Pakistan*, 70 C4
Fakfak, *Indonesia*, 65 H4
Falkland Islands, *Atlantic Ocean*, 45 F10
Farasan Islands, *Saudi Arabia*, 73 D8
Farewell, Cape, *New Zealand*, 55 P8
Fargo, *U.S.A.*, 33 G1
Fargona, *Uzbekistan*, 70 C2
Farmington, *U.S.A.*, 32 E3
Faro, *Portugal*, 89 C7
Farquhar Group, *Seychelles*, 105 K1
Faxafloi, *Iceland*, 86 N2
Faya-Largeau, *Chad*, 98 E5
Federated States of Micronesia, *Oceania, country*, 52 C3
Feira de Santana, *Brazil*, 44 L2
Feodosiya, *Ukraine*, 91 K2
Fernandina, *Ecuador*, 42 N10
Ferrara, *Italy*, 90 D2
Fes, *Morocco*, 100 E2
Fianarantsoa, *Madagascar*, 105 J4
Fiji, *Oceania, country*, 55 Q3
Finland, *Europe, country*, 86 H2
Finland, Gulf of, *Europe*, 86 H4
Flagstaff, *U.S.A.*, 32 D3
Flensburg, *Germany*, 88 G3
Flinders Island, *Australia*, 55 J7
Flin Flon, *Canada*, 30 J3
Florence, *Italy*, 90 D3
Florencia, *Colombia*, 42 C3
Flores, *Azores*, 100 J10
Flores, *Indonesia*, 65 F5
Flores Sea, *Indonesia*, 65 F5
Floresta, *Brazil*, 43 L5
Floriano, *Brazil*, 43 K5

Florianopolis, *Brazil*, **44 J5**
Florida, *U.S.A., internal admin. area*,
   33 K5
Florida Keys, *U.S.A.*, **33 K6**
Florida, Straits of, *North America*, **33 K6**
Focsani, *Romania*, **91 H2**
Foggia, *Italy*, **90 E3**
Fogo, *Cape Verde*, **101 M12**
Fomboni, *Comoros*, **105 H2**
Formosa, *Argentina*, **44 G5**
Fort Albany, *Canada*, **31 L3**
Fort Chipewyan, *Canada*, **30 H3**
Fort-de-France, *Martinique*, **34 M5**
Fort Lauderdale, *U.S.A.*, **33 K5**
Fort McMurray, *Canada*, **30 H3**
Fort Nelson, *Canada*, **30 G3**
Fort Peck Lake, *U.S.A.*, **32 E1**
Fort Providence, *Canada*, **30 H2**
Fort St. John, *Canada*, **30 G3**
Fort Severn, *Canada*, **31 L3**
Fort Vermilion, *Canada*, **30 H3**
Fort Wayne, *U.S.A.*, **33 J2**
Fort Worth, *U.S.A.*, **32 G4**
Foumban, *Cameroon*, **102 B2**
Foxe Basin, *Canada*, **31 M2**
Foxe Peninsula, *Canada*, **31 M2**
Fox Islands, *U.S.A.*, **31 C3**
Foz do Cunene, *Angola*, **104 B3**
Foz do Iguacu, *Brazil*, **44 H5**
France, *Europe, country*, **89 E5**
Franceville, *Gabon*, **102 B4**
Francistown, *Botswana*, **104 E4**
Frankfort, *U.S.A., internal capital*, **33 K3**
Frankfurt, *Germany*, **88 G4**
Franz Josef Land, *Russia*, **74 C1**
Fraser Island, *Australia*, **55 K5**
Fredericton, *Canada, internal capital*,
   31 N4
Fredrikstad, *Norway*, **86 D4**
Freeport City, *The Bahamas*, **33 L5**
Freetown, *Sierra Leone, national capital*,
   101 C7
Freiburg, *Germany*, **88 F4**
French Guiana, *South America,*
   dependency, **43 H3**
French Polynesia, *Oceania, dependency*,
   53 J6
Fresno, *U.S.A.*, **32 C3**
Frisian Islands, *Europe*, **88 F3**
Froya, *Norway*, **86 D3**
Fuerteventura, *Canary Islands*, **100 B3**
Fuji, Mount, *Japan*, **69 N3**
Fukui, *Japan*, **69 N3**
Fukuoka, *Japan*, **69 M4**
Fukushima, *Japan*, **69 P3**
Funafuti, *Tuvalu, national capital*, **52 E5**
Funchal, *Madeira*, **100 B2**
Furnas Reservoir, *Brazil*, **44 J4**
Fushun, *China*, **69 K2**
Fuxin, *China*, **69 K2**
Fyn, *Denmark*, **87 D5**

g
Gabes, *Tunisia*, **98 D2**
Gabes, Gulf of, *Africa*, **98 D2**
Gabon, *Africa, country*, **102 B4**
Gaborone, *Botswana, national capital*,
   104 E4
Gafsa, *Tunisia*, **98 C2**
Gagnoa, *Ivory Coast*, **101 D7**
Gairdner, Lake, *Australia*, **54 F6**
Galapagos Islands, *Ecuador*, **42 N9**
Galati, *Romania*, **91 J2**
Galdhopiggen, *Norway*, **86 D3**
Galle, *Sri Lanka*, **71 E9**
Gallinas, Cape, *Colombia*, **42 D1**
Galveston, *U.S.A.*, **33 H5**
Galway, *Ireland*, **88 B3**
Gambela, *Ethiopia*, **103 F2**
Gambia, The, *Africa, country*, **101 B6**
Ganca, *Azerbaijan*, **72 E3**
Gander, *Canada*, **31 P4**
Ganges, *Asia*, **70 E5**
Ganges, Mouths of the, *Asia*, **71 F6**
Ganzhou, *China*, **69 H5**

Gao, *Mali*, **101 F5**
Garda, Lake, *Italy*, **90 D2**
Garissa, *Kenya*, **103 G4**
Garonne, *France*, **89 E5**
Garoua, *Cameroon*, **102 B2**
Gaspe, *Canada*, **31 N4**
Gatchina, *Russia*, **86 J4**
Gavle, *Sweden*, **86 F3**
Gaza, *Israel*, **73 B5**
Gaziantep, *Turkey*, **72 C4**
Gdansk, *Poland*, **87 F5**
Gdansk, Gulf of, *Poland*, **87 F5**
Gdynia, *Poland*, **87 F5**
Gedaref, *Sudan*, **99 J6**
Geelong, *Australia*, **54 H7**
Gejiu, *China*, **68 F6**
Gemena, *Democratic Republic of Congo*,
   102 C3
General Roca, *Argentina*, **45 E7**
General Santos, *Philippines*, **67 J6**
General Villegas, *Argentina*, **44 F7**
Geneva, *Switzerland*, **90 C2**
Geneva, Lake, *Europe*, **90 C2**
Genoa, *Italy*, **90 D2**
Genoa, Gulf of, *Italy*, **90 D2**
Gent, *Belgium*, **88 E4**
Georgetown, *Guyana, national capital*,
   43 G2
George Town, *Malaysia*, **64 B2**
Georgia, *Asia, country*, **72 D3**
Georgia, *U.S.A., internal admin. area*,
   33 K4
Gera, *Germany*, **88 H4**
Geraldton, *Australia*, **54 B5**
Gerlachovsky stit, *Slovakia*, **87 G6**
Germany, *Europe, country*, **88 G4**
Gerona, *Spain*, **89 E6**
Ghadamis, *Libya*, **98 C2**
Ghana, *Africa, country*, **101 E7**
Ghardaia, *Algeria*, **100 F2**
Gharyan, *Libya*, **98 D2**
Ghat, *Libya*, **98 D3**
Gibraltar, *Europe*, **89 C7**
Gibson Desert, *Australia*, **54 E4**
Gijon, *Spain*, **89 C6**
Gilbert Islands, *Kiribati*, **52 E5**
Gilgit, *Pakistan*, **70 C3**
Girardeau, Cape, *U.S.A.*, **33 J3**
Giza, Pyramids of, *Egypt*, **99 H3**
Gladstone, *Australia*, **55 K4**
Glama, *Norway*, **86 D3**
Glasgow, *United Kingdom*, **88 C3**
Glazov, *Russia*, **85 G2**
Glorioso Islands, *Africa*, **105 J2**
Gloucester, *United Kingdom*, **88 D4**
Gobabis, *Namibia*, **104 C4**
Gobi Desert, *Asia*, **68 F3**
Gochas, *Namibia*, **104 C4**
Godavari, *India*, **71 D7**
Gode, *Ethiopia*, **103 H2**
Goiania, *Brazil*, **44 J3**
Gold Coast, *Australia*, **55 K5**
Golmud, *China*, **70 G3**
Goma, *Democratic Republic of Congo*,
   102 E4
Gonaives, *Haiti*, **35 K4**
Gonder, *Ethiopia*, **103 G1**
Gongga Shan, *China*, **68 F5**
Good Hope, Cape of, *South Africa*,
   104 C6
Goose Lake, *U.S.A.*, **32 B2**
Gorakhpur, *India*, **71 E5**
Gorgan, *Iran*, **72 F4**
Gori, *Georgia*, **72 D3**
Gorki Reservoir, *Russia*, **84 E2**
Gorontalo, *Indonesia*, **65 F3**
Gorzow Wielkopolski, *Poland*, **87 E5**
Gothenburg, *Sweden*, **87 E4**
Gotland, *Sweden*, **87 F4**
Gottingen, *Germany*, **88 G4**
Gouin Reservoir, *Canada*, **33 L1**
Goundam, *Mali*, **101 E5**
Governador Valadares, *Brazil*, **44 K3**
Graaff-Reinet, *South Africa*, **104 D6**
Grafton, *Australia*, **55 K5**
Grahamstown, *South Africa*, **104 E6**

Granada, *Spain*, **89 D7**
Gran Canaria, *Canary Islands*, **100 B3**
Gran Chaco, *South America*, **44 F4**
Grand Bahama, *The Bahamas*, **33 L5**
Grand Canal, *China*, **69 J4**
Grand Canyon, *U.S.A.*, **32 D3**
Grand Comoro, *Comoros*, **105 H2**
Grande Bay, *Argentina*, **45 E10**
Grande Prairie, *Canada*, **30 H3**
Grand Forks, *U.S.A.*, **33 G1**
Grand Island, *U.S.A.*, **32 G2**
Grand Junction, *U.S.A.*, **32 E3**
Grand Rapids, *Canada*, **31 K3**
Grand Rapids, *U.S.A.*, **33 J2**
Grand Teton, *U.S.A.*, **32 D2**
Graskop, *South Africa*, **104 F5**
Graz, *Austria*, **90 E2**
Great Australian Bight, *Australia*, **54 F6**
Great Barrier Reef, *Australia*, **54 J3**
Great Basin, *U.S.A.*, **32 C2**
Great Bear Lake, *Canada*, **30 G2**
Great Dividing Range, *Australia*, **55 J6**
Great Eastern Erg, *Algeria*, **100 G3**
Greater Antilles, *North America*, **35 J4**
Greater Khingan Range, *China*, **69 J1**
Greater Sunda Islands, *Asia*, **64 C4**
Great Falls, *U.S.A.*, **32 D1**
Great Inagua, *The Bahamas*, **35 K3**
Great Karoo, *South Africa*, **104 D6**
Great Plains, *U.S.A.*, **32 F2**
Great Rift Valley, *Africa*, **103 F5**
Great Salt Desert, *Iran*, **72 F5**
Great Salt Lake, *U.S.A.*, **32 D2**
Great Salt Lake Desert, *U.S.A.*, **32 D2**
Great Sandy Desert, *Australia*, **54 D4**
Great Slave Lake, *Canada*, **30 H2**
Great Victoria Desert, *Australia*, **54 D5**
Great Wall of China, *China*, **68 F3**
Great Western Erg, *Algeria*, **100 E2**
Greece, *Europe, country*, **91 G4**
Green Bay, *U.S.A.*, **33 J2**
Greenland, *North America, dependency*,
   108 P3
Greenland Sea, *Atlantic Ocean*, **108 M3**
Greensboro, *U.S.A.*, **33 L3**
Greenville, *U.S.A.*, **33 H4**
Grenada, *North America, country*, **34 M5**
Grenoble, *France*, **89 F5**
Griffith, *Australia*, **54 J6**
Groningen, *Netherlands*, **88 F3**
Groot, *South Africa*, **104 D6**
Groote Eylandt, *Australia*, **54 G2**
Grossglockner, *Austria*, **90 E2**
Groznyy, *Russia*, **72 E3**
Grudziadz, *Poland*, **87 F5**
Grunau, *Namibia*, **104 C5**
Grytviken, *South Georgia*, **45 L10**
Guadalajara, *Mexico*, **34 D3**
Guadalquivir, *Spain*, **89 C7**
Guadalupe Island, *Mexico*, **34 A2**
Guadeloupe, *North America*, **34 M4**
Guadiana, *Europe*, **89 C7**
Gualeguaychu, *Argentina*, **44 G6**
Guam, *Oceania*, **52 B3**
Guangzhou, *China*, **69 H6**
Guantanamo, *Cuba*, **35 J3**
Guapuava, *Brazil*, **44 H5**
Guardafui, Cape, *Somalia*, **103 K1**
Guatemala, *North America, country*,
   34 F4
Guatemala City, *Guatemala,*
   national capital, **34 F5**
Guaviare, *Colombia*, **42 E3**
Guayaquil, *Ecuador*, **42 C4**
Guayaquil, Gulf of, *Ecuador*, **42 B4**
Gueckedou, *Guinea*, **101 C7**
Guelma, *Algeria*, **90 C4**
Guiana Highlands, *Venezuela*, **42 E2**
Guilin, *China*, **68 H5**
Guinea, *Africa, country*, **101 C6**
Guinea-Bissau, *Africa, country*, **101 B6**
Guinea, Gulf of, *Africa*, **101 F8**
Guiria, *Venezuela*, **42 F1**
Guiyang, *China*, **68 G5**
Gujranwala, *Pakistan*, **70 C4**
Gujrat, *Pakistan*, **70 C4**

Gulbarga, *India*, **71 D7**
Gulf, The, *Asia*, **73 F6**
Gulu, *Uganda*, **103 F3**
Gunung Kerinci, *Indonesia*, **64 B4**
Gunung Tahan, *Malaysia*, **64 B3**
Gurupi, *Brazil*, **44 J2**
Gusau, *Nigeria*, **101 G6**
Guwahati, *India*, **70 G5**
Guyana, *South America, country*, **43 G2**
Gwalior, *India*, **70 D5**
Gweru, *Zimbabwe*, **104 E3**
Gympie, *Australia*, **55 K5**
Gyor, *Hungary*, **87 F7**

h
Haapsalu, *Estonia*, **86 G4**
Haarlem, *Netherlands*, **88 F3**
Hadhramaut, *Yemen*, **73 E9**
Ha Giang, *Vietnam*, **66 E3**
Hague, The, *Netherlands, national capital*,
   88 F3
Haifa, *Israel*, **72 B5**
Haikou, *China*, **68 H6**
Hail, *Saudi Arabia*, **73 D6**
Hailar, *China*, **69 J1**
Hainan, *China*, **68 H7**
Hai Phong, *Vietnam*, **66 E3**
Haiti, *North America, country*, **35 K4**
Hakodate, *Japan*, **69 P2**
Halifax, *Canada, internal capital*, **31 N4**
Halmahera, *Indonesia*, **65 G3**
Halmstad, *Sweden*, **87 E4**
Hamadan, *Iran*, **72 E5**
Hamah, *Syria*, **72 C5**
Hamamatsu, *Japan*, **69 N4**
Hamburg, *Germany*, **88 G3**
Hameenlinna, *Finland*, **86 H3**
Hamhung, *North Korea*, **69 L3**
Hami, *China*, **70 G2**
Hamilton, *Canada*, **31 M4**
Hamilton, *New Zealand*, **55 Q7**
Hammerfest, *Norway*, **86 G1**
Handan, *China*, **69 H3**
Hangzhou, *China*, **69 K4**
Hannover, *Germany*, **88 G3**
Hanoi, *Vietnam, national capital*, **66 E3**
Happy Valley-Goose Bay, *Canada*, **31 N3**
Haradh, *Saudi Arabia*, **73 E7**
Harare, *Zimbabwe, national capital*,
   104 F3
Harbin, *China*, **69 L1**
Harer, *Ethiopia*, **103 H2**
Hargeysa, *Somalia*, **103 H2**
Harney Basin, *U.S.A.*, **32 C2**
Harper, *Liberia*, **101 D8**
Harrisburg, *U.S.A., internal capital*, **33 L2**
Harrismith, *South Africa*, **104 E5**
Hartford, *U.S.A., internal capital*, **33 M2**
Hatteras, Cape, *U.S.A.*, **33 L3**
Hattiesburg, *U.S.A.*, **33 J4**
Hat Yai, *Thailand*, **66 D6**
Hauki Lake, *Finland*, **86 J3**
Havana, *Cuba, national capital*, **35 H3**
Hawaii, *Pacific Ocean, internal admin.*
   area, **33 P7**
Hawaiian Islands, *Pacific Ocean*, **33 P7**
Hebrides, *United Kingdom*, **88 C2**
Hefei, *China*, **69 J4**
Hegang, *China*, **69 M1**
Hejaz, *Saudi Arabia*, **73 C6**
Helena, *U.S.A., internal capital*, **32 D1**
Helmand, *Asia*, **70 B5**
Helsingborg, *Sweden*, **87 E4**
Helsinki, *Finland, national capital*, **86 H3**
Hengyang, *China*, **68 H5**
Henzada, *Burma*, **66 C4**
Herat, *Afghanistan*, **70 A4**
Hermosillo, *Mexico*, **34 B2**
Hiiumaa, *Estonia*, **86 G4**
Hilo, *U.S.A.*, **33 P8**
Himalayas, *Asia*, **70 E4**
Hindu Kush, *Asia*, **70 B3**
Hinton, *Canada*, **30 H3**
Hiroshima, *Japan*, **69 M4**
Hispaniola, *North America*, **35 K4**
Hitra, *Norway*, **86 D3**

Hobart, *Australia, internal capital,* 54 J8
Ho Chi Minh City, *Vietnam,* 66 E5
Hohhot, *China,* 68 H2
Hokkaido, *Japan,* 69 P2
Holguin, *Cuba,* 35 J3
Homs, *Syria,* 72 C5
Homyel, *Belarus,* 87 J5
Honduras, *North America, country,* 35 G4
Honduras, Gulf of, *North America,* 35 G4
Honefoss, *Norway,* 86 D3
Hong Kong, *China,* 69 H6
Honiara, *Solomon Islands, national capital,* 52 D5
Honolulu, *U.S.A., internal capital,* 33 P7
Honshu, *Japan,* 69 N3
Horlivka, *Ukraine,* 84 D4
Hormuz, Strait of, *Asia,* 73 G6
Horn, Cape, *Chile,* 45 D11
Horn Lake, *Sweden,* 86 F2
Hotan, *China,* 70 D3
Hotazel, *South Africa,* 104 D5
Houston, *U.S.A.,* 33 G5
Hradec Kralove, *Czech Republic,* 90 E1
Hrodna, *Belarus,* 87 G5
Huacrachuco, *Peru,* 42 C5
Huaihua, *China,* 68 H5
Huancayo, *Peru,* 42 C6
Huang He, *China,* 69 H3
Huanuco, *Peru,* 42 C5
Huascaran, Mount, *Peru,* 42 C5
Hubli, *India,* 71 D7
Hudiksvall, *Sweden,* 86 F3
Hudson Bay, *Canada,* 31 L3
Hudson Strait, *Canada,* 31 M2
Hue, *Vietnam,* 66 E4
Huelva, *Spain,* 89 C7
Hull, *United Kingdom,* 88 D3
Huntsville, *Canada,* 31 M4
Huntsville, *U.S.A.,* 33 J4
Hurghada, *Egypt,* 99 H3
Huron, Lake, *U.S.A.,* 33 K2
Hvannadalshnukur, *Iceland,* 86 P2
Hwange, *Zimbabwe,* 104 E3
Hyderabad, *India,* 71 D7
Hyderabad, *Pakistan,* 70 B5
Hyesan, *North Korea,* 69 L2

i

Iasi, *Romania,* 91 H2
Ibadan, *Nigeria,* 101 F7
Ibague, *Colombia,* 42 C3
Ibarra, *Ecuador,* 42 C3
Ibb, *Yemen,* 73 D9
Iberian Mountains, *Spain,* 89 D6
Ibiza, *Spain,* 89 E7
Ica, *Peru,* 42 C6
Iceland, *Europe, country,* 86 P2
Idaho, *U.S.A., internal admin. area,* 32 C2
Idaho Falls, *U.S.A.,* 32 D2
Ierapetra, *Greece,* 91 H5
Iguacu Falls, *South America,* 44 H5
Ihosy, *Madagascar,* 105 J4
Ikopa, *Madagascar,* 105 J3
Ilagan, *Philippines,* 67 H4
Ilebo, *Democratic Republic of Congo,* 102 D4
Ilheus, *Brazil,* 44 L2
Iliamna Lake, *U.S.A.,* 30 D2
Iligan, *Philippines,* 67 H6
Illapel, *Chile,* 44 D6
Illimani, Mount, *Bolivia,* 44 E3
Illinois, *U.S.A., internal admin. area,* 33 J2
Illizi, *Algeria,* 100 G3
Ilmen, Lake, *Russia,* 86 J4
Iloilo, *Philippines,* 67 H5
Ilonga, *Tanzania,* 103 G5
Ilorin, *Nigeria,* 101 F7
Imeni Ismail Samani, Pik, *Tajikistan,* 70 C3
Imperatriz, *Brazil,* 43 J5
Imphal, *India,* 71 G6
Inari, Lake, *Finland,* 86 H1
Inchon, *South Korea,* 69 L3
Indals, *Sweden,* 86 E3

Inderbor, *Kazakhstan,* 85 G4
India, *Asia, country,* 71 D6
Indiana, *U.S.A., internal admin. area,* 33 J2
Indianapolis, *U.S.A., internal capital,* 33 J3
Indian Ocean, 21
Indonesia, *Asia, country,* 64 C5
Indore, *India,* 71 D6
Indus, *Asia,* 70 B5
Ingolstadt, *Germany,* 88 G4
Inhambane, *Mozambique,* 105 G4
Inner Mongolia, *China,* 69 H2
Innsbruck, *Austria,* 90 D2
Inukjuak, *Canada,* 31 M3
Inuvik, *Canada,* 30 F2
Invercargill, *New Zealand,* 55 N9
Inyangani, *Zimbabwe,* 105 F3
Ioannina, *Greece,* 91 G4
Ionian Sea, *Europe,* 91 F4
Iowa, *U.S.A., internal admin. area,* 33 H2
Ipiales, *Colombia,* 42 C3
Ipoh, *Malaysia,* 64 B3
Ipswich, *United Kingdom,* 88 E3
Iqaluit, *Canada, internal capital,* 31 N2
Iquique, *Chile,* 44 D4
Iquitos, *Peru,* 42 D4
Irakleio, *Greece,* 91 H5
Iran, *Asia, country,* 72 F5
Iranshahr, *Iran,* 73 H6
Iraq, *Asia, country,* 72 D5
Irbid, *Jordan,* 72 C5
Ireland, *Europe, country,* 88 B3
Iringa, *Tanzania,* 103 G5
Irish Sea, *Europe,* 88 C3
Irkutsk, *Russia,* 75 F3
Irrawaddy, *Burma,* 66 C4
Irrawaddy, Mouths of the, *Burma,* 66 B4
Irtysh, *Asia,* 74 D3
Isabela, *Ecuador,* 42 N10
Isafjordhur, *Iceland,* 86 N2
Isiro, *Democratic Republic of Congo,* 102 E3
Islamabad, *Pakistan, national capital,* 70 C4
Isle of Man, *Europe,* 88 C3
Isle of Wight, *United Kingdom,* 88 D4
Ismailia, *Egypt,* 99 H2
Isoka, *Zambia,* 105 F2
Isparta, *Turkey,* 91 J4
Israel, *Asia, country,* 73 B5
Issyk, Lake, *Kyrgyzstan,* 70 D2
Istanbul, *Turkey,* 91 J3
Itaituba, *Brazil,* 43 G4
Itajai, *Brazil,* 44 J5
Italy, *Europe, country,* 90 D2
Itapetininga, *Brazil,* 44 J4
Ivano-Frankivsk, *Ukraine,* 87 H6
Ivanovo, *Russia,* 84 E2
Ivdel, *Russia,* 85 J1
Ivory Coast, *Africa, country,* 101 D7
Ivujivik, *Canada,* 31 M2
Izhevsk, *Russia,* 85 G2
Izmir, *Turkey,* 91 H4

j

Jabalpur, *India,* 71 D6
Jackson, *Mississippi, U.S.A., internal capital,* 33 H4
Jackson, *Tennessee, U.S.A.,* 33 J3
Jacksonville, *U.S.A.,* 33 K4
Jaen, *Spain,* 89 D7
Jaffna, *Sri Lanka,* 71 E9
Jaipur, *India,* 70 D5
Jakarta, *Indonesia, national capital,* 64 C5
Jalalabad, *Afghanistan,* 70 C4
Jalal-Abad, *Kyrgyzstan,* 70 C2
Jamaica, *North America, country,* 35 J4
Jambi, *Indonesia,* 64 B4
James Bay, *Canada,* 31 L3
Jamestown, *U.S.A.,* 33 L2
Jammu, *India,* 70 C4
Jammu and Kashmir, *Asia,* 70 D4
Jamnagar, *India,* 71 C6
Jamshedpur, *India,* 71 F6
Japan, *Asia, country,* 69 N3

Japura, *Brazil,* 42 E4
Jatai, *Brazil,* 44 H3
Java, *Indonesia,* 64 C5
Java Sea, *Indonesia,* 64 C5
Jayapura, *Indonesia,* 65 K4
Jedda, *Saudi Arabia,* 73 C7
Jefferson City, *U.S.A., internal capital,* 33 H3
Jekabpils, *Latvia,* 87 H4
Jelgava, *Latvia,* 87 G4
Jember, *Indonesia,* 64 D5
Jerba, *Tunisia,* 98 D2
Jerez de la Frontera, *Spain,* 89 C7
Jerusalem, *Israel, national capital,* 73 C5
Jhansi, *India,* 70 D5
Jiamusi, *China,* 69 M1
Jilin, *China,* 69 L2
Jima, *Ethiopia,* 103 G2
Jinhua, *China,* 69 J5
Jining, *China,* 69 J3
Jinja, *Uganda,* 103 F3
Jinzhou, *China,* 69 K2
Jixi, *China,* 69 M1
Jizzax, *Uzbekistan,* 70 B2
Joao Pessoa, *Brazil,* 43 M5
Jodhpur, *India,* 70 C5
Johannesburg, *South Africa,* 104 E5
Johnston Atoll, *Oceania,* 52 G3
Johor Bahru, *Malaysia,* 64 B3
Jolo, *Philippines,* 67 H6
Jonesboro, *U.S.A.,* 33 H3
Jonkoping, *Sweden,* 87 E4
Jordan, *Asia, country,* 73 C5
Jorhat, *India,* 70 G5
Jos, *Nigeria,* 102 A2
Juan de Nova, *Africa,* 105 H3
Juazeiro, *Brazil,* 43 K5
Juazeiro do Norte, *Brazil,* 43 L5
Juba, *Africa,* 103 H3
Juba, *South Sudan, national capital* 103 F3
Juchitan, *Mexico,* 34 E4
Juiz de Fora, *Brazil,* 44 K4
Juliaca, *Peru,* 42 D7
Juneau, *U.S.A., internal capital,* 30 F3
Jurmala, *Latvia,* 87 G4
Jurua, *Brazil,* 42 E5
Jutland, *Europe,* 87 C4
Jyvaskyla, *Finland,* 86 H3

k

K2, *Asia,* 70 D3
Kaamanen, *Finland,* 86 H1
Kabinda, *Democratic Republic of Congo,* 102 D5
Kabul, *Afghanistan, national capital,* 70 B4
Kabunda, *Democratic Republic of Congo,* 102 E6
Kabwe, *Zambia,* 104 E2
Kadoma, *Zimbabwe,* 104 E3
Kaduna, *Nigeria,* 101 G6
Kaedi, *Mauritania,* 101 C5
Kafakumba, *Democratic Republic of Congo,* 102 D5
Kafue, *Zambia,* 104 E3
Kagoshima, *Japan,* 69 M4
Kahramanmaras, *Turkey,* 72 C4
Kahului, *U.S.A.,* 33 P7
Kainji Reservoir, *Nigeria,* 101 F6
Kairouan, *Tunisia,* 98 D1
Kajaani, *Finland,* 86 H2
Kakhovske Reservoir, *Ukraine,* 84 C4
Kalahari Desert, *Africa,* 104 D4
Kalamata, *Greece,* 91 G4
Kalemie, *Democratic Republic of Congo,* 102 E5
Kalgoorlie, *Australia,* 54 D6
Kaliningrad, *Russia,* 87 G5
Kalisz, *Poland,* 87 F6
Kalkrand, *Namibia,* 104 C4
Kalmar, *Sweden,* 87 F4
Kaluga, *Russia,* 84 D3
Kamanjab, *Namibia,* 104 B3
Kama Reservoir, *Russia,* 85 H2
Kamativi, *Zimbabwe,* 104 E3
Kamchatka Peninsula, *Russia,* 75 H3

Kamenka, *Russia,* 84 E3
Kamina, *Democratic Republic of Congo,* 102 E5
Kamloops, *Canada,* 30 G3
Kampala, *Uganda, national capital,* 103 F3
Kampong Cham, *Cambodia,* 66 E5
Kampong Chhnang, *Cambodia,* 66 D5
Kampong Saom, *Cambodia,* 66 D5
Kamyanets-Podilskyy, *Ukraine,* 87 H6
Kamyshin, *Russia,* 84 F3
Kananga, *Democratic Republic of Congo,* 102 D5
Kanazawa, *Japan,* 69 N3
Kandahar, *Afghanistan,* 70 B4
Kandalaksha, *Russia,* 86 K2
Kandi, *Benin,* 101 F6
Kandy, *Sri Lanka,* 71 E9
Kang, *Botswana,* 104 D4
Kangaroo Island, *Australia,* 54 G7
Kanggye, *North Korea,* 69 L2
Kankan, *Guinea,* 101 D6
Kano, *Nigeria,* 98 C6
Kanpur, *India,* 70 E5
Kansas, *U.S.A., internal admin. area,* 32 G3
Kansas City, *U.S.A.,* 33 H3
Kanye, *Botswana,* 104 E4
Kaohsiung, *China,* 69 K6
Kaolack, *Senegal,* 101 B6
Kara-Balta, *Kyrgyzstan,* 70 C2
Karabuk, *Turkey,* 91 K3
Karachi, *Pakistan,* 71 B6
Karaj, *Iran,* 72 F4
Karakol, *Kyrgyzstan,* 70 D2
Karakorum Range, *Asia,* 70 D3
Kara Kum Desert, *Turkmenistan,* 72 G3
Karaman, *Turkey,* 91 K4
Karamay, *China,* 70 E1
Kara Sea, *Russia,* 74 D2
Kariba, *Zimbabwe,* 104 E3
Kariba, Lake, *Africa,* 104 E3
Karibib, *Namibia,* 104 C4
Karimata Strait, *Indonesia,* 64 C4
Karlovac, *Croatia,* 90 E2
Karlovy Vary, *Czech Republic,* 90 E1
Karlshamn, *Sweden,* 87 E4
Karlsruhe, *Germany,* 88 G4
Karlstad, *Sweden,* 86 E4
Karmoy, *Norway,* 86 C4
Karonga, *Malawi,* 105 F1
Karora, *Eritrea,* 99 J5
Karpathos, *Greece,* 91 H5
Karratha, *Australia,* 54 C4
Kasai, *Africa,* 102 C4
Kasama, *Zambia,* 104 F2
Kashi, *China,* 70 D3
Kassala, *Sudan,* 99 J5
Kassel, *Germany,* 88 G3
Kasungu, *Malawi,* 105 F2
Kataba, *Zambia,* 104 E3
Kathmandu, *Nepal, national capital,* 70 F5
Katiola, *Ivory Coast,* 101 D7
Katowice, *Poland,* 87 F6
Katsina, *Nigeria,* 101 G6
Kattegat, *Europe,* 87 D4
Kauai, *U.S.A.,* 33 P7
Kaukau Veld, *Africa,* 104 C4
Kaunas, *Lithuania,* 87 G5
Kavala, *Greece,* 91 H3
Kawambwa, *Zambia,* 104 E1
Kayes, *Mali,* 101 C6
Kayseri, *Turkey,* 72 C4
Kazakhstan, *Asia, country,* 74 C3
Kazan, *Russia,* 85 F2
Kaztalovka, *Kazakhstan,* 85 F4
Kebnekaise, *Sweden,* 86 F2
Kecskemet, *Hungary,* 85 F4
Kedougou, *Senegal,* 101 C6
Keetmanshoop, *Namibia,* 104 C5
Kefallonia, *Greece,* 91 F4
Keflavik, *Iceland,* 86 N2
Kelowna, *Canada,* 30 H4
Kempten, *Germany,* 88 G5
Kendari, *Indonesia,* 65 F4
Kenema, *Sierra Leone,* 101 C7

Kenhardt, *South Africa,* 104 D5
Kenitra, *Morocco,* 100 D2
Kenora, *Canada,* 31 K4
Kentucky, *U.S.A., internal admin. area,* 33 J3
Kentucky Lake, *U.S.A.,* 33 J3
Kenya, *Africa, country,* 103 G3
Kenya, Mount, *Kenya,* 103 G4
Kerch, *Ukraine,* 91 L2
Kerema, *Papua New Guinea,* 65 L5
Keren, *Eritrea,* 99 J5
Kerkenah Islands, *Tunisia,* 98 D2
Kermadec Islands, *New Zealand,* 55 Q6
Kerman, *Iran,* 73 G5
Kermanshah, *Iran,* 72 E5
Key West, *U.S.A.,* 33 K6
Khabarovsk, *Russia,* 75 G3
Khanka, Lake, *Asia,* 69 M2
Kharkiv, *Ukraine,* 84 D3
Khartoum, *Sudan, national capital,* 99 H5
Kherson, *Ukraine,* 84 C4
Khmelnytskyy, *Ukraine,* 87 H6
Khon Kaen, *Thailand,* 66 D4
Khorugh, *Tajikistan,* 70 C3
Khouribga, *Morocco,* 100 D2
Khujand, *Tajikistan,* 70 B2
Khulna, *Bangladesh,* 71 F6
Kidal, *Mali,* 100 F5
Kiel, *Germany,* 88 G3
Kielce, *Poland,* 87 G6
Kiev, *Ukraine, national capital,* 87 J6
Kievske Reservoir, *Ukraine,* 84 C3
Kiffa, *Mauritania,* 101 C5
Kigali, *Rwanda, national capital,* 103 F4
Kigoma, *Tanzania,* 102 E4
Kikwit, *Democratic Republic of Congo,* 102 C5
Kilimanjaro, *Africa,* 103 G4
Kilwa, *Democratic Republic of Congo,* 102 E5
Kimberley, *South Africa,* 104 D5
Kimberley Plateau, *Australia,* 54 E3
Kimchaek, *North Korea,* 69 L2
Kindia, *Guinea,* 101 C6
Kindu, *Democratic Republic of Congo,* 102 E4
Kineshma, *Russia,* 84 E2
King George Island, *Atlantic Ocean,* 45 G12
Kingisepp, *Russia,* 86 J4
King Island, *Australia,* 54 H7
Kings Peak, *U.S.A.,* 32 C2
Kingston, *Canada,* 31 M4
Kingston, *Jamaica, national capital,* 35 J4
Kingstown, *St. Vincent and the Grenadines, national capital,* 34 M5
King William Island, *Canada,* 31 K2
Kinkala, *Congo,* 102 B4
Kinshasa, *Democratic Republic of Congo, national capital,* 102 C4
Kipushi, *Democratic Republic of Congo,* 102 E6
Kiribati, *Oceania, country,* 52 F5
Kirikkale, *Turkey,* 91 K4
Kirinyaga, *Kenya,* 103 G4
Kirishi, *Russia,* 86 K4
Kirkenes, *Norway,* 86 J1
Kirkland Lake, *Canada,* 31 L4
Kirkuk, *Iraq,* 72 D4
Kirkwall, *United Kingdom,* 88 D2
Kirov, *Russia,* 85 F2
Kirovohrad, *Ukraine,* 84 C4
Kiruna, *Sweden,* 86 G2
Kisangani, *Democratic Republic of Congo,* 102 E3
Kisii, *Kenya,* 103 F4
Kismaayo, *Somalia,* 103 H4
Kisumu, *Kenya,* 103 F4
Kita, *Mali,* 101 D6
Kitakyushu, *Japan,* 69 M4
Kitale, *Kenya,* 103 G3
Kitwe, *Zambia,* 104 E2
Kiuruvesi, *Finland,* 86 H3
Kivu, Lake, *Africa,* 102 E4
Klagenfurt, *Austria,* 90 E2

Klaipeda, *Lithuania,* 87 G5
Klar, *Europe,* 86 E3
Klintsy, *Russia,* 87 K5
Knittelfeld, *Austria,* 90 E2
Knoxville, *U.S.A.,* 33 K3
Kobar Sink, *Ethiopia,* 99 K6
Koblenz, *Germany,* 88 F4
Kochi, *India,* 71 D9
Kodiak Island, *U.S.A.,* 30 D3
Koforidua, *Ghana,* 101 E7
Kohtla-Jarve, *Estonia,* 86 H4
Kokkola, *Finland,* 86 G3
Kokshetau, *Kazakhstan,* 72 J1
Kola Peninsula, *Russia,* 86 L2
Kolda, *Senegal,* 101 C6
Kolding, *Denmark,* 87 D5
Kolhapur, *India,* 71 C7
Kolkata, *India,* 71 F6
Kolomna, *Russia,* 84 D2
Kolwezi, *Democratic Republic of Congo,* 102 E6
Kolyma Range, *Russia,* 75 H2
Komsomolets, *Kazakhstan,* 85 J3
Komsomolsk, *Russia,* 75 G3
Konduz, *Afghanistan,* 70 B3
Kongur Shan, *China,* 70 D3
Konosha, *Russia,* 84 E1
Konya, *Turkey,* 91 K4
Korce, *Albania,* 91 G3
Korea Bay, *Asia,* 69 K3
Korea Strait, *Asia,* 69 L4
Korhogo, *Ivory Coast,* 101 D7
Korla, *China,* 70 F2
Korosten, *Ukraine,* 87 J6
Kosciuszko, Mount, *Australia,* 55 J7
Kosice, *Slovakia,* 87 G6
Kosovo, *Europe, country,* 91 G3
Kosti, *Sudan,* 99 H6
Kostomuksha, *Russia,* 86 J2
Kostroma, *Russia,* 84 E2
Koszalin, *Poland,* 87 F5
Kota, *India,* 70 D5
Kota Bharu, *Malaysia,* 64 B2
Kota Kinabalu, *Malaysia,* 64 E2
Kotka, *Finland,* 86 H3
Kotlas, *Russia,* 85 F1
Koudougou, *Burkina Faso,* 101 E6
Koutiala, *Mali,* 101 D6
Kouvola, *Finland,* 86 H3
Kovel, *Ukraine,* 87 H6
Kozhikode, *India,* 71 D8
Kragujevac, *Serbia,* 91 G2
Krakatoa, *Indonesia,* 64 C5
Krakow, *Poland,* 87 G6
Kraljevo, *Serbia,* 91 G3
Kramatorsk, *Ukraine,* 84 D4
Kranj, *Slovenia,* 90 E2
Krasnodar, *Russia,* 72 C2
Krasnoyarsk, *Russia,* 74 E3
Kremenchuk, *Ukraine,* 84 C4
Kremenchukske Reservoir, *Ukraine,* 84 C4
Krishna, *India,* 71 D7
Kristiansand, *Norway,* 86 C4
Kristiansund, *Norway,* 86 C3
Krong Kaoh Kong, *Cambodia,* 66 D5
Kroonstad, *South Africa,* 104 E5
Krugersdorp, *South Africa,* 104 E5
Kryvyy Rih, *Ukraine,* 84 C4
Kuala Lumpur, *Malaysia, national capital,* 64 B3
Kuala Terengganu, *Malaysia,* 64 B2
Kuantan, *Malaysia,* 64 B3
Kuching, *Malaysia,* 64 D3
Kuhmo, *Finland,* 86 J2
Kuito, *Angola,* 104 C2
Kulob, *Tajikistan,* 70 B3
Kumamoto, *Japan,* 69 M4
Kumanovo, *Macedonia,* 91 G3
Kumasi, *Ghana,* 101 E7
Kumba, *Cameroon,* 102 A3
Kumo, *Nigeria,* 98 D6
Kunlun Mountains, *China,* 70 E3
Kunming, *China,* 68 F5
Kuopio, *Finland,* 86 H2
Kupang, *Indonesia,* 65 F6

Kuressaare, *Estonia,* 87 G4
Kurgan, *Russia,* 85 K2
Kurikka, *Finland,* 86 G3
Kuril Islands, *Russia,* 75 H3
Kursk, *Russia,* 84 D3
Kushiro, *Japan,* 69 P2
Kutahya, *Turkey,* 91 J4
Kutaisi, *Georgia,* 72 D3
Kutch, Rann of, *India,* 71 B6
Kuujjuaq, *Canada,* 31 N3
Kuusamo, *Finland,* 86 J2
Kuwait, *Asia, country,* 73 E6
Kuwait City, *Kuwait, national capital,* 73 E6
Kuybyshev Reservoir, *Russia,* 85 F3
Kuyto, Lake, *Russia,* 86 K2
Kuytun, *China,* 70 F2
Kwangju, *South Korea,* 69 L3
Kyoga, Lake, *Uganda,* 103 F3
Kyoto, *Japan,* 69 N3
Kyrenia, *Cyprus,* 91 K5
Kyrgyzstan, *Asia, country,* 70 C2
Kythira, *Greece,* 91 G4
Kyushu, *Japan,* 69 M4
Kyzyl, *Russia,* 74 E3

I

Laayoune, *Western Sahara, national capital,* 100 C3
Labe, *Guinea,* 101 C6
Labrador City, *Canada,* 31 N3
Labrador Sea, *North America,* 31 P2
La Chorrera, *Colombia,* 42 D4
La Coruna, *Spain,* 89 B6
Ladoga, Lake, *Russia,* 86 J3
Ladysmith, *South Africa,* 104 E5
Lae, *Papua New Guinea,* 65 L5
Lagdo Reservoir, *Cameroon,* 102 B2
La Gomera, *Canary Islands,* 100 B3
Lagos, *Nigeria,* 101 F7
Lagos, *Portugal,* 89 B7
La Grande Reservoir, *Canada,* 31 M3
Lagunillas, *Venezuela,* 42 D1
Lahat, *Indonesia,* 64 B4
Lahore, *Pakistan,* 70 C4
Lahti, *Finland,* 86 H3
Lai, *Chad,* 102 C2
La Libertad, *Ecuador,* 42 B4
Lambarene, *Gabon,* 102 B4
Lamia, *Greece,* 91 G4
Lancaster Sound, *Canada,* 31 L1
Land's End, *United Kingdom,* 88 C4
Langanes, *Iceland,* 86 Q2
Langsa, *Indonesia,* 64 A3
Lansing, *U.S.A., internal capital,* 33 K2
Lanzarote, *Canary Islands,* 100 C3
Lanzhou, *China,* 68 F3
Laoag, *Philippines,* 67 H4
Lao Cai, *Vietnam,* 66 D3
La Oroya, *Peru,* 42 C6
Laos, *Asia, country,* 66 D4
La Palma, *Canary Islands,* 100 B3
La Palma, *Panama,* 35 J6
La Paz, *Bolivia, national capital,* 44 E3
La Paz, *Mexico,* 34 B3
La Perouse Strait, *Asia,* 69 P1
Lapland, *Europe,* 86 H1
La Plata, *Argentina,* 44 G6
Lappeenranta, *Finland,* 86 J3
Laptev Sea, *Russia,* 75 G2
Larache, *Morocco,* 100 D1
Laredo, *U.S.A.,* 32 G5
La Rioja, *Argentina,* 44 E5
Larisa, *Greece,* 91 G4
Larkana, *Pakistan,* 70 B5
Larnaca, *Cyprus,* 91 K5
La Rochelle, *France,* 89 D5
La Romana, *Dominican Republic,* 35 L4
Larvik, *Norway,* 86 D4
Lashio, *Burma,* 66 C3
Lastoursville, *Gabon,* 102 B4
Las Vegas, *U.S.A.,* 32 C3
Latakia, *Syria,* 72 C4
Latvia, *Europe, country,* 87 H4
Launceston, *Australia,* 54 J8
Lausanne, *Switzerland,* 90 C2

Lautoka, *Fiji,* 55 Q3
Lebanon, *Asia, country,* 72 C5
Lecce, *Italy,* 91 F3
Ledo, Cape, *Angola,* 104 B1
Leeds, *United Kingdom,* 88 D3
Leeuwarden, *Netherlands,* 88 F3
Leeuwin, Cape, *Australia,* 54 B6
Leeward Islands, *North America,* 34 M4
Legaspi, *Philippines,* 67 H5
Legnica, *Poland,* 87 F6
Le Havre, *France,* 88 E4
Leipzig, *Germany,* 88 H4
Leiria, *Portugal,* 89 B7
Le Mans, *France,* 88 E4
Lena, *Russia,* 75 G2
Leon, *Mexico,* 34 D3
Leon, *Nicaragua,* 35 G5
Leon, *Spain,* 89 C6
Leonardville, *Namibia,* 104 C4
Lerida, *Spain,* 89 E6
Lerwick, *United Kingdom,* 88 D1
Les Cayes, *Haiti,* 35 K4
Leshan, *China,* 68 F5
Leskovac, *Serbia,* 91 G3
Lesotho, *Africa, country,* 104 E5
Lesser Antilles, *North America,* 34 M5
Lesser Sunda Islands, *Indonesia,* 64 E5
Lesvos, *Greece,* 91 H4
Lethbridge, *Canada,* 30 H4
Leticia, *Brazil,* 42 E4
Lewiston, *U.S.A.,* 32 C1
Lexington, *U.S.A.,* 33 K3
Lhasa, *China,* 70 G5
Lhokseumawe, *Indonesia,* 64 A2
Lianyungang, *China,* 69 J4
Liaoyuan, *China,* 69 L2
Liberec, *Czech Republic,* 90 E1
Liberia, *Africa, country,* 101 D7
Liberia, *Costa Rica,* 35 G5
Libreville, *Gabon, national capital,* 102 A3
Libya, *Africa, country,* 98 F3
Libyan Desert, *Africa,* 98 F3
Lichinga, *Mozambique,* 105 G2
Lida, *Belarus,* 87 H5
Lidkoping, *Sweden,* 86 E4
Liechtenstein, *Europe, country,* 90 D2
Liege, *Belgium,* 88 F4
Lieksa, *Finland,* 86 J3
Liepaja, *Latvia,* 87 G4
Ligurian Sea, *Europe,* 90 C3
Likasi, *Democratic Republic of Congo,* 102 E6
Lille, *France,* 88 E4
Lillehammer, *Norway,* 86 D3
Lilongwe, *Malawi, national capital,* 105 F2
Lima, *Peru, national capital,* 42 C6
Limassol, *Cyprus,* 91 K5
Limerick, *Ireland,* 88 B3
Limnos, *Greece,* 84 C3
Limoges, *France,* 89 E5
Limon, *Costa Rica,* 35 H5
Limpopo, *Africa,* 104 F4
Linares, *Chile,* 45 D7
Linchuan, *China,* 69 J5
Lincoln, *U.S.A., internal capital,* 33 G2
Lindi, *Tanzania,* 103 G6
Line Islands, *Kiribati,* 53 H4
Linhares, *Brazil,* 44 K3
Linkoping, *Sweden,* 86 E4
Linz, *Austria,* 90 E1
Lions, Gulf of, *Europe,* 89 F6
Lipari Islands, *Italy,* 90 E4
Lipetsk, *Russia,* 84 D3
Lisbon, *Portugal, national capital,* 89 B7
Lithuania, *Europe, country,* 87 G5
Little Andaman, *India,* 71 G8
Little Rock, *U.S.A., internal capital,* 33 H4
Liuzhou, *China,* 68 G6
Liverpool, *United Kingdom,* 88 D3
Livingstone, *Zambia,* 104 E3
Livorno, *Italy,* 90 D3
Liwale, *Tanzania,* 103 G5
Ljubljana, *Slovenia, national capital,* 90 E2

Llanos, *South America*, 42 D2
Lloydminster, *Canada*, 30 J3
Lobamba, *Swaziland, national capital*, 104 F5
Lodz, *Poland*, 87 F6
Lofoten, *Norway*, 86 E1
Logan, Mount, *Canada*, 30 F2
Logrono, *Spain*, 89 D6
Loire, *France*, 88 E5
Loja, *Ecuador*, 42 C4
Lokan Reservoir, *Finland*, 86 H2
Lolland, *Denmark*, 87 D5
Lombok, *Indonesia*, 64 E5
Lome, *Togo, national capital*, 101 F7
London, *Canada*, 31 L4
London, *United Kingdom, national capital*, 88 D4
Londonderry, *United Kingdom*, 88 C3
Londrina, *Brazil*, 44 H4
Long Island, *The Bahamas*, 33 L6
Long Xuyen, *Vietnam*, 66 E5
Lopez, Cape, *Gabon*, 102 A4
Lop Lake, *China*, 70 G2
Lord Howe Island, *Australia*, 55 L6
Los Angeles, *Chile*, 45 D7
Los Angeles, *U.S.A.*, 32 C4
Los Mochis, *Mexico*, 34 C2
Louangphrabang, *Laos*, 66 D4
Loubomo, *Congo*, 102 B4
Louga, *Senegal*, 101 B5
Louisiana, *U.S.A., internal admin. area*, 33 H4
Lower California, *Mexico*, 34 B2
Loyalty Islands, *New Caledonia*, 55 N4
Luacano, *Angola*, 104 D2
Luanda, *Angola, national capital*, 104 B1
Luangwa, *Africa*, 104 F2
Luanshya, *Zambia*, 104 E2
Lubango, *Angola*, 104 B2
Lubbock, *U.S.A.*, 32 F4
Lublin, *Poland*, 87 G6
Lubny, *Ukraine*, 84 C3
Lubumbashi, *Democratic Republic of Congo*, 102 E6
Lucena, *Philippines*, 67 H5
Lucerne, *Switzerland*, 90 D2
Lucira, *Angola*, 104 B2
Lucknow, *India*, 70 E5
Luderitz, *Namibia*, 104 C5
Ludhiana, *India*, 70 D4
Ludza, *Latvia*, 87 H4
Luena, *Angola*, 104 C2
Luganville, *Vanuatu*, 55 N3
Lugo, *Spain*, 89 C6
Luhansk, *Ukraine*, 84 D4
Luiana, *Angola*, 104 D3
Lukulu, *Zambia*, 104 D2
Lumbala Kaquengue, *Angola*, 104 D2
Lumbala Nguimbo, *Angola*, 104 D2
Lundazi, *Zambia*, 105 F2
Lupilichi, *Mozambique*, 105 G2
Lusaka, *Zambia, national capital*, 104 E3
Lutsk, *Ukraine*, 87 H6
Luxembourg, *Europe, country*, 88 F4
Luxembourg, *Luxembourg, national capital*, 88 F4
Luxor, *Egypt*, 99 H3
Luzhou, *China*, 68 G5
Luzon, *Philippines*, 67 H4
Luzon Strait, *Philippines*, 67 H4
Lviv, *Ukraine*, 87 H6
Lyon, *France*, 89 F5
Lysychansk, *Ukraine*, 84 D4

m

Maan, *Jordan*, 73 C5
Maastricht, *Netherlands*, 88 F4
Macae, *Brazil*, 44 K4
Macapa, *Brazil*, 43 H3
Macau, *China*, 69 H6
Macedonia, *Europe, country*, 91 G3
Maceio, *Brazil*, 43 L5
Machakos, *Kenya*, 103 G4
Machala, *Ecuador*, 42 C4
Machu Picchu, *Peru*, 42 D6
Mackay, *Australia*, 55 J4

Mackenzie, *Canada*, 30 G2
Mackenzie Bay, *Canada*, 30 F2
Mackenzie Mountains, *Canada*, 30 F2
Macon, *U.S.A.*, 33 K4
Madagascar, *Africa, country*, 105 J4
Madang, *Papua New Guinea*, 65 L5
Madeira, *Atlantic Ocean*, 100 B2
Madeira, *Brazil*, 42 F5
Madingou, *Congo*, 102 B4
Madison, *U.S.A., internal capital*, 33 J2
Madras, *India*, 71 E8
Madrid, *Spain, national capital*, 89 D6
Madurai, *India*, 71 D9
Maevatanana, *Madagascar*, 105 J3
Mafeteng, *Lesotho*, 104 E5
Mafia Island, *Tanzania*, 103 H5
Magadan, *Russia*, 75 H3
Magangue, *Colombia*, 42 D2
Magdalena, *Bolivia*, 44 F2
Magdeburg, *Germany*, 88 G3
Magellan, Strait of, *South America*, 45 E10
Magnitogorsk, *Russia*, 85 H3
Mahajanga, *Madagascar*, 105 J3
Mahalapye, *Botswana*, 104 E4
Mahilyow, *Belarus*, 87 J5
Mahon, *Spain*, 89 F7
Maiduguri, *Nigeria*, 98 D6
Mai-Ndombe, Lake, *Democratic Republic of Congo*, 102 C4
Maine, *U.S.A., internal admin. area*, 33 N1
Maine, Gulf of, *U.S.A.*, 33 N2
Maio, *Cape Verde*, 101 M11
Majorca, *Spain*, 89 E7
Majuro, *Marshall Islands, national capital*, 52 E4
Makarikari, *Botswana*, 104 D4
Makassar Strait, *Indonesia*, 65 E4
Makeni, *Sierra Leone*, 101 C7
Makgadikgadi Pans, *Botswana*, 104 D4
Makhachkala, *Russia*, 72 E3
Makkovik, *Canada*, 31 P3
Makokou, *Gabon*, 102 B3
Makumbako, *Tanzania*, 103 F5
Makurdi, *Nigeria*, 102 A2
Mala, *Peru*, 42 C6
Malabo, *Equatorial Guinea, national capital*, 102 A3
Maladzyechna, *Belarus*, 87 H5
Malaga, *Spain*, 89 C7
Malaimbandy, *Madagascar*, 105 J4
Malakal, *South Sudan*, 103 F2
Malakula, *Vanuatu*, 55 N3
Malang, *Indonesia*, 64 D5
Malanje, *Angola*, 104 C1
Malar, Lake, *Sweden*, 86 F4
Malatya, *Turkey*, 72 C4
Malawi, *Africa, country*, 105 F2
Malawi, Lake, *Africa*, 103 F6
Malaysia, *Asia, country*, 64 B2
Maldives, *Asia, country*, 71 C9
Male, *Maldives, national capital*, 71 C10
Malegaon, *India*, 71 C6
Mali, *Africa, country*, 100 E5
Malindi, *Kenya*, 103 H4
Malmo, *Sweden*, 87 E5
Malpelo Island, *Colombia*, 42 B3
Malta, *Europe, country*, 90 E4
Mamoudzou, *Mayotte*, 105 J2
Mamuno, *Botswana*, 104 D4
Man, *Ivory Coast*, 101 D7
Manado, *Indonesia*, 65 F3
Managua, *Nicaragua, national capital*, 35 G5
Manakara, *Madagascar*, 105 J4
Manama, *Bahrain, national capital*, 73 F6
Manaus, *Brazil*, 43 G4
Manchester, *United Kingdom*, 88 D3
Manchuria, *China*, 69 K2
Mandalay, *Burma*, 66 C3
Mandera, *Kenya*, 103 H3
Mandritsara, *Madagascar*, 105 J3
Mandurah, *Australia*, 54 C6
Mangalore, *India*, 71 C8
Mania, *Madagascar*, 105 J3
Manicouagan Reservoir, *Canada*, 31 N3

Manila, *Philippines, national capital*, 67 H5
Manisa, *Turkey*, 91 H4
Man, Isle of, *Europe*, 88 C3
Manitoba, *Canada, internal admin. area*, 31 K3
Manitoba, Lake, *Canada*, 31 K3
Manizales, *Colombia*, 42 C2
Manja, *Madagascar*, 105 H4
Mannar, *Sri Lanka*, 71 E9
Mannar, Gulf of, *Asia*, 71 D9
Mannheim, *Germany*, 88 G4
Mansa, *Zambia*, 104 E2
Manta, *Ecuador*, 42 B4
Manzhouli, *China*, 75 F3
Mao, *Chad*, 98 E6
Maoke Range, *Indonesia*, 65 J4
Maputo, *Mozambique, national capital*, 105 F5
Maraba, *Brazil*, 43 J5
Maracaibo, *Venezuela*, 42 D1
Maracaibo, Lake, *Venezuela*, 42 D2
Maracay, *Venezuela*, 42 E1
Maradi, *Niger*, 98 C6
Maranon, *Peru*, 42 C4
Marathon, *Canada*, 31 L4
Mar del Plata, *Argentina*, 45 G7
Margarita Island, *Venezuela*, 42 F1
Margherita Peak, *Africa*, 102 E3
Marib, *Yemen*, 73 E8
Maribor, *Slovenia*, 90 E2
Marie Byrd Land, *Antarctica*, 109 Q3
Mariental, *Namibia*, 104 C4
Marijampole, *Lithuania*, 87 G5
Marilia, *Brazil*, 44 J4
Marimba, *Angola*, 104 C1
Mariupol, *Ukraine*, 84 D4
Marka, *Somalia*, 103 H3
Marmara, Sea of, *Turkey*, 91 J3
Maroantsetra, *Madagascar*, 105 J3
Maroua, *Cameroon*, 102 B1
Marquesas Islands, *French Polynesia*, 53 K5
Marrakech, *Morocco*, 100 D2
Marra, Mount, *Sudan*, 98 F6
Marsa Matruh, *Egypt*, 99 G2
Marseille, *France*, 89 F6
Marshall Islands, *Oceania, country*, 52 D3
Martapura, *Indonesia*, 64 D4
Martinique, *North America*, 34 M5
Mary, *Turkmenistan*, 72 H4
Maryland, *U.S.A., internal admin. area*, 33 L3
Masaka, *Uganda*, 103 F4
Masasi, *Tanzania*, 103 G6
Masbate, *Philippines*, 67 H5
Maseru, *Lesotho, national capital*, 104 E5
Mashhad, *Iran*, 72 G4
Masirah Island, *Oman*, 73 G7
Massachusetts, *U.S.A., internal admin. area*, 33 M2
Massangena, *Mozambique*, 105 F4
Massawa, *Eritrea*, 99 J5
Massif Central, *France*, 89 E5
Massinga, *Mozambique*, 105 G4
Masvingo, *Zimbabwe*, 104 F4
Matagalpa, *Nicaragua*, 35 G5
Matala, *Angola*, 104 B2
Matamoros, *Mexico*, 34 E2
Matanzas, *Cuba*, 35 H3
Mataram, *Indonesia*, 64 E5
Mataro, *Spain*, 89 E6
Matehuala, *Mexico*, 34 D3
Mato Grosso, Plateau of, *Brazil*, 43 G6
Matsuyama, *Japan*, 69 M4
Maturin, *Venezuela*, 42 F2
Maui, *U.S.A.*, 33 P7
Maun, *Botswana*, 104 D3
Mauritania, *Africa, country*, 100 C5
Mauritius, *Indian Ocean, country*, 105 L3
Mavinga, *Angola*, 104 D3
Mayotte, *Africa*, 105 J2
Mazar-e Sharif, *Afghanistan*, 70 B3
Mazatlan, *Mexico*, 34 C3
Mazyr, *Belarus*, 87 J5
Mbabane, *Swaziland, national capital*, 104 F5

Mbala, *Zambia*, 104 F1
Mbale, *Uganda*, 103 F3
Mbandaka, *Democratic Republic of Congo*, 102 C3
Mbarara, *Uganda*, 103 F4
Mbeya, *Tanzania*, 103 F5
Mbuji-Mayi, *Democratic Republic of Congo*, 102 D5
McClintock Channel, *Canada*, 30 J1
McClure Strait, *Canada*, 30 G1
McKinley, Mount, *U.S.A.*, 30 D2
Mead, Lake, *U.S.A.*, 32 D3
Mecca, *Saudi Arabia*, 73 C7
Mecula, *Mozambique*, 105 G2
Medan, *Indonesia*, 64 A3
Medellin, *Colombia*, 42 C2
Medford, *U.S.A.*, 32 B2
Medina, *Saudi Arabia*, 73 C7
Mediterranean Sea, *Africa/Europe*, 21
Medvezhyegorsk, *Russia*, 86 K3
Meerut, *India*, 70 D5
Meiktila, *Burma*, 66 C3
Meizhou, *China*, 69 J6
Mekele, *Ethiopia*, 103 G1
Meknes, *Morocco*, 100 D2
Mekong, *Asia*, 66 E5
Melaka, *Malaysia*, 64 B3
Melamo, Cape, *Mozambique*, 105 H2
Melanesia, *Oceania*, 52 D5
Melbourne, *Australia, internal capital*, 54 H7
Melekeok, *Palau, national capital*, 52 A4
Melilla, *Africa*, 89 D7
Melitopol, *Ukraine*, 84 D4
Melo, *Uruguay*, 44 H6
Melville Island, *Australia*, 54 F2
Melville Island, *Canada*, 30 H1
Melville Peninsula, *Canada*, 31 L2
Memphis, *U.S.A.*, 33 J4
Mendoza, *Argentina*, 44 E6
Menongue, *Angola*, 104 C2
Mentawai Islands, *Indonesia*, 64 A4
Menzel Bourguiba, *Tunisia*, 98 C1
Mergui, *Burma*, 66 C5
Mergui Archipelago, *Burma*, 66 C5
Merida, *Mexico*, 34 G3
Meridian, *U.S.A.*, 33 J4
Merlo, *Argentina*, 44 E6
Mersin, *Turkey*, 72 B4
Meru, *Kenya*, 103 G3
Messina, *Italy*, 90 E4
Messina, *South Africa*, 104 F4
Metz, *France*, 88 F4
Mexicali, *Mexico*, 34 A1
Mexico, *North America, country*, 34 D3
Mexico City, *Mexico, national capital*, 34 E4
Mexico, Gulf of, *North America*, 34 F3
Mexico, Plateau of, *Mexico*, 34 D2
Miami, *U.S.A.*, 33 K5
Michigan, *U.S.A., internal admin. area*, 33 J2
Michigan, Lake, *U.S.A.*, 33 J2
Michurinsk, *Russia*, 84 E3
Micronesia, *Oceania*, 52 C4
Micronesia, Federated States of, *Oceania, country*, 52 C4
Middlesbrough, *United Kingdom*, 88 D3
Midway Islands, *Pacific Ocean*, 52 F2
Mikkeli, *Finland*, 86 H3
Milan, *Italy*, 90 D2
Milange, *Mozambique*, 105 G3
Mildura, *Australia*, 54 H6
Milwaukee, *U.S.A.*, 33 J2
Minas, *Uruguay*, 44 G6
Mindanao, *Philippines*, 67 H6
Mindelo, *Cape Verde*, 101 M11
Mindoro, *Philippines*, 67 H5
Mingacevir, *Azerbaijan*, 72 E3
Minna, *Nigeria*, 101 G7
Minneapolis, *U.S.A.*, 33 H2
Minnesota, *U.S.A., internal admin. area*, 33 G1
Minorca, *Spain*, 89 E6
Minot, *U.S.A.*, 32 F1

Nuuk, *Greenland, national capital*, 108 P2
Nyala, *Sudan*, 98 F6
Nyasa, Lake, *Africa*, 103 F6
Nyeri, *Kenya*, 103 G4
Nykobing, *Denmark*, 87 D5
Nzerekore, *Guinea*, 101 D7
Nzwani, *Comoros*, 105 H2

O

Oahu, *U.S.A.*, 33 P7
Oaxaca, *Mexico*, 34 E4
Ob, *Russia*, 74 D2
Obi, *Indonesia*, 65 G4
Obninsk, *Russia*, 84 D2
Obo, *Central African Republic*, 102 E2
Odda, *Norway*, 86 C3
Odemis, *Turkey*, 91 J4
Odense, *Denmark*, 87 D5
Oder, *Europe*, 87 E5
Odesa, *Ukraine*, 84 C4
Odienne, *Ivory Coast*, 101 D7
Ogbomoso, *Nigeria*, 101 F7
Ogden, *U.S.A.*, 32 D2
Ohio, *U.S.A.*, 33 J3
Ohio, *U.S.A., internal admin. area*, 33 K2
Ojinaga, *Mexico*, 34 D2
Ojos del Salado, Mount, *South America*, 44 E5
Oka, *Russia*, 84 E2
Okahandja, *Namibia*, 104 C4
Okaukuejo, *Namibia*, 104 C3
Okavango, *Africa*, 104 D3
Okavango Swamp, *Botswana*, 104 D3
Okayama, *Japan*, 69 M4
Okeechobee, Lake, *U.S.A.*, 33 K5
Okhotsk, Sea of, *Asia*, 75 H3
Okinawa, *Japan*, 69 L5
Oklahoma, *U.S.A., internal admin. area*, 32 G4
Oklahoma City, *U.S.A., internal capital*, 32 G3
Oktyabrskiy, *Russia*, 85 G3
Oland, *Sweden*, 87 F4
Olavarria, *Argentina*, 45 F7
Olbia, *Italy*, 90 D3
Oleksandriya, *Ukraine*, 84 C4
Ollague, *Chile*, 44 E4
Olomouc, *Czech Republic*, 90 F1
Olongapo, *Philippines*, 67 H5
Olsztyn, *Poland*, 87 G5
Olympia, *U.S.A., internal capital*, 32 B1
Olympus, Mount, *Greece*, 91 G3
Omaha, *U.S.A.*, 33 G2
Oman, *Asia, country*, 73 G7
Oman, Gulf of, *Asia*, 73 G7
Omdurman, *Sudan*, 99 H5
Omsk, *Russia*, 74 D3
Ondangwa, *Namibia*, 104 C3
Onega, Lake, *Russia*, 86 K3
Onitsha, *Nigeria*, 101 G7
Ontario, *Canada, internal admin. area*, 31 L3
Ontario, Lake, *U.S.A.*, 33 L2
Opochka, *Russia*, 87 J4
Opole, *Poland*, 87 F6
Oporto, *Portugal*, 89 B6
Oppdal, *Norway*, 86 D3
Opuwo, *Namibia*, 104 B3
Oradea, *Romania*, 91 G2
Oral, *Kazakhstan*, 85 G3
Oran, *Algeria*, 100 E1
Orange, *Africa*, 104 C5
Orange, Cape, *Brazil*, 43 H3
Orapa, *Botswana*, 104 E4
Orebro, *Sweden*, 86 E4
Oregon, *U.S.A., internal admin. area*, 32 B2
Orel, *Russia*, 84 D3
Orenburg, *Russia*, 85 H3
Orense, *Spain*, 89 C6
Orinoco, *Venezuela*, 42 F2
Orinoco Delta, *Venezuela*, 42 F2
Oristano, *Italy*, 90 D4
Orizaba, *Mexico*, 34 E4
Orkney, *South Africa*, 104 E5

Orkney Islands, *United Kingdom*, 88 D2
Orlando, *U.S.A.*, 33 K5
Orleans, *France*, 88 E5
Orsha, *Belarus*, 87 J5
Orsk, *Russia*, 85 H3
Oruro, *Bolivia*, 44 E3
Osaka, *Japan*, 69 N4
Osh, *Kyrgyzstan*, 70 C2
Osijek, *Croatia*, 91 F2
Oskarshamn, *Sweden*, 87 F4
Oskemen, *Kazakhstan*, 74 E3
Oslo, *Norway, national capital*, 86 D4
Osnabruck, *Germany*, 88 G3
Osorno, *Chile*, 45 D8
Ostersund, *Sweden*, 86 E3
Ostrava, *Czech Republic*, 91 F1
Otavi, *Namibia*, 104 C3
Otjiwarongo, *Namibia*, 104 C4
Ottawa, *Canada, national capital*, 31 M4
Ouadda, *Central African Republic*, 102 D2
Ouagadougou, *Burkina Faso, national capital*, 101 E6
Ouahigouya, *Burkina Faso*, 101 E6
Ouargla, *Algeria*, 100 G2
Ouarzazate, *Morocco*, 100 D2
Oudtshoorn, *South Africa*, 104 D6
Ouesso, *Congo*, 102 C3
Oujda, *Morocco*, 100 E2
Oulu, *Finland*, 86 H2
Oulu Lake, *Finland*, 86 H2
Ovalle, *Chile*, 44 D6
Oviedo, *Spain*, 89 C6
Owando, *Congo*, 102 C4
Owen Sound, *Canada*, 31 L4
Owo, *Nigeria*, 101 G7
Oxford, *United Kingdom*, 88 D4
Oyem, *Gabon*, 102 B3
Ozark Plateau, *U.S.A.*, 33 H3

P

Paarl, *South Africa*, 104 C6
Pacasmayo, *Peru*, 42 C5
Pacific Ocean, 20–21
Padang, *Indonesia*, 64 B4
Pafuri, *Mozambique*, 104 F4
Pagadian, *Philippines*, 67 H6
Paijanne Lake, *Finland*, 86 H3
Pakistan, *Asia, country*, 70 B5
Pakxe, *Laos*, 66 E4
Palangkaraya, *Indonesia*, 64 D4
Palau, *Oceania, country*, 52 A4
Palawan, *Philippines*, 67 G6
Palembang, *Indonesia*, 64 B4
Palencia, *Spain*, 89 C6
Palermo, *Italy*, 90 E4
Palikir, *Federated States of Micronesia, national capital*, 52 C4
Palk Strait, *Asia*, 71 D9
Palma, *Mozambique*, 105 H2
Palma, *Spain*, 89 E7
Palmas, Cape, *Africa*, 101 D8
Palmyra Atoll, *Oceania*, 52 G4
Palopo, *Indonesia*, 65 F4
Palu, *Indonesia*, 65 E4
Pampas, *Argentina*, 45 F7
Pamplona, *Colombia*, 42 D2
Pamplona, *Spain*, 89 D6
Panama, *North America, country*, 35 H6
Panama Canal, *Panama*, 35 J6
Panama City, *Panama, national capital*, 35 J6
Panama, Gulf of, *North America*, 35 J6
Panay, *Philippines*, 67 H5
Panevezys, *Lithuania*, 87 H5
Pangkalpinang, *Indonesia*, 64 C4
Panjgur, *Pakistan*, 70 A5
Pantelleria, *Italy*, 90 E4
Panzhihua, *China*, 68 F5
Papeete, *French Polynesia*, 53 J6
Paphos, *Cyprus*, 91 K5
Papua, Gulf of, *Papua New Guinea*, 65 K5
Papua New Guinea, *Oceania, country*, 65 L5
Paracel Islands, *Asia*, 67 F4
Paraguaipoa, *Venezuela*, 42 D1

Paraguay, *South America*, 44 G4
Paraguay, *South America, country*, 44 F4
Parakou, *Benin*, 101 F7
Paramaribo, *Suriname, national capital*, 43 G2
Parana, *South America*, 44 G6
Paranagua, *Brazil*, 44 J5
Parepare, *Indonesia*, 65 E4
Paris, *France, national capital*, 88 E4
Parma, *Italy*, 90 D2
Parnaiba, *Brazil*, 43 K4
Parnu, *Estonia*, 86 H4
Parry Islands, *Canada*, 30 J1
Pasadena, *U.S.A.*, 32 C4
Passo Fundo, *Brazil*, 44 H5
Pasto, *Colombia*, 42 C3
Patagonia, *Argentina*, 45 E9
Pathein, *Burma*, 66 B4
Patna, *India*, 70 F5
Patos de Minas, *Brazil*, 44 J3
Patos Lagoon, *Brazil*, 44 H6
Patra, *Greece*, 91 G4
Pattaya, *Thailand*, 66 D5
Pau, *France*, 89 D6
Pavlodar, *Kazakhstan*, 74 D3
Paysandu, *Uruguay*, 44 G6
Peace River, *Canada*, 30 H3
Pecos, *U.S.A.*, 32 F4
Pecs, *Hungary*, 87 F7
Pedro Juan Caballero, *Paraguay*, 44 G4
Pegu, *Burma*, 70 F5
Peipus, Lake, *Europe*, 86 H4
Peiraias, *Greece*, 91 G4
Pekanbaru, *Indonesia*, 64 B3
Pelagian Islands, *Italy*, 90 E5
Peleng, *Indonesia*, 65 F4
Pelotas, *Brazil*, 44 H6
Pematangsiantar, *Indonesia*, 64 A3
Pemba, *Mozambique*, 105 H2
Pemba Island, *Tanzania*, 103 G5
Penang, *Malaysia*, 64 B2
Penas, Gulf of, *Chile*, 45 C9
Pennsylvania, *U.S.A., internal admin. area*, 33 L2
Pensacola, *U.S.A.*, 33 J4
Penza, *Russia*, 84 F3
Penzance, *United Kingdom*, 88 C4
Peoria, *U.S.A.*, 33 J2
Pereira, *Colombia*, 42 C3
Perm, *Russia*, 85 H2
Perpignan, *France*, 89 E6
Persepolis, *Iran*, 73 F6
Persian Gulf, *Asia*, 73 F6
Perth, *Australia, internal capital*, 54 C6
Peru, *South America, country*, 42 C5
Perugia, *Italy*, 90 E3
Pescara, *Italy*, 90 E3
Peshawar, *Pakistan*, 70 C4
Petauke, *Zambia*, 104 F2
Petra, *Jordan*, 73 C5
Petrolina, *Brazil*, 43 K5
Petropavlovsk-Kamchatskiy, *Russia*, 75 H3
Petrozavodsk, *Russia*, 86 K3
Philadelphia, *U.S.A.*, 33 L3
Philippine Sea, *Asia*, 67 H5
Philippines, *Asia, country*, 67 J5
Phitsanulok, *Thailand*, 66 D4
Phnom Penh, *Cambodia, national capital*, 66 D5
Phoenix, *U.S.A., internal capital*, 32 D4
Phongsali, *Laos*, 66 D3
Piatra Neamt, *Romania*, 91 H2
Pica, *Chile*, 44 E4
Pico, *Azores*, 100 K10
Pietermaritzburg, *South Africa*, 104 F5
Pietersburg, *South Africa*, 104 E4
Pihlaja Lake, *Finland*, 86 J3
Pik Pobedy, *Asia*, 70 E2
Pilcomayo, *South America*, 44 F4
Pilsen, *Czech Republic*, 90 E1
Pinar del Rio, *Cuba*, 35 H3
Pindus Mountains, *Greece*, 91 G4
Pingdingshan, *China*, 69 H4
Pinsk, *Belarus*, 87 H5

Pisa, *Italy*, 90 D3
Pitcairn Islands, *Oceania*, 53 L7
Pitesti, *Romania*, 91 H2
Pittsburgh, *U.S.A.*, 33 L2
Piura, *Peru*, 42 B5
Platte, *U.S.A.*, 32 F2
Pleven, *Bulgaria*, 91 H3
Plock, *Poland*, 87 F5
Ploiesti, *Romania*, 91 H2
Plovdiv, *Bulgaria*, 91 H3
Plumtree, *Zimbabwe*, 104 E4
Plymouth, *United Kingdom*, 88 C4
Po, *Italy*, 90 D2
Pocos de Caldas, *Brazil*, 44 J4
Podgorica, *Montenegro, national capital*, 84 C4
Podolsk, *Russia*, 84 D2
Pointe-Noire, *Congo*, 102 B4
Poitiers, *France*, 89 E5
Pokhara, *Nepal*, 70 E5
Poland, *Europe, country*, 87 F6
Polatsk, *Belarus*, 87 J5
Poltava, *Ukraine*, 84 C4
Polynesia, *Oceania*, 52 G5
Pompeii, *Italy*, 90 E3
Ponta Delgada, *Azores*, 100 K10
Ponta Pora, *Brazil*, 44 G4
Pontianak, *Indonesia*, 64 C4
Poole, *United Kingdom*, 88 D4
Poona, *India*, 71 C7
Poopo, Lake, *Bolivia*, 44 E3
Popayan, *Colombia*, 42 C3
Porbandar, *India*, 71 B6
Pori, *Finland*, 86 G3
Porlamar, *Venezuela*, 34 M5
Port-au-Prince, *Haiti, national capital*, 35 K4
Port Blair, *India*, 71 G8
Port Elizabeth, *South Africa*, 104 E6
Port-Gentil, *Gabon*, 102 A4
Port Harcourt, *Nigeria*, 101 G8
Port Hardy, *Canada*, 30 G3
Port Hedland, *Australia*, 54 C4
Portland, *Australia*, 54 H7
Portland, *Maine, U.S.A.*, 33 M2
Portland, *Oregon, U.S.A.*, 32 B1
Port Louis, *Mauritius, national capital*, 105 L4
Port Macquarie, *Australia*, 55 K6
Port McNeill, *Canada*, 30 G3
Port Moresby, *Papua New Guinea, national capital*, 65 L6
Porto Alegre, *Brazil*, 44 H5
Port-of-Spain, *Trinidad and Tobago, national capital*, 34 M5
Porto-Novo, *Benin, national capital*, 101 F7
Porto-Vecchio, *France*, 89 G6
Porto Velho, *Brazil*, 42 F5
Port Said, *Egypt*, 99 H2
Portsmouth, *United Kingdom*, 88 D4
Port Sudan, *Sudan*, 99 J5
Portugal, *Europe, country*, 89 B7
Port Vila, *Vanuatu, national capital*, 55 N3
Porvenir, *Chile*, 45 D10
Posadas, *Argentina*, 44 G5
Poti, *Georgia*, 72 D3
Potiskum, *Nigeria*, 98 D6
Potosi, *Bolivia*, 44 E3
Potsdam, *Germany*, 88 H3
Poyang Lake, *China*, 69 J5
Poznan, *Poland*, 87 F5
Prachuap Khiri Khan, *Thailand*, 66 C5
Prague, *Czech Republic, national capital*, 90 E1
Praia, *Cape Verde, national capital*, 101 M12
Presidente Prudente, *Brazil*, 44 H4
Presov, *Slovakia*, 87 G6
Pretoria, *South Africa, national capital*, 104 E5
Preveza, *Greece*, 91 G4
Prieska, *South Africa*, 104 D5
Prilep, *Macedonia*, 91 G3
Prince Albert, *Canada*, 30 J3

Prince Edward Island, *Canada, internal admin. area,* **31 N4**
Prince George, *Canada,* **30 G3**
Prince of Wales Island, *Canada,* **31 K1**
Prince Rupert, *Canada,* **30 F3**
Principe, *Sao Tome and Principe,* **101 G8**
Pripet, *Europe,* **87 J6**
Pripet Marshes, *Europe,* **87 H5**
Pristina, *Kosovo, national capital,* **91 G3**
Providence, *Seychelles,* **105 K1**
Providence, *U.S.A., internal capital,* **33 M2**
Providence, Cape, *New Zealand,* **55 N9**
Provo, *U.S.A.,* **32 D2**
Prudhoe Bay, *U.S.A.,* **30 E1**
Pskov, *Russia,* **87 J4**
Pskov, Lake, *Europe,* **86 J4**
Pucallpa, *Peru,* **42 D5**
Puebla, *Mexico,* **34 E4**
Pueblo, *U.S.A.,* **32 F3**
Puerto Ayora, *Ecuador,* **42 N10**
Puerto Cabezas, *Nicaragua,* **35 H5**
Puerto Deseado, *Argentina,* **45 E9**
Puerto Inirida, *Colombia,* **42 E3**
Puerto Leguizamo, *Colombia,* **42 D4**
Puerto Maldonado, *Peru,* **42 E6**
Puerto Montt, *Chile,* **45 D8**
Puerto Natales, *Chile,* **45 D10**
Puerto Paez, *Venezuela,* **42 E2**
Puerto Princesa, *Philippines,* **67 G6**
Puerto Rico, *North America,* **34 L4**
Puerto Suarez, *Bolivia,* **44 G3**
Puerto Vallarta, *Mexico,* **34 C3**
Pula, *Croatia,* **90 E2**
Pulog, Mount, *Philippines,* **67 H4**
Puncak Jaya, *Indonesia,* **65 J4**
Pune, *India,* **71 C7**
Puno, *Peru,* **42 D7**
Punta Arenas, *Chile,* **45 D10**
Puntarenas, *Costa Rica,* **35 H5**
Purus, *Brazil,* **42 E5**
Pusan, *South Korea,* **69 L3**
Pushkin, *Russia,* **86 J4**
Putrajaya, *Malaysia, national capital,* **64 B3**
Puula Lake, *Finland,* **86 H3**
Pweto, *Democratic Republic of Congo,* **102 E5**
Pya, Lake, *Russia,* **86 J2**
Pye, *Burma,* **66 C4**
Pyongyang, *North Korea, national capital,* **69 L3**
Pyramids of Giza, *Egypt,* **99 H3**
Pyrenees, *Europe,* **89 D6**
Pyrgos, *Greece,* **91 G4**

q
Qaidam Basin, *China,* **70 G3**
Qaraghandy, *Kazakhstan,* **74 D3**
Qatar, *Asia, country,* **73 F6**
Qattara Depression, *Egypt,* **99 G3**
Qazvin, *Iran,* **72 E4**
Qena, *Egypt,* **99 H3**
Qingdao, *China,* **69 K3**
Qinghai Lake, *China,* **68 F3**
Qinhuangdao, *China,* **69 J3**
Qiqihar, *China,* **69 K1**
Qom, *Iran,* **72 F5**
Qostanay, *Kazakhstan,* **85 J3**
Quanzhou, *China,* **69 J6**
Quebec, *Canada, internal admin. area,* **31 M3**
Quebec, *Canada, internal capital,* **31 M4**
Queen Charlotte Islands, *Canada,* **30 F3**
Queen Elizabeth Islands, *Canada,* **30 H1**
Queen Maud Land, *Antarctica,* **109 C3**
Queensland, *Australia, internal admin. area,* **54 H4**
Quelimane, *Mozambique,* **105 G3**
Quellon, *Chile,* **45 D8**
Quetta, *Pakistan,* **70 B4**
Quetzaltenango, *Guatemala,* **34 F4**
Quevedo, *Ecuador,* **42 C4**
Quillabamba, *Peru,* **42 D6**
Quimper, *France,* **88 C5**
Quincy, *U.S.A.,* **33 H3**

Qui Nhon, *Vietnam,* **66 E5**
Quirima, *Angola,* **104 C2**
Quito, *Ecuador, national capital,* **42 C4**
Qurghonteppa, *Tajikistan,* **70 B3**
Qyzylorda, *Kazakhstan,* **72 J3**

r
Raahe, *Finland,* **86 H2**
Rabat, *Morocco, national capital,* **100 D2**
Rabaul, *Papua New Guinea,* **65 M4**
Rabnita, *Moldova,* **91 J2**
Radisson, *Canada,* **31 M3**
Radom, *Poland,* **87 G6**
Ragusa, *Italy,* **90 E4**
Rahimyar Khan, *Pakistan,* **70 C5**
Rainier, Mount, *U.S.A.,* **32 B1**
Raipur, *India,* **71 E6**
Rajahmundry, *India,* **71 E7**
Rajkot, *India,* **71 C6**
Rajshahi, *Bangladesh,* **71 F6**
Rakops, *Botswana,* **104 D4**
Raleigh, *U.S.A., internal capital,* **33 L3**
Ralik Islands, *Marshall Islands,* **52 D3**
Ramnicu Valcea, *Romania,* **91 H2**
Rancagua, *Chile,* **44 D6**
Ranchi, *India,* **71 F6**
Randers, *Denmark,* **87 D4**
Rangoon, *Burma, national capital,* **66 C4**
Rangpur, *Bangladesh,* **70 F5**
Rapid City, *U.S.A.,* **32 F2**
Ras Dashen, *Ethiopia,* **103 G1**
Rasht, *Iran,* **72 E4**
Ratak Islands, *Marshall Islands,* **52 E3**
Rat Islands, *U.S.A.,* **31 A3**
Rauma, *Finland,* **86 G3**
Ravenna, *Italy,* **90 E2**
Rawson, *Argentina,* **45 E8**
Rechytsa, *Belarus,* **87 J5**
Recife, *Brazil,* **43 M5**
Reconquista, *Argentina,* **44 G5**
Red, *Asia,* **68 F6**
Red, *U.S.A.,* **33 G4**
Red Deer, *Canada,* **30 H3**
Redding, *U.S.A.,* **32 B2**
Red Sea, *Africa/Asia,* **99 J4**
Regensburg, *Germany,* **88 H4**
Regina, *Canada, internal capital,* **30 J3**
Regina, *French Guiana,* **43 H3**
Rehoboth, *Namibia,* **104 C4**
Reims, *France,* **88 F4**
Reindeer Lake, *Canada,* **30 J3**
Rennell Island, *Solomon Islands,* **55 M2**
Rennes, *France,* **88 D4**
Reno, *U.S.A.,* **32 C3**
Reunion, *Indian Ocean,* **105 L4**
Revelstoke, *Canada,* **30 H3**
Revillagigedo Islands, *Mexico,* **34 B4**
Reykjavik, *Iceland, national capital,* **86 N2**
Rhine, *Europe,* **88 F4**
Rhode Island, *U.S.A., internal admin. area,* **33 M2**
Rhodes, *Greece,* **91 J4**
Rhone, *Europe,* **89 F5**
Riau Islands, *Indonesia,* **64 B3**
Ribeirao Preto, *Brazil,* **44 J4**
Riberalta, *Bolivia,* **44 E2**
Richards Bay, *South Africa,* **104 F5**
Richmond, *U.S.A., internal capital,* **33 L3**
Riga, *Latvia, national capital,* **87 H4**
Riga, Gulf of, *Europe,* **87 G4**
Rijeka, *Croatia,* **90 E2**
Rimini, *Italy,* **90 E2**
Rio Branco, *Brazil,* **42 E5**
Rio Cuarto, *Argentina,* **44 F6**
Rio de Janeiro, *Brazil,* **44 K4**
Rio Gallegos, *Argentina,* **45 E10**
Rio Grande, *Argentina,* **45 E10**
Rio Grande, *Brazil,* **44 H6**
Rio Grande, *U.S.A.,* **32 F5**
Riohacha, *Colombia,* **42 D1**
Rivas, *Nicaragua,* **35 G5**
Rivera, *Uruguay,* **44 G6**
Riverside, *U.S.A.,* **32 C4**
Rivne, *Ukraine,* **87 H6**
Riyadh, *Saudi Arabia, national capital,* **73 E7**
Roanoke, *U.S.A.,* **33 L3**

Robson, Mount, *Canada,* **30 H3**
Rochester, *U.S.A.,* **33 L2**
Rockford, *U.S.A.,* **33 J2**
Rockhampton, *Australia,* **55 K4**
Rocky Mountains, *U.S.A.,* **32 D1**
Romania, *Europe, country,* **91 G2**
Rome, *Italy, national capital,* **90 E3**
Rondonopolis, *Brazil,* **44 H3**
Ronne, *Denmark,* **87 E5**
Ronne Ice Shelf, *Antarctica,* **109 S3**
Roraima, Mount, *South America,* **42 F2**
Rosario, *Argentina,* **44 F6**
Roseau, *Dominica, national capital,* **34 M4**
Roslavl, *Russia,* **87 K5**
Ross Ice Shelf, *Antarctica,* **109 M4**
Rosso, *Mauritania,* **101 B5**
Rostock, *Germany,* **88 H3**
Rostov, *Russia,* **84 D4**
Roti, *Indonesia,* **65 F6**
Rotorua, *Australia,* **55 Q7**
Rotterdam, *Netherlands,* **88 F4**
Rouen, *France,* **88 E4**
Rovaniemi, *Finland,* **86 H2**
Roxas, *Philippines,* **67 H5**
Rub al Khali, *Asia,* **73 E8**
Rudnyy, *Kazakhstan,* **85 J3**
Rufino, *Argentina,* **44 F6**
Rufunsa, *Zambia,* **104 E3**
Rukwa, Lake, *Tanzania,* **103 F5**
Rundu, *Namibia,* **104 C3**
Rurrenabaque, *Bolivia,* **44 E2**
Ruse, *Bulgaria,* **91 H3**
Russia, *Asia/Europe, country,* **74 E3**
Ruvuma, *Africa,* **103 G6**
Rwanda, *Africa, country,* **102 E4**
Ryazan, *Russia,* **84 D3**
Rybinsk, *Russia,* **84 D2**
Rybinsk Reservoir, *Russia,* **84 D2**
Rybnik, *Poland,* **87 F6**
Ryukyu Islands, *Japan,* **69 L5**
Rzeszow, *Poland,* **87 G6**
Rzhev, *Russia,* **84 C2**

s
Saarbrucken, *Germany,* **88 F4**
Saarijarvi, *Finland,* **86 H3**
Sabha, *Libya,* **98 D3**
Sabzevar, *Iran,* **72 G4**
Sacramento, *U.S.A., internal capital,* **32 B3**
Sadah, *Yemen,* **73 E8**
Safi, *Morocco,* **100 D2**
Sahara, *Africa,* **98 C5**
Saharanpur, *India,* **70 D5**
Sahel, *Africa,* **98 C6**
Sahiwal, *Pakistan,* **70 C4**
Saida, *Algeria,* **100 F2**
Saigon, *Vietnam,* **66 E5**
Saimaa Lake, *Finland,* **86 H3**
St. Andrew, Cape, *Madagascar,* **105 H3**
St. Denis, *Reunion,* **105 L4**
St. Etienne, *France,* **89 F5**
St. Francis, Cape, *South Africa,* **104 D6**
St. George, *U.S.A.,* **32 D3**
St. George's, *Grenada, national capital,* **34 M5**
St. Helier, *Channel Islands,* **88 D4**
Saint John, *Canada,* **31 N4**
St. John's, *Antigua and Barbuda, national capital,* **34 M4**
St. John's, *Canada, internal capital,* **31 P4**
St. Kitts and Nevis, *North America, country,* **34 M4**
St. Lawrence, *Canada,* **31 M4**
St. Lawrence, Gulf of, *Canada,* **31 N4**
St. Lawrence Island, *U.S.A.,* **30 B2**
St. Louis, *Senegal,* **101 B5**
St. Louis, *U.S.A.,* **33 H3**
St. Lucia, *North America, country,* **34 M5**
St. Lucia, Cape, *South Africa,* **105 F5**
St. Malo, *France,* **88 D4**
St. Martha, Cape, *Angola,* **104 B2**
St. Martin, *North America,* **34 M4**
St. Mary, Cape, *Madagascar,* **105 J5**
St. Paul, *U.S.A., internal capital,* **33 H1**

St. Petersburg, *Russia,* **86 J4**
St. Petersburg, *U.S.A.,* **33 K5**
St. Pierre, *Seychelles,* **105 J1**
St. Pierre and Miquelon, *North America,* **31 P4**
St. Polten, *Austria,* **90 E1**
St. Vincent and the Grenadines, *North America, country,* **34 M5**
St. Vincent, Cape, *Portugal,* **89 B7**
Sakhalin, *Russia,* **75 H3**
Saki, *Azerbaijan,* **72 E3**
Saki, *Nigeria,* **101 F7**
Sakishima Islands, *Japan,* **69 K6**
Sal, *Cape Verde,* **101 M11**
Salado, *Argentina,* **44 F5**
Salalah, *Oman,* **73 F8**
Salamanca, *Spain,* **89 C6**
Salem, *India,* **71 D8**
Salem, *U.S.A., internal capital,* **32 B1**
Salerno, *Italy,* **90 E3**
Salihorsk, *Belarus,* **87 H5**
Salinas, *U.S.A.,* **32 B3**
Salta, *Argentina,* **44 E4**
Saltillo, *Mexico,* **34 D2**
Salt Lake City, *U.S.A., internal capital,* **32 D2**
Salto, *Uruguay,* **44 G6**
Salton Sea, *U.S.A.,* **32 C4**
Salvador, *Brazil,* **43 L6**
Salween, *Asia,* **66 C4**
Salzburg, *Austria,* **90 E2**
Samar, *Philippines,* **67 J5**
Samara, *Russia,* **85 G3**
Samarinda, *Indonesia,* **64 E4**
Samarqand, *Uzbekistan,* **70 B3**
Sambalpur, *India,* **71 E6**
Samoa, *Oceania, country,* **52 F6**
Sampwe, *Democratic Republic of Congo,* **102 E5**
Sam Rayburn Reservoir, *U.S.A.,* **33 H4**
Samsun, *Turkey,* **72 C3**
San, *Mali,* **101 E6**
Sana, *Yemen, national capital,* **73 D8**
Sanandaj, *Iran,* **72 E4**
San Andres Island, *Colombia,* **35 H5**
San Antonio, *U.S.A.,* **32 G5**
San Antonio, Cape, *Argentina,* **45 G7**
San Antonio Oeste, *Argentina,* **45 F8**
San Cristobal, *Ecuador,* **42 P10**
San Cristobal, *Venezuela,* **42 D2**
Sandakan, *Malaysia,* **65 E2**
San Diego, *U.S.A.,* **32 C4**
Sandoway, *Burma,* **66 B4**
San Fernando, *Chile,* **44 D6**
San Fernando de Apure, *Venezuela,* **42 E2**
San Francisco, *Argentina,* **44 F6**
San Francisco, *U.S.A.,* **32 B3**
San Francisco, Cape, *Ecuador,* **42 B3**
Sangihe Islands, *Indonesia,* **65 G3**
San Jorge, Gulf of, *Argentina,* **45 E9**
San Jose, *Costa Rica, national capital,* **35 H6**
San Jose, *U.S.A.,* **32 B3**
San Jose de Chiquitos, *Bolivia,* **44 F3**
San Jose del Guaviare, *Colombia,* **42 D3**
San Juan, *Argentina,* **44 E6**
San Juan, *Puerto Rico,* **34 L4**
San Julian, *Argentina,* **45 E9**
Sanliurfa, *Turkey,* **72 C4**
San Lucas, Cape, *Mexico,* **34 B3**
San Luis, *Argentina,* **44 E6**
San Luis Obispo, *U.S.A.,* **32 B3**
San Luis Potosi, *Mexico,* **34 D3**
San Marino, *Europe, country,* **90 E3**
San Matias, Gulf of, *Argentina,* **45 F8**
San Miguel de Tucuman, *Argentina,* **44 E5**
San Nicolas de los Arroyos, *Argentina,* **44 F6**
San Pedro, *Ivory Coast,* **101 D8**
San Pedro de Atacama, *Chile,* **44 E4**
San Rafael, *Argentina,* **44 E6**
San Remo, *Italy,* **90 C3**
San Salvador, *Ecuador,* **42 N10**
San Salvador, *El Salvador, national capital,* **34 G5**
San Salvador de Jujuy, *Argentina,* **44 E4**

San Sebastian, *Spain*, 89 D6
Santa Clara, *Cuba*, 35 H3
Santa Cruz, *Bolivia*, 44 F3
Santa Cruz, *Ecuador*, 42 N10
Santa Cruz Islands, *Solomon Islands*, 55 N2
Santa Elena, *Venezuela*, 42 F3
Santa Fe, *Argentina*, 44 F6
Santa Fe, *U.S.A., internal capital*, 32 E3
Santa Maria, *Brazil*, 44 H5
Santa Marta, *Colombia*, 42 D1
Santander, *Spain*, 89 D6
Santarem, *Brazil*, 43 H4
Santiago, *Chile, national capital*, 44 D6
Santiago, *Dominican Republic*, 35 K4
Santiago, *Panama*, 35 H6
Santiago de Compostela, *Spain*, 89 B6
Santiago de Cuba, *Cuba*, 35 J3
Santiago del Estero, *Argentina*, 44 F5
Santo Antao, *Cape Verde*, 101 L11
Santo Domingo, *Dominican Republic, national capital*, 35 L4
Santo Domingo de los Colorados, *Ecuador*, 42 C4
San Valentin, Mount, *Chile*, 45 D9
Sanya, *China*, 68 G7
Sao Francisco, *Brazil*, 43 L5
Sao Jose do Rio Preto, *Brazil*, 44 J4
Sao Luis, *Brazil*, 43 K4
Sao Miguel, *Azores*, 100 K10
Sao Nicolau, *Cape Verde*, 101 M11
Sao Paulo, *Brazil*, 44 J4
Sao Roque, Cape, *Brazil*, 43 L4
Sao Tiago, *Cape Verde*, 101 M11
Sao Tome, *Sao Tome and Principe, national capital*, 101 G8
Sao Tome and Principe, *Africa, country*, 101 G8
Sapporo, *Japan*, 69 P2
Saqqara, *Egypt*, 99 H3
Sarajevo, *Bosnia and Herzegovina, national capital*, 91 F3
Saransk, *Russia*, 84 F3
Sarapul, *Russia*, 85 G2
Saratov, *Russia*, 85 F3
Saratov Reservoir, *Russia*, 85 F3
Sardinia, *Italy*, 90 D3
Sargodha, *Pakistan*, 70 C4
Sarh, *Chad*, 102 C2
Sarremaa, *Estonia*, 86 G4
Saskatchewan, *Canada, internal admin. area*, 30 J3
Saskatoon, *Canada*, 30 J3
Sassari, *Italy*, 90 D3
Sault Ste. Marie, *Canada*, 31 L4
Saurimo, *Angola*, 104 D1
Savannah, *U.S.A.*, 33 K4
Savannakhet, *Laos*, 66 D4
Sawu, *Indonesia*, 65 F6
Sawu Sea, *Indonesia*, 65 F5
Schwerin, *Germany*, 88 G3
Scotland, *United Kingdom, internal admin. area*, 88 C2
Seattle, *U.S.A.*, 32 B1
Seeheim, *Namibia*, 104 C5
Sefadu, *Sierra Leone*, 101 C7
Seg, Lake, *Russia*, 86 K3
Segou, *Mali*, 101 D6
Seine, *France*, 88 E4
Sekondi-Takoradi, *Ghana*, 101 E8
Selebi-Phikwe, *Botswana*, 104 E4
Selibabi, *Mauritania*, 101 C5
Selvas, *Brazil*, 42 E5
Semarang, *Indonesia*, 64 D5
Semenov, *Russia*, 84 E2
Semiozernoe, *Kazakhstan*, 85 J3
Sendai, *Japan*, 69 P3
Senegal, *Africa*, 101 C5
Senegal, *Africa, country*, 101 B6
Seoul, *South Korea, national capital*, 69 L3
Serang, *Indonesia*, 64 C5
Serbia, *Europe, country* 91 G2
Seremban, *Malaysia*, 64 B3

Sergiyev Posad, *Russia*, 84 D2
Serov, *Russia*, 85 J2
Serowe, *Botswana*, 104 E4
Serpukhov, *Russia*, 84 D3
Serres, *Greece*, 91 G3
Sesheke, *Zambia*, 104 D3
Setif, *Algeria*, 100 G1
Setubal, *Portugal*, 89 B7
Sevastopol, *Ukraine*, 91 K2
Severn, *United Kingdom*, 88 D3
Severnaya Zemlya, *Russia*, 75 F2
Severomorsk, *Russia*, 86 K1
Sevettijarvi, *Finland*, 86 J1
Seville, *Spain*, 89 C7
Seward, *U.S.A.*, 30 E2
Seward Peninsula, *U.S.A.*, 30 C2
Seychelles, *Indian Ocean, country*, 105 J1
Seydhisfjordhur, *Iceland*, 86 Q2
Sfax, *Tunisia*, 98 D2
Shalqar, *Kazakhstan*, 72 G2
Shanghai, *China*, 69 K4
Shannon, *Ireland*, 88 C3
Shantou, *China*, 69 J6
Shaoguan, *China*, 69 H6
Sharjah, *United Arab Emirates*, 73 G6
Sharm el Sheikh, *Egypt*, 99 H3
Shasta, Mount, *U.S.A.*, 32 B2
Sheffield, *United Kingdom*, 88 D3
Shenyang, *China*, 69 K2
Shepetivka, *Ukraine*, 87 H6
Shetland Islands, *United Kingdom*, 88 D1
Shieli, *Kazakhstan*, 72 J3
Shihezi, *China*, 70 F2
Shijiazhuang, *China*, 69 H3
Shikoku, *Japan*, 69 M4
Shillong, *India*, 70 G5
Shiraz, *Iran*, 73 F6
Shishaldin Volcano, *U.S.A.*, 31 C3
Shiyan, *China*, 68 H4
Shizuoka, *Japan*, 69 N3
Shkoder, *Albania*, 91 F3
Shreveport, *U.S.A.*, 33 H4
Shumen, *Bulgaria*, 91 H3
Shymkent, *Kazakhstan*, 70 B2
Sialkot, *Pakistan*, 70 C4
Siauliai, *Lithuania*, 87 G5
Sibiti, *Congo*, 102 B4
Sibiu, *Romania*, 91 H2
Sibolga, *Indonesia*, 64 A3
Sibu, *Malaysia*, 64 D3
Sicily, *Italy*, 90 E4
Sicuani, *Peru*, 42 D6
Sidi-Bel-Abbes, *Algeria*, 100 E1
Sidon, *Lebanon*, 72 C5
Sidra, Gulf of, *Africa*, 98 E2
Sierra Leone, *Africa, country*, 101 C7
Sierra Morena, *Spain*, 89 C7
Sierra Nevada, *Spain*, 89 D7
Sierra Nevada, *U.S.A.*, 32 B3
Siglufjordhur, *Iceland*, 86 P2
Siguiri, *Guinea*, 101 D6
Sikasso, *Mali*, 101 D6
Sikhote Alin Range, *Russia*, 69 N1
Siling Lake, *China*, 70 F4
Simao, *China*, 68 F6
Simeulue, *Indonesia*, 64 A3
Simferopol, *Ukraine*, 91 K2
Simpson Desert, *Australia*, 54 G4
Sinai, *Egypt*, 99 H3
Sinai, Mount, *Egypt*, 99 H3
Sincelejo, *Colombia*, 42 C2
Sines, *Portugal*, 89 B7
Singapore, *Asia, country*, 64 B3
Singapore, *Singapore, national capital*, 64 B3
Sinnamary, *French Guiana*, 43 H2
Sinuiju, *North Korea*, 69 K2
Sioux City, *U.S.A.*, 33 G2
Sioux Falls, *U.S.A.*, 33 G2
Sirjan, *Iran*, 73 G6
Sittwe, *Burma*, 66 B3
Sivas, *Turkey*, 72 C4
Skagen, *Denmark*, 87 D4
Skagerrak, *Europe*, 87 C4
Skelleftea, *Sweden*, 86 G2
Skikda, *Algeria*, 100 G1

Skopje, *Macedonia, national capital*, 91 G3
Skyros, *Greece*, 91 H4
Slavonski Brod, *Croatia*, 90 F2
Sligo, *Ireland*, 88 B3
Sliven, *Bulgaria*, 91 H3
Slovakia, *Europe, country*, 87 F6
Slovenia, *Europe, country*, 90 E2
Slovyansk, *Ukraine*, 84 D4
Slupsk, *Poland*, 87 F5
Slutsk, *Belarus*, 87 H5
Smallwood Reservoir, *Canada*, 31 N3
Smola, *Norway*, 86 C3
Smolensk, *Russia*, 87 J5
Sobradinho Reservoir, *Brazil*, 43 K6
Sobral, *Brazil*, 43 K4
Sochi, *Russia*, 72 C3
Society Islands, *French Polynesia*, 53 J6
Socotra, *Yemen*, 73 F9
Sodankyla, *Finland*, 86 H2
Sodertalje, *Sweden*, 86 F4
Sofia, *Bulgaria, national capital*, 91 G3
Sohag, *Egypt*, 99 H3
Sokhumi, *Georgia*, 72 D3
Sokode, *Togo*, 101 F7
Sokoto, *Nigeria*, 101 G6
Solapur, *India*, 71 D7
Solikamsk, *Russia*, 85 H2
Solomon Islands, *Oceania, country*, 52 D5
Solomon Sea, *Papua New Guinea*, 65 M5
Solwezi, *Zambia*, 104 E2
Somalia, *Africa, country*, 103 J2
Somerset Island, *Canada*, 31 K1
Songea, *Tanzania*, 103 G6
Songo, *Mozambique*, 105 F3
Son La, *Vietnam*, 66 D3
Sorong, *Indonesia*, 65 H4
Soroti, *Uganda*, 103 F3
Soroya, *Norway*, 86 G1
Sotra, *Norway*, 86 C3
Souk Ahras, *Algeria*, 90 C4
Sousse, *Tunisia*, 98 D1
South Africa, *Africa, country*, 104 D6
South America, 20
Southampton, *United Kingdom*, 88 D4
Southampton Island, *Canada*, 31 L2
South Australia, *Australia, internal admin. area*, 54 F5
South Bend, *U.S.A.*, 33 J2
South Carolina, *U.S.A., internal admin. area*, 33 K4
South China Sea, *Asia*, 67 F5
South Dakota, *U.S.A., internal admin. area*, 32 F2
South East Cape, *Australia*, 54 J8
Southend-on-Sea, *United Kingdom*, 88 E4
Southern Ocean, 20–21
Southern Sierra Madre, *Mexico*, 34 D4
South Georgia, *Atlantic Ocean*, 45 L10
South Island, *New Zealand*, 55 N8
South Korea, *Asia, country*, 69 L3
South Orkney Islands, *Atlantic Ocean*, 45 J12
South Sandwich Islands, *Atlantic Ocean*, 45 N10
South Shetland Islands, *Atlantic Ocean*, 45 G12
South Sudan, *Africa, country*, 102 E2
South West Cape, *New Zealand*, 55 N9
Spain, *Europe, country*, 89 D7
Split, *Croatia*, 90 F3
Spokane, *U.S.A.*, 32 C1
Spratly Islands, *Asia*, 67 F5
Springfield, *Illinois, U.S.A., internal capital*, 33 J3
Springfield, *Massachusetts, U.S.A.*, 33 M2
Springfield, *Missouri, U.S.A.*, 33 H3
Springs, *South Africa*, 104 E5
Sri Jayewardenepura Kotte, *Sri Lanka, national capital*, 71 E9
Sri Lanka, *Asia, country*, 71 E9
Srinagar, *India*, 70 C4
Standerton, *South Africa*, 104 E5
Stanley, *Falkland Islands*, 45 G10

Stara Zagora, *Bulgaria*, 91 H3
Staryy Oskol, *Russia*, 84 D3
Stavanger, *Norway*, 86 C4
Stavropol, *Russia*, 72 D2
Steinkjer, *Norway*, 86 D2
Stellenbosch, *South Africa*, 104 C6
Sterlitamak, *Russia*, 85 H3
Stewart Island, *New Zealand*, 55 N9
Stockholm, *Sweden, national capital*, 86 F4
Stoeng Treng, *Cambodia*, 66 E5
Stoke-on-Trent, *United Kingdom*, 88 D3
Stora Lule Lake, *Sweden*, 86 F2
Storavan Lake, *Sweden*, 86 F2
Stor Lake, *Sweden*, 86 E3
Stornoway, *United Kingdom*, 88 C2
Stranraer, *United Kingdom*, 88 C3
Strasbourg, *France*, 88 F4
Sturt Stony Desert, *Australia*, 54 G5
Stuttgart, *Germany*, 88 G4
Subotica, *Serbia*, 91 F2
Suceava, *Romania*, 91 H2
Sucre, *Bolivia, national capital*, 44 E3
Sudan, *Africa, country*, 99 G5
Sudbury, *Canada*, 31 L4
Suez, *Egypt*, 99 H3
Suez Canal, *Egypt*, 99 H2
Suhar, *Oman*, 73 G7
Sukkur, *Pakistan*, 70 B5
Sukses, *Namibia*, 104 C4
Sula, *Norway*, 86 C3
Sula Islands, *Indonesia*, 65 G4
Sullana, *Peru*, 42 B4
Sulu Archipelago, *Philippines*, 67 H6
Sulu Sea, *Asia*, 67 G6
Sumatra, *Indonesia*, 64 B3
Sumba, *Indonesia*, 65 E5
Sumbawa, *Indonesia*, 64 E5
Sumqayit, *Azerbaijan*, 72 E3
Sumy, *Ukraine*, 84 C3
Sunderland, *United Kingdom*, 88 D3
Sundsvall, *Sweden*, 86 F3
Superior, Lake, *U.S.A.*, 33 J1
Sur, *Oman*, 73 G7
Surabaya, *Indonesia*, 64 D5
Surakarta, *Indonesia*, 64 D5
Surat, *India*, 71 C6
Surgut, *Russia*, 74 D2
Surigao, *Philippines*, 67 J6
Suriname, *South America, country*, 43 G3
Surt, *Libya*, 98 E2
Sutherland Falls, *New Zealand*, 55 N8
Suva, *Fiji, national capital*, 55 Q3
Suwalki, *Poland*, 87 G5
Suwon, *South Korea*, 69 L3
Svalbard, *Norway*, 74 A2
Svolvaer, *Norway*, 86 E1
Svyetlahorsk, *Belarus*, 87 J5
Swakopmund, *Namibia*, 104 B4
Swan Islands, *Honduras*, 35 H4
Swansea, *United Kingdom*, 88 D4
Swaziland, *Africa, country*, 104 F5
Sweden, *Europe, country*, 86 E3
Swift Current, *Canada*, 30 J3
Swindon, *United Kingdom*, 88 D4
Switzerland, *Europe, country*, 90 C2
Sydney, *Australia, internal capital*, 55 K6
Sydney, *Canada*, 31 N4
Syktyvkar, *Russia*, 85 G1
Sylhet, *Bangladesh*, 71 G6
Syracuse, *Italy*, 90 E4
Syracuse, *U.S.A.*, 33 L2
Syr Darya, *Asia*, 72 H2
Syria, *Asia, country*, 72 C4
Syrian Desert, *Asia*, 73 C5
Syzran, *Russia*, 85 F3
Szczecin, *Poland*, 87 E5
Szeged, *Hungary*, 87 G7
Szekesfehervar, *Hungary*, 87 F7
Szombathely, *Hungary*, 87 F7

t

Tabora, *Tanzania*, 103 F5
Tabriz, *Iran*, 72 E4
Tabuk, *Saudi Arabia*, 73 C6
Tacloban, *Philippines*, 67 J5

ACKNOWLEDGEMENTS

Every effort has been made to trace the copyright holders of the material in this book. If any rights have been omitted, the publishers offer to rectify this in any subsequent edition, following notification. The publishers are grateful to the following organizations and individuals for their contributions and permission to reproduce material (t=top, m=middle, b=bottom, l=left, r=right):

Cover (globe) © Don Farrall/Photodisc; **Endpapers** © Ric Ergenbright/CORBIS; **p1** © Jim Zuckerman/CORBIS; **p2–3** © Art Wolfe/ Science Photo Library; **p4–5** Stephen Moncrieff, Digital Vision; **p4** (tr) © Geospace/Science Photo Library; **p6** (bl) © CNES, 1988 Distribution SPOT Image/Science Photo Library; (mr) Stephen Moncrieff; **p7** (tm & tr) European Map Graphics Ltd; (b) © Paul A. Souders/CORBIS; **p8–9** (background) © Digital Vision; **p8** (mr) PHOTO ESA; **p9** (tl) © NERC Satellite Station, University of Dundee www.sat.dundee.ac.html; (br) Science Photo Library/European Space Agency; **p10** (b) Stephen Moncrieff; (tr) © Dan Guravich/ CORBIS; **p11** (bl) European Map Graphics Ltd; (tr) © W. Perry Conway/CORBIS; **p12** (b) © Christopher Cormack/CORBIS; **p13** Stephen Moncrieff, Craig Asquith; **p14** (tr) © Bill Ross/CORBIS; (b) Craig Asquith; **p15** Craig Asquith; **p16–17** European Map Graphics Ltd; **p22–23** © Richard Cummins/CORBIS; **p23** (br) © W. Perry Conway/CORBIS; **p24** (tr) © Worldsat International/Science Photo Library; (m) © NASA/JSC; (b) © Raymond Gehman/CORBIS; **p25** © NASA/CORBIS; **p26–27** (b) © Richard Cummins/CORBIS; **p26** (t) © Dave G. Houser/CORBIS; **p27** (tr) © Joe McDonald/CORBIS; **p28** (l) © Angelo Hornak/CORBIS; (tr) © Carl & Ann Purcell/CORBIS; **p29** (tl) © Schafer & Hill/GettyImages; (br) © Michael & Patricia Fogden/CORBIS; **p36–37** © Galen Rowell/CORBIS; **p37** (tr) © Eye Ubiquitous/ CORBIS; **p38** (m) © Julian Baum & David Angus/Science Photo Library; (bl) © Yann Arthus-Bertrand/CORBIS; (mr) © NASA/JSC; **p39** (r) © CNES, 1986 Distribution SPOT Image/Science Photo Library; (bl) © CNES, Distribution SPOT Image/Science Photo Library; **p40–41** (b) © Robert Frederick/GettyImages; **p40** (tr) Claus Meyer/Taxi/GettyImages; **p41** (tl) Walter Bibikow/GettyImages; (tr) Peter Oxford/BBC Wild; **p46–47** © Still Pictures/Pascal Kobeh; **p47** (br) © Bates Littlehales/CORBIS; **p48–49** (b) © Amos Nachoum/CORBIS; **p48** (ml) © 1995, Worldsat International and J. Knighton/Science Photo Library; (t) © NASA/JSC; **p49** (r) © CNES, Distribution SPOT Image/ Science Photo Library; (ml) © CORBIS; **p50** © Robert Harding Picture Library/SuperStock ; **p51** (tr) © J.L. Klein and M.L. Hubert/ Biosphoto/ Specialist Stock, Still Pictures; (bl) © Imagestate Media Partners Limited – Impact Photos/Alamy; **p57** (br) © Keren Su/ CORBIS; **p58** (tr) © Worldsat International/Science Photo Library; (m) © CNES, 1986 Distribution SPOT Image/Science Photo Library; (b) © Liu Liqun/CORBIS; **p59** (t) © NASA JPL; (br) © CNES, 1987 Distribution SPOT Image/Science Photo Library; **p60** (l) © Keren Su/ CORBIS; (tr) © Keren Su/China Span/Alamy; **p61** (tl) © DAJ/amana images/Getty Images; (b) © Papilio/CORBIS; **p62** (tr) © Richard T. Nowitz/CORBIS; (b) © Design Pics/CORBIS; **p63** (ml) © www.pictor.com; (tr) © Wolfgang Kaehler/CORBIS; (b) © Brian & Cherry Alexander Photography; **p76–77** © Digital Vision; **p77** (br) Agripicture/ © Peter Dean; **p78–79** (b) © Peter Adams/GettyImages; **p78** (tr) NASA/GSFC/MITI/ERSDAC/JAROS, & U.S./Japan ASTER Science Team; (ml) © NASA GSFC Scientific Visualization Studio; **p79** (tr) © CNES, 1994 Distribution SPOT Image/Science Photo Library; (m) © German Remote Sensing Data Center; **p80** (tr) © The Art Archive/ Historiska Muséet Stockholm/Dagli Orti; (bl) © Enzo & Paolo Ragazzini/CORBIS; **p81** (t) © Zefa visual media; (br) © Frans Lanting/ Minden Pictures; **p82** © Paul Hardy/corbisstockmarket.com; **p83** (t) © Bob Krist/CORBIS; (b) © Araldo de Luca/CORBIS; **p92–93** © Tom Brakefield/CORBIS; **p93** (br) © Gallo Images/CORBIS; **p94** (tr) © Worldsat International/Science Photo Library; (bl) © Yann Arthus-Bertrand/CORBIS; (br) © NASA JPL; **p95** (r) © Jacques Descloitres, MODIS Land Science Team; (bl) © NASA/JSC; **p96** © Roger Wood/ CORBIS; **p97** (ml) © Charles O'Rear/CORBIS; (tr) © Wolfgang Kaehler/CORBIS; (b) © Karl Ammann/CORBIS; **p106** (tr) © Worldsat International/Science Photo Library; (m) © Pixonnet.com/Alamy; **p107** (t) © NRSC Ltd/Science Photo Library; (b) © Digital Vision; **p110–111** (b) © Iain Masterton/Alamy; **p110** (tl) © Peter M. Wilson/CORBIS; (tm) © Joe McDonald/CORBIS; (ml) © Charles O'Rear/ CORBIS; (mr) © Vanni Archive/CORBIS; **p111** (br) Galen Rowell/CORBIS; **p112–125** (background) © Digital Vision; (Afghanistan, Bahrain, Comoros, Rwanda, Turkmenistan and East Timor flags) © Shipmate Flags, Vlaardingen, The Netherlands; (all other flags) © Flag Enterprises Ltd; **p125** (b) UN/Mark Garten; **p126** (b) Craig Asquith.

Managing editor: Gillian Doherty
Managing designer: Mary Cartwright
This edition updated by Phil Clarke
Cover design by Tom Lalonde
Internet research by Jacqui Clark
With thanks to Ruth King